u19

EVALUATING NEW LABOUR'S WELFARE REFORMS

Edited by Martin Powell

D0242295

First published in Great Britain in July 2002 by

The Policy Press
34 Tyndall's Park Road
Bristol BS8 1PY
UK

Tel +44 (0)117 954 6800
Fax +44 (0)117 973 7308
e-mail tpp@bristol.ac.uk
www.policypress.org.uk

© The Policy Press 2002

British Library Cataloguing in Publication Data
A catalogue record for this book is available from the British Library

ISBN 1 86134 335 3 paperback
A hardcover version of this book is also available

Martin Powell is Senior Lecturer in Social Policy in the Department of Social and Policy Sciences, University of Bath

Cover design by Qube Design Associates, Bristol
Front cover: photograph supplied by kind permission of Third Avenue Photography, www.third-avenue.co.uk

Printed and bound in Great Britain by Bell & Bain Ltd, Glasgow.

Contents

List of tables

Notes on contributors

Mark Baldwin is Senior Lecturer in Social Work at the University of Bath. His main research interest is the development of professional practice in social welfare organisations, and the way that the use and misuse of discretion skews or constructs policies. The extent to which effective practice can be developed through reflective practice in learning organisations is a practical focus, through the use of participative action research methods. In 2000 he published *Care management and community care: Social work discretion and the construction of policy* (Ashgate).

Edward Brunsdon is Principal Lecturer at London Guildhall University where he teaches a range of courses in welfare management and social policy. His main research interests are private welfare and the management of welfare services, on which he has published widely. A past editor of the *Social Policy Review*, he has recently co-edited *Understanding social problems* (Blackwell, 2001) and is currently (with Margaret May) completing a study of occupational and commercial welfare in the UK for publication in 2003.

Sarah Charman is currently Senior Lecturer at the Institute of Criminal Justice Studies, University of Portsmouth. She has published widely in the area of pressure groups in criminal justice policy making, the role of the Association of Chief Police Officers and the politics of criminal justice policy. Sarah is co-author (with Stephen P. Savage and Stephen Cope) of *Policing and the power of persuasion* (Blackstone Press, 2000)

Martin Hewitt lectured in social policy at the University of Hertfordshire before joining the Institute of Actuaries in 2001 as Programme Manager for the Social Policy Board. His publications include *Welfare and human nature* (Macmillan, 2000) and *Welfare state and welfare change* (with Martin Powell, Open University Press, 2002). His research interests include social security, financial exclusion and welfare ideology.

Brian Lund is Principal Lecturer in Social Policy at the Manchester Metropolitan University. He is author of *Housing problems and housing policy* (Longman, 1996), *Towards integrated living: Housing strategies and community care* (with Mark Foord, The Policy Press, 1997) and *Understanding state welfare: Social justice or social exclusion* (Sage Publications, 2002).

Margaret May is Principal Lecturer at London Guildhall University where she teaches a range of courses in welfare management and social policy. Her main research interests are private welfare and the management of welfare services, on which she has published widely. She is co-editor of the *Student's* *companion to social policy* (Blackwell, 1998) and *The dictionary of social policy* (Blackwell, 2002). She is currently (with Edward Brunsdon) completing a study of occupational and commercial welfare in the UK for publication in 2003.

Jane Millar is Professor of Social Policy at the University of Bath, with research interests in social security and family policy, poverty and social exclusion. Recent publications include an edited volume, *Lone parents, employment and social policy: Cross-national comparisons* (with Karen Rowlingson, The Policy Press, 2001), and a literature review, *Families, poverty, work and care: A review of the literature on lone parents and low-income couple families with children* (with Tess Ridge, Department for Work and Pensions, 2001).

Yolande Muschamp is Senior Lecturer in Education at the University of Bath. Her research is in the area of policy for primary education, and teaching and learning in the middle years. Her publications include *Work and identity in the primary school* (with Ian Mentor, Peter Nicholls, Jenny Ozga and Andrew Pollard, Open University Press, 1996).

Rajani Naidoo lectures in the School of Education at the University of Bath. She has held a range of management, consultancy and teaching positions in South African and British higher education institutions. She is also a member of the Governing Council of the Society for Research into Higher Education. Her research interests include the impact of marketisation and managerialism on higher education and the relationship between globalisation, higher education and skills in developing countries.

Calum Paton is Professor of Health Policy at Keele University's Centre for Health Planning and Management. He has published widely on health policy and political economy, most recently *World, class, Britain* (Macmillan, 2000) and *Competition and planning in the NHS* (2nd edn, Stanley Thornes, 1998). He is Editor of the *International Journal of Health Planning and Management* and has advised British political parties and governments overseas. He has recently directed two EU projects on health reform and the effect of the EU on healthcare systems.

Martin Powell is Senior Lecturer in Social Policy in the Department of Social and Policy Sciences, University of Bath. He has published in the areas of health policy and on New Labour. He is the author of *Evaluating the NHS* (Open University Press, 1997) and the editor of *New Labour, new welfare state? The 'third way' in British social policy* (The Policy Press, 1999).

Tess Ridge is a lecturer and researcher in the Department of Social and Policy Sciences at the University of Bath. Her research interests are childhood poverty and family policy, particularly how children fare within the policy process.

She is currently engaged on a three-year ESRC Research Fellowship. Recent publications include *Families, poverty, work and care: A review of the literature on lone parents and low-income couple families with children* (with Jane Millar, Department for Work and Pensions, 2001) and has a forthcoming book, *Childhood poverty and social exclusion: From a child's perspective* (The Policy Press, 2002).

John Rouse is Professor of Public Services Management and Dean of the Faculty of Law and Social Sciences at the University of Central England in Birmingham. His main teaching, research interests and publications are in the fields of public services, performance management and local governance. His most recent work is on Best Value in local government, and the police.

Stephen P. Savage is Professor of Criminology and Director of the Institute of Criminal Justice Studies, University of Portsmouth. He has published widely in the areas of policing and criminal justice. His most recent publications include *Policing and the power of persuasion* (with Sarah Charman and Stephen Cope, Blackstone Press, 2000), *Policy networks in criminal justice* (co-edited with Mick Ryan and David Wall, Palgrave, 2001), *Public policy under Blair* (co-edited with Rob Atkinson, Palgrave, 2001) and *Core issues in policing* (co-edited with Frank Leishman and Barry Loveday, 2nd edn, Pearson Education, 2001).

George Smith lectures in social policy in the Department of Sociology at University of Central England in Birmingham. He has also worked in a central government ministry and in a new town development corporation. His publications have been on innovation and change in higher education, and on various aspects of contemporary social policy.

ONE

Introduction

Martin Powell

Introduction

A central concern of the New Labour government was to modernise the welfare state. Welfare reform featured heavily in the 1997 Manifesto, and it has been a major feature of government policy ever since (for example, Powell, 1999; Burden et al, 2000; Timmins, 2001). The main aim of this text is to evaluate the welfare policies of the first term of the New Labour government (1997-2001). It is concerned with evaluation *of* policy rather than evaluation *for* policy. The government has invested heavily in the latter, commissioning a significant amount of research with the main aim of improving the policy process. For example, it has set up many area-based policies such as Action Zones in education, health and employment. Changes in these zones are evaluated in order to 'mainstream' any improvements to the national level. Similarly, policies such as the New Deal have been subject to evaluation (see Chapters Five and Ten of this volume). Moreover, it has encouraged evidence-based approaches in health, education and social care in order to determine 'what works' (for example, Davies et al, 2000).

However, this text is concerned with evaluation of policy. There is a rapidly growing literature that examines the changes that New Labour has made to social policy. Some of this literature is implicitly evaluative in that it gives a broadly positive (for example, Glennerster, 1999) or negative (for example, Hay, 1999; Burden et al, 2000; *Critical Social Policy*, 2001) verdict on the changes. However, there is much less material that is explicitly evaluative in that it gives a clear verdict (for example, Glennerster, 2001; Toynbee and Walker, 2001; Boyne et al, 2003: forthcoming). Toynbee and Walker (2001) is perhaps the most developed and best-known account. In order to answer their question of 'Did things get better?', they:

> ... tried to strip away the hyperbole, the claims and boasts, to look as cooly as we could at what Labour has achieved in four years. We needed a baseline on which to measure New Labour but none exists, dry and objective, to be taken down from history's shelf.... The fairest judgements must be made on what New Labour itself promised. (Toynbee and Walker, 2001, p 232)

There are two main differences between Toynbee and Walker (2001) and this text. First, while they cover the whole area of government activity, this present account focuses on social policy. Second, this text aims to locate social policy evaluation within a wider template of evaluation. In particular, it differentiates between *intrinsic* evaluation and *extrinsic* evaluation (see below). The former examines progress against the government's own stated aims, while the latter takes a broader perspective.

This chapter begins by introducing the notion of evaluation, focusing on the key differences between intrinsic and extrinsic evaluation that run through the book. The next section demonstrates the importance of evaluation to New Labour, pointing to its pledges, promises and targets made in the Election Manifesto, White and Green Papers, Annual Reports, Public Service Agreements (PSAs) and Performance Assessment Frameworks (PAFs). This is followed by a short section that places these targets in the wider context of the policy process. The final section gives a brief overview of the main issues and areas that will be covered in the remainder of the book.

Evaluating the welfare state

The welfare state has always been subject to scrutiny. At one extreme, some judgements have been wildly enthusiastic. With reference to the NHS, Hennessy (1992, pp 143-4) writes that "The fifth of July 1948 was one of the greatest days in British history.... The NHS was and remains one of the finest institutions ever built by anyone anywhere". However, writing of the same institution, Green and Benedict (2001, p 82) compare the NHS with the healthcare systems of France and Germany, concluding that it is "embarrassing for a nation to admit that it has been wrong for fifty years".

There are two very broad dimensions of evaluation of public services. The first is associated with government and its associated agencies, which are concerned with official or internal evaluations. As Carter et al (1992, p 2) point out, issues such as what counts as good performance, how we define the various dimensions of performance, and who determines what is good performance are fundamental questions of governance. Hood et al (1999) focus on the rise of regulation, which includes audit bodies (for example, Audit Commission, National Audit Office; see also Pollitt et al, 1999; Day and Klein, 2001), Inspectorates (for example, SSI, OFSTED; see also Hughes et al, 1996), ombudsmen and equivalents (for example, NHS Commissioner, Police Complaints Authority), central agency regulators (for example, Citizen's Charter Unit) and funder-regulators (for example, HEFCE, Housing Corporation). Hood et al (1999) claim that these diverse bodies may be separated into seven types. Public audit bodies' main responsibilities are to monitor and enforce probity and efficiency. Professional Inspectorates oversee specific services, monitoring performance and often enforcing standards in a specialised domain. The ombudsmen's main role is in the handling of individual grievances, but has extended in some cases to the explication of general principles of 'good' administration. Central agency regulators set, monitor and/or enforce rules for the conduct of central government. Funder-regulators set, monitor and enforce conditions for the provision of public services by local public bodies. Departmental regulators of agencies are those sections of core departments that regulate organisations within their own department's domain. Finally, central regulators of local public bodies and the NHS regulate local authorities and the NHS. Neither the precise details nor the accuracy of the classification are of great relevance here. What matters is that each of these types of agencies – 'waste-watchers, quality police and sleaze-busters' (Hood et al, 1999) – may address different issues, ask different questions, and use different methods, but are fundamentally concerned with judgement and evaluation.

The second main dimension is associated with external, unofficial and academic evaluations (see, for example, Phillips et al, 1994; Clarke, 1999). There have been evaluations of governments (for example, Townsend and Bosanquet, 1972; Bosanquet and Townsend, 1980; Walker and Walker, 1997; Seldon, 2001), programme areas (for example, Powell, 1997; Carrier and Kendall, 1998) and reforms (for example, Butler et al, 1994; Le Grand et al, 1998; Boyne et al, 2003: forthcoming). However, in spite of much activity, our knowledge of evaluation remains fairly limited, with significant conceptual and methodological problems.

A useful starting point may be found in the systems approach of Easton (1965), who views the policy process in terms of the transformation of inputs into outputs. Within social policy, there are some similarities in the 'production of welfare' model (Knapp, 1984; Hill and Bramley, 1986) or the production process model (Powell, 1997; Glennerster and Hills, 1998). In simple terms, these models see inputs (for example, expenditure) purchasing outputs (for example, patients treated) to influence outcomes (for example, better health).

However, there are two main problems. First, we have limited understanding of the production process. While we know that certain chemicals combine under certain conditions, we are less certain about constructing policy packages to reduce mortality or increase educational qualifications. Our knowledge of 'evidence-based policy' and 'what works?' remains limited (Davies et al, 2000; Klein, 2000). The traditional response to this problem has been 'more of the same', where problems were addressed by increasing expenditure (Powell, 1997). Little thought was given to issues of efficiency and effectiveness, and better outcomes were sought largely by increasing inputs more or less across the board in a similar pattern. The target was hit by a blunderbuss rather than by a shotgun. Even if we know that a policy works, we are often less certain about *why* it works. This fits with the work of Chen (1990, p 40; see also Boyne et al, 2003: forthcoming) on 'theory-driven evaluation', which is based on a specification of what must be done to achieve the desired goals, what other important impacts may be anticipated, and how these goals and impacts would be generated. It is also important to identify the contextual and intervening factors that hinder or facilitate programme processes and outcomes (Chen, 1990, p 45). This emphasis is also present in 'realistic evaluation' (Pawson and Tilley, 1997), which was developed to reach a better understanding of why a programme worked, for whom and in what circumstances. Outcome depends on both context and mechanism. Policy levers that work in one situation may not work in another.

The second problem concerns the aims and objectives of the process. At a basic level, we can distinguish between intrinsic and extrinsic evaluation (cf Powell, 1997). The former is based on assessing progress in terms of each government's own stated objectives (Glennerster and Hills, 1998, p 6). The latter examines a standard set of evaluation criteria, irrespective of a government's stated objectives (for example, Le Grand and Robinson, 1984; Le Grand and Bartlett, 1993). A useful analogy is Bradshaw's (1972) taxonomy of need: 'felt need' examines need in terms of the individual's own views, while 'normative need' superimposes an external, third-party view, irrespective of the person's own views (see Plant et al, 1980). Intrinsic evaluation examines performance in its own terms, with reference to stated goals. Extrinsic evaluation is based on a 'third-party' specification of criteria, and may result in criticising a government for failing to achieve something that it has not set as an objective, but which the third party thinks should be an objective.

Intrinsic evaluation

This is based on comparing stated aims and objectives with achievements. In other words, it involves measuring success on the government's own terms. Glennerster and Hills (1998, p 10) argue that if politicians set objectives and justify a policy with public statements of intention, a necessary part of the democratic process should be to see how far the stated intentions have been fulfilled. This form of 'democratic audit' is analogous to a voters' 'Which?' or 'Watchdog', protecting the public from false political advertising. A section of political science literature focuses on the politics of manifestos (Topf, 1994), mandate theory (Budge et al, 1987; Hofferbert and Budge, 1992), or the 'manifesto model of party government' (Rose, 1984). Rose explains that when two parties alternate in office, then for a given party, opposition intention ($t1$) is equal to government practice ($t2$). In opposition a party will set out its policy intentions, and then put these into practice upon entering office. It starts from the assumption that elections should offer voters a choice between alternative ways of governing the country. For an election to be meaningful in policy terms, the parties must not only pledge different policies but also practice what they preach.

Some writers have argued that writing manifestos is a waste of paper and examining manifestos is a waste of time: politics does not matter, either because there are no differences between 'bourgeois' parties or because external events shape policies. However, Hofferbert and Budge (1992) conclude that parties appear to perform broadly as called for by the mandate theory of democracy. Moreover, whether mandate theory is valid, many voters believe that it should be valid. In a democratic society, the ultimate test of political success is election. In short, there is an assumption of a contract (see below). It seems reasonable that for this contract to be valid, it should be enforceable in that it should contain only feasible pledges that can be carried out within a five-year term of government. However, some pledges may be heavily dependent on external events such as the state of the world economy. Some may be long-term. Others may be vague and immeasurable. Topf (1994, p 153) states that we have no clear criterion against which to measure what is to count as an 'election promise'.

However, unlike money-back guarantees that are available in some high street stores, there are no clear means of redress for the electorate other than changing their vote at the next election. Moreover, it does not follow that election indicates that all manifesto pledges are popular, nor that re-election shows that all pledges were carried out. An election is not a referendum on dozens of manifesto pledges but a crude choice between two bundles of party politics, that may include some pledges disliked by a majority of the electorate (Rose, 1984, p 28). This position is central to the new right critique of government provision (for example, Harris and Seldon, 1979). The political market sells policies at the wholesale level. In elections, voters are asked to judge between two broad policy baskets. The economic market, on the other hand, sells policies at the retail level. It offers choice through a 'daily referendum', and consumers may choose any combination of goods and services from an 'à la carte', rather than set, menu.

Although manifestos give the broad shape of parties' intentions and some detailed pledges, more specific commitments emerge over a government's term of office. Ministers make speeches. Green and White Papers are produced. In some ways, these elaborate original intentions, putting policy flesh on manifesto bones. In other ways, they may reflect different directions, perhaps arising in response to events. Of course, they should not generally indicate opposite directions, or a u-turn from the original manifesto. In short, it seems reasonable to examine how governments' rhetoric compares with reality (cf Fairclough, 2000).

Extrinsic evaluation

Extrinsic evaluation means evaluation from some external reference point. This may be comparative (for example, comparing expenditure with the EU average) or temporal (for example, comparing waiting lists with the previous government). The main problem here is that these external targets may not be accepted as legitimate by the government. In short, it examines targets that a third party considers that the government *should* be trying to achieve rather than a stated aim. For example, New Labour rejects 'old' redistribution of income through the tax and benefit system. It considers old 'full employment' through Keynesian demand management is no longer feasible in a global economy. Unlike Old Labour, it tends not to concentrate on poverty, with the exception of the pledge to abolish child poverty. Neither does it say much about the Old Labour versions of equality and redistribution of income. Some have criticised New Labour on this count (for example, Levitas, 1998; Lister, 1998, 2000), but it is possible that some parts of New Labour's inclusion and redistribution of opportunities agenda are more complex and ambitious (see Chapter Two of this volume; Powell, 2000; Glennerster, 2001; Powell et al, 2001).

While a sole emphasis on extrinsic evaluation is therefore not wise, it can provide a useful complement to intrinsic evaluation. There are three main reasons for this. First, governments may choose targets that they consider to be easily achievable (for example, extrapolations of existing trends) rather than desirable but more difficult targets. Second, there are opportunity costs in choosing targets. For example, a pledge to reduce class sizes in primary schools may be achieved by diverting resources, and allowing class sizes in other parts of the system (for example, secondary and higher education) to expand. Similarly, reducing inpatient waiting lists may be achieved at the expense of longer outpatient waiting lists. Therefore it is necessary to examine the whole picture, including trade-offs, rather than the partial picture of stated targets. Third, examining the same measures allows comparisons over time and space. For example, are New Labour's education policies more equitable than those of the Conservatives? Are New Labour's health policies more efficient than those of the US?

However, there is the problem of choosing the broad domains as well as specific measures as these inevitably reflect normative value-judgements. For example, some neoliberals generally reject equality as a goal of government. Some regard 'equality of opportunity' but not 'equality of outcome' as legitimate objectives (see, for example, George and Wilding, 1985). It is sometimes difficult to reach a consensus about legitimate objectives within political parties (for example, compare the left and right of the Labour and Conservative parties), let alone between them. Similarly, what is 'equitable' for one observer may be 'inequitable' for another.

There is a fairly standard set of criteria for evaluating welfare states such as equality, efficiency, accountability and so on (for example, Le Grand and Robinson, 1984; Hill and Bramley, 1986; Le Grand and Bartlett, 1993; Le Grand et al, 1998; Boyne et al, 2003: forthcoming), but problems remain concerning the operationalisation of these concepts and any trade-offs between them. For example, is technical efficiency more important than allocative efficiency? Is there a trade-off between an efficient and an equitable healthcare system? Given these difficulties, any analysis must make clear its criteria for others to accept or reject.

Evaluating New Labour

Intrinsic evaluation is particularly appropriate for the New Labour government. New Labour's approach highlights the importance of delivery and results. It stresses meeting pledges in the 1997 Manifesto. Loyal party members still carry their pledge cards close to their hearts. It has introduced new PAFs in services such as the NHS and social services. It has pioneered the government's Annual Reports and PSAs with SMART (specific, measurable, achievable, relevant, timed) targets. It has stressed the importance of Inspectorates in areas such as health, housing and education, and has 'zero tolerance' for 'failing' schools and hospitals. In short, New Labour has probably set itself more targets than any previous government in history. It has asked the electorate to judge the government on its results. It has manufactured huge amounts of ammunition either to fire a celebratory salute, or to shoot itself in the foot.

In his introduction to the 1997 General Election Manifesto, Tony Blair stated that he wanted to renew the country's faith in politics by:

> ... making a limited set of important promises and achieving them. This is the purpose of the bond of trust I set out ... in which ten specific commitments are put before you. Hold us to them. They are our covenant with you. (Labour Party, 1997, p 1)

This is contrasted with the 'gross breaches of faith' under the Conservative government of John Major. Blair continues that:

> The Conservatives' broken promises taint all politics. That is why we have made it our guiding rule not to promise what we cannot deliver; and to deliver what we promise. (p 2)

Blair then sets out 10 commitments:

> ... that form our bond of trust with the people. They are specific. They are real. Judge us on them. Have trust in us and we will repay that trust. (p 4)

He goes on to present 'our contract with the people'. Over the five years of a Labour government:

1. Education will be our number one priority, and we will increase the share of national income spent on education as we decrease it on the bills of economic and social failure.

2. There will be no increase in the basic or top rates of income tax.

3. We will provide stable economic growth with low inflation, and promote dynamic and competitive business and industry at home and abroad.

4. We will get 250,000 young unemployed off benefit and into work.

5. We will rebuild the NHS, reducing spending on administration and increasing spending on patient care.

6. We will be tough on crime and tough on the causes of crime, and halve the time it takes persistent juvenile offenders to come to court.

7. We will help build strong families and strong communities, and lay the foundations of a modern welfare state in pensions and community care.

8. We will safeguard our environment, and develop an integrated transport policy to fight congestion and pollution.

9. We will clean up politics, decentralise political power throughout the United Kingdom and put the funding of political parties on a proper and accountable basis.

10. We will give Britain the leadership in Europe which Britain and Europe need. (p 5)

The document ends by claiming that:

We have promised only what we know we can deliver. Britain deserves better and the following five election pledges will be the first step towards a better Britain:

- cut class sizes to 30 or under for 5, 6 and 7 year-olds by using money from the assisted places scheme;

- fast-track punishment for persistent young offenders by halving the time from arrest to sentencing;

- cut NHS waiting lists by treating an extra 100,000 patients as a first step by releasing £100 M saved from NHS red tape;

- get 250,000 under-25 year-olds off benefit and into work by using money from a windfall levy on the privatised utilities;

- no rise in income tax rates, cut VAT on heating to 5 per cent and inflation and interest rates as low as possible. (p 40)

These commitments feature heavily in many government documents (see below), and will be examined in more detail later. For the moment, it is sufficient to highlight the importance of delivery and the prominence of social policy in New Labour's discourse.

Early in its term of office, the government set up a Comprehensive Spending Review (CSR). Every spending department was required to reassess its budget from a zero base. The CSR was an attempt to move from an incremental to a more rational pattern of spending. In other words, instead of giving each department incremental annual increases in spending, there would be a return to first principles, examining how best departmental programmes can contribute to the achievement of the government's objectives (HM Treasury, 1998a; Burchardt and Hills, 1999). Rather than 'needing' to spend $x\%$ more than last year, each department would have to justify why it needed $£y$ in total in order to achieve its objectives. This resulted in changes in spending priorities both between and within departments, with the most obvious feature being large increases in spending on the government's priorities such as health and education to deliver its Manifesto commitments. Spending plans were agreed for three-year periods. The key principle was 'money for modernisation': a 'contract' that "we will invest more money but that money comes with strings attached. In return for investment there must be reform" (HM Treasury, 1998a, p 1). There is an obligation on those spending that money to do wisely in pursuit of agreed and ambitious targets. The report stressed the importance of meeting the five key election pledges. It outlined the government's key objectives, and set out challenging targets for key public services. For example, the Departmental Review for the Department of Health stated that by the end of the Parliament, the government would: reduce waiting lists by 100,000; begin to reduce avoidable illness, disease and injury; improve cooperation between the NHS, social services and other services; and improve the educational achievement for children in care.

Some six months later a White Paper delivered the commitments of the earlier document by publishing "for the first time, measurable targets for the full range of the government's objectives for public services in the form of ground-breaking new Public Service Agreements (PSAs)" (HM Treasury, 1998b, p 1). The document focused on results. Expenditure or numbers employed are measures of inputs to a service but they do not show what is being achieved. Programmes and legislation are only a means to an end to delivering the real improvements on the ground that the government wants to see. What really matters is the effectiveness and efficiency of the service the public receives. That is what really makes a difference to the quality of people's lives.

> The targets published in this White Paper are therefore of a new kind. As far as possible, they are expressed either in terms of the end results that taxpayers' money is intended to deliver – for example, improvements in health and educational achievement and reductions in crime – or service standards – for example, smaller class sizes, reduced waiting lists, swifter justice. The government is therefore setting specific, measurable, achievable, relevant and timed (ie SMART) targets, related to outcomes wherever possible. (HM Treasury, 1998b, p 1)

The main elements of PSAs – aims and objectives and performance targets – were applied to each department. For example, the Department of Health's overall aim is to improve the health and well-being of the people of England, through improving health and providing health and social care. The key objectives in pursuing these aims are: reducing the incidence of avoidable illness, disease and injury; treating people quickly and effectively on the basis of need; enabling people who are unable to perform essential activities of daily living to live as full and normal lives as possible; and maximising the social development of children within stable family settings. Finally, relating to the objectives, 14 key performance targets, including some with subsidiary targets, were set out. For example, key target (2) was the waiting list commitment, while key target (14) involved reducing the proportion of children reregistered on the child protection register by 10% from the baseline figure of March 1997.

The *Modernising government* White Paper (Prime Minister, 1999a, p 40) insisted that public service must "compare actual performance with promises, and learn by benchmarking policymaking and services between organisations, between regions, between sectors and between countries".

The Annual Reports are intended to give a "progress report on how we are doing in meeting our manifesto commitments, the values that guide us, and the targets we are trying to achieve" (Prime Minister, 2000, p 4).

New Labour has stressed PAFs in a number of sectors. For example, a new PAF was introduced in the NHS (see Chapter Seven of this volume). The government claims that it is superior to the Conservatives' emphasis on narrow measures of financial efficiency (see, for example, Carter et al, 1992; Powell, 1997). The new PAF examines the dimensions of health improvement, fair access, effective delivery of appropriate healthcare, efficiency, patient/care experience and health outcomes of NHS care. In June 1999 "a package of high level performance indicators and clinical indicators [and] a new way of assessing and improving quality and performance in the NHS" (DoH, 1999a) was launched. According to the then Secretary of State for Health, Frank Dobson, "In the past, there was too much meaningless bean-counting combined with a narrow focus on efficiency. Now ... we have made a start in assessing the outcome of treatment and the effectiveness of services" (DoH, 1999a).

In November 1999, the first national set of performance figures for social services were issued (see Chapter Nine of this volume). The PAF is part of a wider system for social services, built around the Best Value regime (discussed later in this chapter) which was introduced on 1 April 1999 for all parts of local government. According to the then Health Minister, John Hutton, "This marks the start, for the very first time, of being able to produce a national picture of the quality of social services provided" (DoH, 1999b). Hutton said that the indicators showed wide and unacceptable variation in services. Poorly performing authorities were given four months to 'get their house in order' or, under powers to be introduced in April 2000, the government would not hesitate to intervene and, in the last instance, change the authority running those services. Following poor inspection reports by the Social Services Inspectorate and Audit Commission, and unrelated to the indicators, the then Health Minister named 17 authorities on 'special measures'. These authorities are being kept under special scrutiny and are required to report direct to ministers (Brindle, 1999).

The Best Value regime may be seen as the local version of the central concern with performance. The Election Manifesto (Labour Party, 1997) stated that the Conservatives' Compulsory Competitive Tendering would be replaced with Best Value: "councils should not be forced to put their services out to tender, but will be required to obtain best value. Every council will be required to publish a local performance plan with targets for service improvement, and be expected to achieve them" (p 34). The government identifies five key aspects of performance: cost, efficiency, effectiveness, quality and fair access (DETR, 1998). As Boyne (1999) notes, while the last two dimensions seem to signal a broadening of the '3Es' framework of the previous Conservative government (economy, effectiveness and efficiency), New Labour places an emphasis on targets and continuous improvement. Local authorities must publish an annual performance plan, and over a longer term, probably at least once every five years, must take fundamental reviews of their services. Each review must contain the '4Cs': to *challenge* why and how a service is being provided; to *compare* performance with other organisations; to *consult* with local taxpayers, service users and the business community; and to use *competition* as a means of enhancing performance.

Local evaluation is a key part of New Labour's desire to 'mainstream' or 'spread best practice'. For example, 'what works' in area-based initiatives such as the Health Action Zones (HAZs) is being examined with a view to inform wider policy making. The NHS Plan (DoH, 2000) points out that "Good and bad practice are stuck in their own ghettos because there has been no means of meeting the challenge Aneurin Bevan set out in 1948: how to universalise the best" (p 29).

In addition to the government's general stress on performance, some Green and White Papers contain elements of performance targets. For example, the Green Paper on welfare reform (DSS, 1998, p 7) sets out the framework for welfare reform, based on eight principles, together with 32 success measures which will help to guide progress over a 10 to 20 year time horizon. *The NHS Plan* (DoH, 2000) states that a key message from consultation was that the NHS needs a small, focused set of targets to drive change. Too many targets simply overwhelm the service. Therefore a small core of targets (seven for the NHS; three for the NHS in partnership with social services; four for social services) form the Department of Health's PSA with the Treasury.

Moreover, some ad hoc promises have arisen along the way. For example, in March 1999 the Prime Minister stated that child poverty would be abolished within a generation (Walker, 1999; see Chapter Five of this volume). Similarly, in January 2000 he interrupted the nation's cornflakes by announcing on a breakfast television programme that NHS spending would be brought up to the EU average (see Chapter Seven of this volume). It is reported that, like Mrs Thatcher's announcement of a fundamental review of the NHS on television, this took the Cabinet by surprise, particularly spoiling Chancellor Gordon Brown's breakfast. Subsequent debate focused on whether the announcement was a 'pledge' or an 'aspiration'. Although there is a pledge of significant extra money in the NHS, this specific pledge does not appear in *The NHS Plan* (DoH, 2000) some six months later. On the other hand, the Plan did contain "for the first time" (p 106) a national target on health inequalities.

In addition to the emphasis on quantitative targets, New Labour has placed great stress on inspection. "External scrutiny plays a key part in ensuring that the providers of public services are held accountable" (HM Treasury, 1998a, p 37). With an emphasis on regulation, New Labour has strengthened existing Inspectorates such as OFSTED and has introduced new ones, such as the

Commission for Health Improvement (CHI), and a new Housing Inspectorate (Hughes et al, 1996; Hood et al, 1999; Day and Klein, 2001).

Frameworks of policy success

New Labour's third way makes a clear distinction between policy ends and means. In his introduction to the Manifesto, Blair claims that:

> What counts is what works. The objectives are radical. The means will be modern.... Our values are the same ... but we recognise also that the policies of 1997 cannot be those of 1947 or 1967. (Labour Party, 1997)

This theme of modernisation, achieving traditional objectives by modern means is central to the third way (for example, DoH, 1997; Blair, 1998; DSS, 1998; see Fairclough, 2000). According to *The NHS Plan* (DoH, 2000), the NHS is a 1940s system operating in a 21st-century world. The principles of the NHS are sound but its practices need to change. In some ways, it has parallels with the separation of ends and means in Croslandite revisionism (Crosland, 1964; Leonard, 1999). Crosland (1964) argued that equality was the main end of socialism, but questioned whether traditional Labour policies such as nationalisation were the best means to achieve that end.

However, the separation of means and ends is more complex than New Labour's sleight of hand implies for two main reasons (cf Parsons, 1995; Levin, 1997). First, in the 'ideal type' sense policy is seen as a linear process. The policy process consists of a number of stages such as problem identification, goal selection and so on. In this rational model, policies flow from values as Blair (1998) implies. However, it has been suggested that in the 'real world' policy making is more incremental. This has parallels with the literature on historical institutionalism or path dependency that argues that it is difficult to change paths. While policies are not written on tablets of stone, neither can they be written on a blank sheet of paper. Second, the process implies a much deeper understanding of 'evidence-based policy making' and 'what works?' than we have (Davies et al, 2000; Klein, 2000). Policy making is more an 'art' than a laboratory experiment. While we know how to combine iron ore, limestone and coke in order to produce iron, we are less certain of the way to combine policy ingredients to ensure outcomes such as equality of health status (for example, Wolman, 1981; Exworthy and Powell, 2000). The translation of traditional values into new policies must show that the traditional policy was failing; identify the reason why it was failing; show that it was not possible to improve the traditional policy through incremental means; and prove that the new policy will show better returns (Powell, 2000).

These points come together to suggest that the first term of 1997-2001 saw an implementation deficit. As Timmins (2001, p 601) puts it, the government was stronger on policy and planning than on delivery. Whatever the merits of government policy on paper and regardless of what the academic evaluations might say, the public perceived few improvements on the ground. In the view of the most important stakeholders, things did not appear to get a lot better. There are a number of possible reasons for this implementation deficit (for example, Wolman, 1981; Marsh and Rhodes, 1992; Parsons, 1995). First, the policies may have problems that make successful implementation difficult. Second, governments may command, but find it more difficult to control, especially when the main agencies of delivery such as the local authorities and the health agencies have various degrees of independence. This problem may increase in the future, given New Labour's stress on increasing use of commercial and voluntary sectors (see Chapter Four of this volume). Third, improving outcomes may be a long-term process. While some policies showed results in the short term, targets such as abolishing child poverty and reducing health inequalities will take longer to achieve. Many critics argue that New Labour's first term was a 'short Parliament'. Given the spending constraints in the first two years, the decision to seek a General Election after four rather than five years, and the time-lag in the publication of government statistics, there was very little time for New Labour's belated largesse to show dividends. It has been claimed that Tony Blair has stated that the key themes for the second term must be 'delivery, delivery, delivery'.

Content outline

The following chapters provide an evaluation of the welfare reforms of the first term of the New Labour government. The starting point is intrinsic evaluation, focusing on the government's stated aims, such as the Election Manifesto, the 'pledge card 5', the 'covenant 10' promises and the 177 pledges as detailed in the Annual Reports. In addition, some chapters point to aims that evolved through White and Green Papers. In some areas, there are also a host of measures contained in the PSAs and the PAFs. There are obvious questions over the consistency of these measures. Are they consistent over time? Is there evidence of backtracking or rewriting the promise if it appears difficult to deliver? Are these consistent between themselves? Are the PSA measures compatible with those of the PAF? This exercise provides an alternative, independent examination of success. The views of the contributors to this volume may be compared with those of the civil servants who considered that most of 177 pledges were successfully carried out. The focus then moves towards the wider sphere of extrinsic evaluation. Does New Labour neglect any wider criteria (for example, 'old' equality of outcome) or parts of system (for example, trade-offs such as that between primary and secondary education). Finally, developments in the early months of the government's second term are examined. This brings the picture up to date (to early 2002), and allows some speculation about the evolving shape of welfare in the future.

The initial chapters provide a broad contextual examination of welfare reforms. Chapters Two to Five focus on cross-cutting areas such as social justice, accountability, independent welfare provision and family policy. In Chapters Six to Eleven, the focus moves to individual service areas such as housing, health, education, social care, social security and criminal justice. Finally, a concluding chapter brings together some of the main conclusions contributing to the evaluation of the New Labour government's welfare reforms of its first term.

References

Blair, T. (1998) *The third way*, London: Fabian Society.

Bosanquet, N. and Townsend, P. (eds) (1980) *Labour and equality: A Fabian study of Labour in power, 1974-79*, London: Heinemann.

Boyne, G. (1999) 'Processes, performance and Best Value in local government', *Local Government Studies*, vol 29, no 3, pp 1-15.

Boyne, G., Farrell, C., Law, J., Powell, M. and Walker, R. (2003: forthcoming) *Evaluating public management reforms*, Buckingham: Open University Press.

Bradshaw, J. (1972) 'The concept of social need', *New Society*, 30 March, pp 640-3.

Brindle, D. (1999) 'Minister warns over poor social service', *The Guardian*, 24 November.

Budge, I., Robertson, D. and Hearl, D. (eds) (1987) *Ideology, strategy and party movement*, Cambridge: Cambridge University Press.

Burchardt, T. and Hills, J. (1999) 'Public expenditure and the public/private mix', in M. Powell (ed) *New Labour, new welfare state?: The 'third way' in British social policy*, Bristol: The Policy Press, pp 29-49.

Burden, T., Cooper, C. and Petrie, S. (2000) *'Modernising' social policy: Unravelling New Labour's welfare reforms*, Aldershot: Ashgate.

Butler, D., Adonis, A. and Travers, T. (1994) *Failure in British government: The politics of the Poll Tax*, Oxford: Oxford University Press.

Carrier, J. and Kendall, I. (1998) *Health and the National Health Service*, London: Athlone Press.

Carter, N., Klein, R. and Day. P. (1992) *How organisations measure success*, London: Routledge.

Chen, H. (1990) *Theory-driven evaluation*, London: Sage Publications.

Clarke, A. (1999) *Evaluation research*, London: Sage Publications.

Critical Social Policy (2001) Special Issue on 'In and against New Labour', vol 21, no 4.

Crosland, C.A.R. (1964) *The future of socialism* (abridged edition, first published 1956), London: Jonathan Cape.

Davies, H., Nutley, S. and Smith, P. (eds) (2000) *What works?: Evidence-based policy and practice in public services*, Bristol: The Policy Press.

Day, P. and Klein, R. (2001) *Auditing the auditors*, London: Nuffield Trust/The Stationery Office.

DETR (Department of the Environment, Transport and the Regions) (1998) *Modernising local government: Improving local services through Best Value*, London: DETR.

DoH (Department of Health) (1997) *The new NHS*, London: The Stationery Office.

DoH (1999a) 'New figures give picture of clinical care in the NHS', Press Release 99/355, 16 June.

DoH (1999b) 'Figures must be used to benchmark and identify areas for improvement', Press Release 99/690, 24 November.

DoH (2000) *The NHS Plan*, London: The Stationery Office.

DSS (Department for Social Security) (1998) *A new contract for welfare: New ambitions for our country*, London: The Stationery Office.

Easton, D. (1965) *A systems approach to political life*, New York, NY: John Wiley.

Exworthy, M. and Powell, M. (2000) 'Variations on a theme: New Labour, health inequalities and policy failure', in A. Hann (ed) *Analysing health policy*, Aldershot: Avebury, pp 45-62.

Fairclough, N. (2000) *New Labour, new language?*, London: Routledge.

George, V. and Wilding, P. (1985) *Ideology and social welfare*, London: Routledge and Kegan Paul.

Glennerster, H. (1999) 'A third way?', in H. Dean and R. Woods (eds) *Social Policy Review 11*, Luton: Social Policy Association, pp 28-44.

Glennerster, H. (2001) 'Social policy', in A. Seldon (ed) *The Blair effect*, London: Little, Brown & Company, pp 383-403.

Glennerster, H. and Hills, J. (eds) (1998) *The state of welfare*, Oxford: Oxford University Press.

Green, D. and Benedict, I. (2001) *Health care in France and Germany: Lessons for the UK*, London: Civitas.

Harris, R. and Seldon, A. (1979) *Over-ruled on welfare*, London: IEA.

Hay, C. (1999) *The political economy of New Labour*, Manchester: Manchester University Press.

Hennessy, P. (1992) *Never again: Britain 1945-51*, London: Jonathan Cape.

Hill, M. and Bramley, G. (1986) *Analysing social policy*, Oxford: Basil Blackwell.

HM Treasury (1998a) *Modern public services for Britain*, London: The Stationery Office.

HM Treasury (1998b) *Public services for the future*, London: The Stationery Office.

Hofferbert, R. and Budge, I. (1992) 'The party mandate and the Westminster model', *British Journal of Political Science*, vol 22, pp 151-82.

Hood, C., James, O., Jones, G., Scott, C. and Travers, T. (1999) *Regulation inside government*, Oxford: Oxford University Press.

Hughes, G., Mears, R. and Winch, C. (1996) 'An inspector calls?', *Policy & Politics*, vol 25, no 3, pp 299-313.

Klein, R. (2000) 'From evidence-based medicine to evidence-based policy?', *Journal of Health Services Research and Policy*, vol 5, no 2, pp 65-6.

Knapp, M. (1984) *The economics of social care*, Oxford: Martin Robertson.

Labour Party (1997) *New Labour because Britain deserves better* (Election Manifesto), London: Labour Party.

Le Grand, J. and Bartlett, W. (eds) (1993) *Quasi-markets and social policy*, Basingstoke: Macmillan.

Le Grand, J. and Robinson, R. (eds) (1984) *The economics of social problems*, Basingstoke: Macmillan.

Le Grand, J., Mays, N. and Mulligan, J.-A. (eds) (1998) *Learning from the NHS internal market*, London: King's Fund.

Leonard, D. (ed) (1999) *Crosland and New Labour*, Basingstoke: Macmillan.

Levin, P. (1997) *Making social policy*, Buckingham: Open University Press.

Levitas, R. (1998) *The inclusive society?*, Basingstoke: Macmillan.

Lister, R. (1998) 'From equality to social inclusion: New Labour and the welfare state', *Critical Social Policy*, vol 18, no 2, pp 215-25.

Lister, R. (2000) 'To RIO via the Third Way', *Renewal*, vol 8, no 4, pp 9-20.

Marsh, D. and Rhodes, R. (eds) (1992) *Implementing Thatcherite policies*, Buckingham: Open University Press.

Newman, J. (2000) 'Beyond the new public management? Modernizing public services', in J. Clarke, S. Gewirtz and E. McLaughlin (eds) *New managerialism, new welfare?*, London: Sage Publications, pp 45-61.

Parsons, W. (1995) *Public policy*, Aldershot: Edward Elgar.

Pawson, R. and Tilley, N. (1997) *Realistic evaluation*, London: Sage Publications.

Phillips, C., Palfrey, C. and Thomas, P. (1994) *Evaluating health and social care*, Basingstoke: Macmillan.

Plant, R., Lesser, H. and Taylor-Gooby, P. (1980) *Political philosophy and social welfare*, London: Routledge and Kegan Paul.

Pollitt, C., Girre, X. and Lonsdale, J. (1999) *Performance or compliance?*, Oxford: Oxford University Press.

Powell, M. (1997) *Evaluating the National Health Service*, Buckingham: Open University Press.

Powell, M. (ed) (1999) *New Labour, new welfare state?: The 'third way' in British social policy*, Bristol: The Policy Press.

Powell, M. (2000) 'Something old, something new, something borrowed, something blue', *Renewal*, vol 8, no 4, pp 21-31.

Powell, M., Boyne, G. and Ashworth, R. (2001) 'Towards a geography of people poverty and place poverty', *Policy & Politics*, vol 29, no 3, pp 243-58.

Prime Minister (1998) *The Government's Annual Report 97/98*, London: The Stationery Office.

Prime Minister (1999) *Modernising government*, London: The Stationery Office.

Prime Minister (2000) *The Government's Annual Report 99/00*, London: The Stationery Office.

Rose, R. (1984) *Do parties make a difference?*, London: Macmillan.

Seldon, A. (2001) 'The net Blair Effect', in A. Seldon (ed) *The Blair effect*, London: Little, Brown & Company, pp 593-600.

Timmins, N. (2001) *The five giants* (2nd edn), London: HarperCollins.

Topf, R. (1994) 'Party manifestos', in A. Heath, R. Jowell and J. Curtice (eds) *Labour's last chance?*, Aldershot: Dartmouth, pp 149-72.

Townsend, P. and Bosanquet, N. (eds) (1972) *Labour and inequality*, London: Fabian Society.

Toynbee, P. and Walker, D. (2001) *Did things get better?*, Harmondsworth: Penguin.

Walker, A. and Walker, C. (eds) (1997) *Divided Britain*, London: CPAG.

Walker, R. (ed) (1999) *Ending child poverty: Popular welfare for the 21st century*, Bristol: The Policy Press.

Wolman, H. (1981) 'The determinants of program success and failure', *Journal of Public Policy*, vol 1, no 4, pp 433-64.

TWO

New Labour and social justice

Martin Powell[1]

Introduction

Equality and social justice are central concepts to social policy (for example, Weale, 1978, 1983; Plant et al, 1980; Le Grand, 1982; Edwards, 1987; Powell, 1995) and Old Labour (for example, Townsend and Bosanquet, 1972; Bosanquet and Townsend, 1980; Hattersley, 1987; Sullivan, 1999). It has been claimed that New Labour's third way has diluted its social justice and equality agenda. However, White (1999, p 168) notes that a fundamental weakness of much third-way philosophising lies in the tendency to regard basic concepts such as 'fairness' and 'social justice' as having self-evident and clear, unequivocal meanings.

This chapter explores the social justice of New Labour's social policy. After outlining social justice in the context of social policy and New Labour respectively, it illustrates the government's social justice agenda in its own terms and (briefly) in the wider extrinsic sense.

Social policy and social justice

There are two major problems in applying social justice to social policy. First, social justice is generally undertheorised, and sometimes even undefined. It is simply a 'good thing', and whatever supports the author's (often undefined or vague) view of social justice is regarded positively. In short, with the major exception of Hayek (1976), who regards social justice as a 'mirage' or an entirely empty and meaningless term (Plant et al, 1980, pp 58-62; George and Wilding, 1985, p 25; Lund, 2002, pp 4-6), everyone is in favour of (their view) of social justice and against social injustice.

Second, there have been few attempts to bridge the divide between the two cultures of the philosophical and empirical worlds (Miller, 1976; Le Grand, 1991; but see Phelps Brown, 1991; Powell et al, 2001). Many discussions of social justice show considerable conceptual elegance (for example, Phillips, 1999; Callinicos, 2000; Dworkin, 2000), but little empirical application. There are few examples of a "moral scrutiny of a policy practice" (Edwards, 1987). Edwards (1987, p 1) argues that there is a wide gap in British academic and non-academic thinking between the substance of social policies on the one hand and moral thought on the other. All too rarely are social policies and the ideas behind them subjected to critical moral thought. And all too often the substance of policy has been the 'football' between one unthinking political reaction and another.

Although 'social justice' and 'equality' are often used interchangeably, it is important to differentiate the terms. At a simple level, social justice may be compatible with some versions of equality but not with others. Aristotle made a distinction between arithmetic and proportional equality (see, for example, Fitzpatrick, 2001). Arithmetic simply divides a cake into *n* slices. This simple equality has relevance for issues such as votes – 'one person one vote'. Proportional equality, on the other hand, divides the cake unequally in accordance with some criteria of distribution. One person may 'need' a larger slice of cake because they are hungry, or 'deserve' a larger slice because they have been good. Some writers prefer to describe this in the language of social justice, while others (for example, Sen, 1992) use the language of equality. As Saunders (1990) puts it, inequality is not necessarily unfair, or in the terms of the Commission on Social Justice (1994) there are justifiable inequalities.

At the risk of considerable oversimplification, it is possible to contrast two different theories of justice. The work of Rawls (1972) has been variously termed 'patterned', 'justice as contract', or 'justice as fairness', while the work of Nozick (1974) may be seen in terms of process, procedural or justice as entitlement (Miller, 1976; Weale, 1978, 1983; Plant et al, 1980; Callinicos, 2000; Dworkin, 2000; Drake, 2001; Fitzpatrick, 2001; Lund, 2001b, 2002).

Rawls' (1972) theory of justice attempts to justify the 'patterned' approach to distribution. To establish the basic principles of justice, Rawls constructs a hypothetical 'original position' in which individuals are placed behind a 'veil of ignorance'. Rawls claims that participants will agree two principles in priority order. The first principle is that each person is to have an equal right to the most extensive total system of equal basic liberties compatible with a similar system of liberty for all. The second principle is that social and economic inequalities are to be arranged so that they are both (a) to the greatest benefit of the least advantaged, and (b) attached to offices and positions open to all under conditions of fair equality of opportunity.

Nozick (1974) argues against any patterned principle of distribution. In its most extreme version (which has subsequently been modified: Nozick, 1990), he argues that taxation is on a par with forced labour or the appropriation of bodily parts. In effect, this violates people, giving other people partial property rights in them which is incompatible with the principle of respect for persons. Nozick argues for a historical entitlement conception of justice that is the only conception compatible with the principle of inviolability. If holdings have been justly acquired (justice in acquisition), an individual is entitled to his or her holdings and has property rights in them. These can be freely transferred, but not compulsorily redistributed.

The most familiar conception of social justice is probably 'patterned'. This means that goods and services are distributed according to certain criteria.

Commentators have pointed to a wide variety of distributive criteria (Miller, 1976; Plant et al, 1980; Weale, 1983; Drake, 2001; Fitzpatrick, 2001). Edwards (1987, pp 46-9) surveys 11 writers on social justice, concluding that only need and deserts are mentioned by all 11 writers. Patterned distributions simply require information on the relevant end-state. For example, perhaps the best-known patterned distribution is the Communist Manifesto's to each according to his or her need. Process distributions, on the other hand, require some knowledge of how people came to be in the end-state. Two people may have an identical level of need, but it might be decided that one should be helped while the other should not. Le Grand (1991) sets out the case that equity depends on the level of choice behind decisions. Similarly, Dworkin (2001) advances the principles that people's fates should be, so far as governments can achieve this, insensitive to who they are but, again as far as governments can achieve this, sensitive to the choices they have made. There are still, of course, big questions about these issues, such as what constitute 'choices' and how to treat children of parents who make poor choices. However, in polar terms, there are two sets of issues focusing on the existence of inequalities and the rationale for those inequalities.

One approach to these complex issues is through the work of Walzer, who claims that "different political arrangements enforce, and different ideologies justify, different distributions of membership, power, honor, ritual eminence, divine grace, kinship and love, knowledge, wealth, physical security, work and leisure, rewards and punishments, and a host of goods more narrowly and materially conceived ..." (1985, p 30). This multiplicity of goods is matched by a multiplicity of distributive procedures, agents and criteria. Walzer focuses on different spheres of justice, and on complex rather than simple equality. No citizen's standing in one sphere or with regard to one social good can be undercut by their standing in some other sphere, with regard to some other good. For example, X may be chosen over Y for political office, but X's office should give him or her no advantage over Y in any other sphere – such as superior medical care or access to better schools for their children and so on. In general, "No social good x should be distributed to men and women who possess some other good y merely because they possess y and without regard to the meaning of x" (p 20). Fair shares therefore involve two different questions: the range of goods that ought to be shared, and the distributive principles appropriate within the relevant sphere (p 75). However, Walzer admits that he simply provides a general structure that still leave problems of judgements and of detail, with no a priori stipulation of what needs ought to be recognised, nor any a priori way of determining appropriate levels of provision.

New Labour and social justice

In Britain the Labour Party has tended to use more of an equality, rather than a social justice, discourse. The main points of reference have tended to be to classic texts such as Tawney (1964) and Crosland (1964) that discuss equality (see, for example, Hattersley, 1987; Franklin, 1997; Leonard, 1999; Sullivan, 1999). However, New Labour does tend to draw more on a social justice discourse (CSJ, 1994; Franklin, 1998). Blair (1998, p 1) claims that the third way is "passionate in its commitment to social justice". Moreover, the third way reconciles the false choice between social justice and economic efficiency, which are two sides of the same coin (CSJ, 1994; cf Blair, 1998; Brown, 1999; Blair and Schroeder, 1999). Many commentators argue that New Labour has diluted the party's traditional equality and social justice agenda (for example, Cohen, 1997; Daniel, 1997; Callinicos, 2000). Le Grand (1998, p 27) claims that unlike social democracy, the third way is not egalitarian. There is undoubtedly a commitment to social justice, but it is the kind of social justice that relies on ensuring minimum standards and equality of opportunity rather than on redistribution and equality of outcome. Dworkin (2001, p 172) writes that equality is the endangered species of political ideals, with left-of-centre politicians rejecting the very idea of equality. Once minimum standards are met, government has no further obligation to make people equal in anything. However, the recent debate on social justice and equality is more complex and multidimensional than these claims suggest.

A useful starting point is the Commission on Social Justice (CSJ). This was a body set up by the then Labour leader, John Smith, as a semi-independent, arm's-length temporary think-tank to generate new thinking for debate. According to the report of the CSJ (1994), the values of social justice are: equal worth of all citizens; their equal rights to be able to meet their basic needs; the need to spread opportunities and life chances as widely as possible; and the requirement that we reduce and where possible eliminate unjustified inequalities. Social justice is seen as a hierarchy of four ideas. The most important element of equal worth is regarded largely in terms of political and civil liberties. The second level is mainly concerned with social citizenship. The third level involves the distribution of opportunity, *as well as* redistribution (my emphasis). The fourth level stresses that social justice does not mean taking things away from successful people and giving to the unsuccessful. In other words, redistribution is for a purpose, not for its own sake. In this changing world with its economic, social and political revolutions, we face three alternative futures. The first scenario is associated with the 'Levellers' or the 'old left', who seek social justice primarily through the tax and benefit system. The second is associated with the 'Deregulators' or 'new right', who see the free market as delivering social justice. The Commission's preferred alternative involved the 'Investors', who combine the ethics of community with the dynamics of a market economy. Investment in people's human and social capital is the top priority. Subsequent chapter headings in the report are concerned with investment, opportunity, security and responsibility.

In the 1996 John Smith Memorial Lecture, Gordon Brown, then Labour's Shadow Chancellor, argued that "the essence of equality is equality of opportunity" (1999, p 161). A few weeks later he claimed that "The search for equalities of outcome, and even to talk as if that is the aim of the Labour Party, has led us up the wrong roads. The pursuit of equality of outcome is someone else's nightmare about socialism rather than a genuine socialist dream. I would prefer to look at equality in terms of opportunities for all" (in Kellner, 1999, p 161). Subsequently, Brown (1999) has developed this argument. He claimed that "our commitment to equality is as strong as ever", and rooted in the views of Crosland (see Plant, 1999a, 1999b; Callinicos, 2000). Brown (1999, p 37) sought to translate, into the context of the 1990s, Crosland's idea of democratic equality – a concept that offers more than equality of opportunity, but something other than equality of outcome. In other words, Brown argues for a 'radical' or 'maximalist' version of equality of opportunity. We reject – as Crosland did – both an unrealisable equality of outcome and a narrow view of opportunity. Indeed, we reject equality of outcome not because it is too radical but because it is neither desirable nor feasible.

According to Blair (1998, p 3), four values are essential to a just society: equal worth, opportunity for all, responsibility and community. Social justice must be founded on the equal worth of each individual, whatever their background, capability, creed or race. Talent and effort should be encouraged to flourish in all quarters, and governments must act decisively to end discrimination and prejudice. Opportunity is a key value in the new politics. At worst, the left has stifled opportunity in the name of abstract equality. The progressive left must robustly tackle the obstacles to true equality of opportunity. Blair and Schroder (1999) assert that fairness and social justice, liberty and equality of opportunity, solidarity and responsibility to others – these are timeless values. Social democracy will never sacrifice them, but the third way aims to combine social justice and economic dynamism. The promotion of social justice was sometimes confused with the imposition of equality of outcome. The result was neglect of the importance of rewarding effort and responsibility, and the association of social democracy with conformity and mediocrity rather than the celebration of creativity, diversity and excellence. Our objective is the widening of equality of opportunity regardless of race, age or disability, to fight social exclusion and ensure equality between men and women. Blair's speech to the Labour Party Conference in 1999 was a "morality tale based on the life chances of two babies" (Rawnsley, 2001, p 319). This was used to illustrate Blair's discussion of 'true equality', which was seen in terms of equal worth and opportunity. New Labour represented the 'forces of modernity' standing against the 'forces of conservatism', invoked 17 times in the speech, which were blamed for everything from stopping women rising in the workplace to keeping bright children out of university. The speech drew a dividing line through the media, attacked by the right-wing press, but termed by *The Guardian* as Blair's "best yet as leader" (Rawnsley, 2001, p 321). According to Blair (2001), social justice remains an important part (or half?) of the third way, which combines values traditionally associated with Europe, such as fairness and solidarity, with the economic dynamism traditionally associated with the US. He points to the challenge of inequality and social mobility. Tackling exclusion is not only about preventing the development of an underclass. It is also about developing genuine social mobility throughout society: opening up the professions, rewarding merit and fostering entrepreneurship. In his introduction to the 2001 Election Manifesto, 'Ambitions for Britain', Blair states that "My passion is to continue the modernisation of Britain in favour of hard-working families, so that all our children, wherever they live, whatever their background, have an equal chance to benefit from the opportunities our country has to offer and to share in its wealth ... to extend opportunity to all". He offers a deal: "if you put in a fair day's work, the government will ensure that you are able to support yourself and your family" (Labour Party, 2001). According to Lister (2001a), Blair has declared meritocracy as "the true radical second term agenda", but has conceded that on its own meritocracy is insufficient. It needs to be coupled with recognition both of "talent in all its forms" and of the "equal worth of all our citizens". This has been described, as claimed by Lister, as the 'new egalitarianism'.

Labour Minister Margaret Hodge (2000) suggests that equality is a central part of our vision for a better society and should form a central theme in our programme for a second term. She states that after necessarily securing public confidence over fiscal prudence, in 1999 Blair was able to make equality a central theme of his conference speech (see Rawnsley, 2001). According to Hodge, the underpinning context for the modern equality agenda is our belief that economic prosperity and social justice (a term we use to encompass equality) are not competing objectives, but are inextricably linked ambitions. She argues that this is a comfortable thesis that appeals to middle Britain, yet it is also 'pretty convincing'. In contrast,

> ... the Old Labour mantra that income redistribution of itself creates equality was flawed, and it has even less pertinence in the global economy. Redistribution of wealth alone will not deliver equality – either equality of respect and worth, or equality of opportunity and the ability to enjoy equal access to social and material goods. As poverty is linked to other disadvantages, some redistribution is required but this should not only be from the tax and benefit system, but also through public service programmes or modern forms of redistribution. We need to win the argument for tax and spend – but taxing fairly and spending efficiently. (p 35)

> A modern redistributive principle is not about 'punishing' the rich by curtailing ambitions and aspirations. It is not about crippling tax burdens on successful entrepreneurs. We are redistributing tax, but in a new and different way, that is contingent on the individual who is able to work getting a job. We are evolving a new instrument, as we strive for equality based on the hand up, not the hand out. Discrimination based on race, gender and age. The Labour Party has always believed that we could create equality through public services. (pp 36-7)

Hodge concludes that equality is our core vision and what binds New and Old Labour together (pp 39-40; but see, for example, Cohen, 1997; Callinicos, 2000).
Giddens (1998) considers that strong egalitarianism was a key defining

characteristic of 'old-style' social democracy. The pursuit of equality has been a major concern of all social democrats, including the British Labour Party, and is still at the core of what remains of the left–right division. However, equality is a relative concept. We have to ask: equality between whom, of what and in what degree? (p 40). Equality remains a key value of the third way, but in the sense of equality as inclusion. Similarly, there is still a role for redistribution, but redistribution of possibilities rather than redistribution of resources. Giddens is clear that equality of opportunity/meritocracy alone is not tenable. He expands on the 'question of inequality' (2000, ch 4). Social democrats must revise not only their approach to, but also their concept of, equality in the wake of the decline of socialism. There is no future for the 'egalitarianism at all costs' that absorbed leftists for so long. He quotes Walzer that "simple equality of that sort is the bad utopianism of the old left" (p 85). The contemporary left needs to develop a dynamic, life-chances approach to equality, placing the prime stress on equality of opportunity, but his emphasis on equality of opportunity still presumes a redistribution of wealth and income. The traditional social democratic solution of taking from the rich and giving to the poor can and should be applied today. However, this is not a simple question. There is the problem of defining the 'rich'. It is no longer feasible or desirable to have very steeply graduated income tax of the sort that existed in many countries up to 30 years ago. Finally, Giddens (2001, p 8) reiterates his view that we must not give up on the objective of creating an egalitarian society. The pursuit of equality has to be at the core of third-way politics. However, he acknowledges that it is on this issue that many on the old left express their strongest reservations about third-way politics.

There have been many criticisms of these moves. However, they are often conducted at a fairly high level of abstraction, with a loose grip on conceptual definitions, policy details and the historical record. For example, there is a potential paradox that while some proponents such as Blair and Brown and critics such as Hattersley claim that New Labour has rejected equality of outcome, other commentators argue that New Labour's linking of the old left with equality of outcome was a caricature (for example, Lund, 2001a, 2002).

As I mentioned earlier, there is no one unequivocal New Labour or third-way statement on social justice. There are clearly some variations between these accounts. For example, as Driver and Martell (2000) note, Giddens is more egalitarian than Blair, and launches a stern attack on the inadequacy of meritocracy and equality of opportunity alone. Nevertheless, they are sufficiently similar to draw out some of the main themes. First, there have been moves from a general discourse based on equality to one based on social justice. Lund (2001a) argues that although 'social justice' and 'equality' were used interchangeably throughout the 20th century, New Labour has attempted to establish a clear distinction between the two concepts. This is often seen in terms of moves from equality to inclusion (Levitas, 1998; Lister, 1998). Certainly, 'social inclusion' is an important component of recent rhetoric (see, for example, SEU, 1998; DSS, 1999; Howarth et al, 2001; see Lund, 2002). However, this disguises more complex shifts. At one level, this may be seen in terms of spheres of justice and the recognition that equality is complex. Paid work is central to New Labour, and inclusion through work in what Levitas (1998) has termed a 'social integrationist discourse' (SID) is more important than equality per se. Blair (1998, p 12) states that we seek a diverse but inclusive society. According to the Labour MP Tony Wright, 'liberal socialism' will be "diverse, pluralistic and variegated, both politically and economically. It will be egalitarian enough to be socially inclusive, so that all its citizens are within reach of each other, but this will not be confused with identify of treatment or uniformity of provision" (1996, p 143). There is tolerance of greater inequalities in income, provided that incomes are above a basic floor and that the larger incomes are deserved (see Lund, 2001a, 2001b). As Peter Mandelson puts it, New Labour has no quarrel with rich rewards when they result from "genuine initiative and creative dynamism" (in Driver and Martell, 1998, p 90). Goodhart (1999) points to the problem of the old fixation with the gap between rich and poor. He argues that a third-way theory of fairness should state that the gap does not matter – or at least that it matters less than the life chances of the people at the bottom. If these are rising steadily, then it does not matter that the rich are getting even richer. Marquand (1998, p 19) argues that New Labour is unshocked by huge and growing income disparities. It sees no reason why successful meritocrats should not enjoy the full fruits of their success: it is for widening opportunity, not for redistributing reward. It wants inclusion or integration, and is relaxed about winners and losers. In other words, the stress is on 'fair' outcomes rather than equal outcomes. It is unclear to what extent this is distinctive from the old left. Only George Bernard Shaw advocated equal incomes (for example, Daniel, 1997, p 13; Drake, 2001, p 49). Old Labour advocated *more equal*, not equal incomes. The problem is that while there has been much philosophising, more concrete suggestions such as the level of income equality and the level and type of taxation have rarely been justified. The 'New Liberals' (for example, Lund, 2001a, 2001b) and the Labour Party (for example, Jay, 1938; Durbin, 1940; Dell, 2000) were always more in favour of the taxation of 'unearned income', such as that from land or inheritance, than 'earned income'. For example, Crosland argued that the Labour Party should 'bash the rich' by a wealth tax, a gifts tax, higher death duties and the public ownership of land (in Dell, 2000, pp 404-5). Even the 'penal' tax rates of the 1970s – when Chancellor Denis Healy promised to 'squeeze the rich until the pips squeaked' – saw higher rates for 'unearned' than 'earned' incomes. Although Crosland is correctly characterised as favouring progressive taxation, he was aware of the limits of this strategy and believed more in increasing the social dividend through the engine of economic growth (see, for example, Sullivan, 1999; Dell, 2000). Orwell (1982) considered a ratio of maximum to minimum tax-free income as 10 to one. Within these limits some sense of equality is possible: "A man with £3 a week and a man with £1,500 a year can feel themselves fellow creatures, which the Duke of Westminster and the sleepers on the Embankment benches cannot" (p 107). Miller (1997, p 97) suggests that a society with top incomes of £80,000 and bottom incomes of £10,000 could be socially egalitarian in circumstances of equal citizenship and Walzerian complex equality.

However, it is possible to challenge Lund's (2001a) claim that New Labour's 'model of the citizen-worker' is at odds with Walzer's idea of different spheres of justice. Lund claims that 'citizens' are to be valued in terms of a solitary 'sphere of justice', with loss of autonomy, financial exclusion and potential stigmatisation the consequence for those unable to achieve the elevated status of 'worker-citizen'. Indeed, it can be argued that New Labour's strategy more clearly separates the existing spheres. Marshall's (1963) social citizenship aimed progressively to divorce real and money incomes. His discussion of the difficulties of combining the principles of social equality and the price system for social services in general and legal aid in particular may be seen in terms of spheres of justice. Similarly, Durbin (1940) differentiated the 'relevant spheres' of ameliorative measures of the social services and the egalitarian measures primarily of taxation. For Marshall, the welfare state was to secure equality of status and qualitative class abatement or class fusion: "the extension of the social services is not primarily a means of equalizing incomes ... equality of status is more important than equality of income" (1963, p 107). It may be possible to challenge Marshall's optimism, but not his clarity. Recent formulations such as civic liberalism (Kaus, 1992), social equality or equality of status (Miller, 1997), equality of access (Kellner, 1999) and civic equality (Prowse, 2000) are clearly linked to the writings of Tawney, Marshall and Crosland in the traditional strategy of equality of the welfare state (Powell, 1995). Services such as education have been central for previous socialists such as Tawney on public schools and Crosland on grammar schools. Concentration on work and cash incomes misses the importance of the 'social wage' of in-kind benefits of public services (CSJ, 1994; DSS, 1998; Powell et al, 2001). When they have focused on services, critics have concentrated on the moves to selection in education, but tended to neglect New Labour's pledges of reducing health inequalities: *if* the latter are achieved, a redistribution of mortality can be seen as more radical and important than increasing benefits by a few pounds. However, critics might point out that the extra years of life produced might be spent in poverty.

Second, although the terms are not fully defined, there have been moves from equality of outcome towards equality of opportunity. However, it is stressed that this is not simply the liberal removal of legal barriers but a 'real', 'maximalist', or 'democratic' equality of opportunity that is in line with some past left thinking. Moreover, this is regarded as 'dynamic' rather than a 'once-off' (for example, Brown, 1999). According to the CSJ (1994, p 119), "equality of opportunity is often dismissed as a weak aspiration. But if every child and every adult is to fulfil his or her potential, we need a social and economic revolution". Simple assertions that New Labour has abandoned Croslandite equality are wide of the mark (for example, Plant, 1999a, 1999b). As Driver and Martell (1998, p 80) note, Crosland's view of equality was by no means straightforward. Certainly, he considered liberal equality of opportunity as insufficient, but also rejected equality of outcome. He desired greater equality in terms of income and wealth, and in public services, but warned that a "definite limit exists to the degree of equality which is desirable ... but where en route, before we reach some drab extreme, we shall wish to stop, I have no idea" (in Driver and Martell, 1998, p 81). As Dell (2000, pp 229-30) argues, Labour's vague objective of 'equality' could mean a great variety of things. Moreover, there were usually differences between opposition intentions and achievements in governments: "Equality remained the proclaimed but neglected objective of Labour governments" (p 230; cf Townsend and Bosanquet, 1972; Bosanquet and Townsend, 1980).

Third, and linked, responsibility is seen as the other side of the coin from opportunity. At a seminar held under the auspices of the Smith Institute, Brown claimed that Smith believed passionately in equality of opportunity, which had to be distinguished from equality of outcome. Equality of opportunity involved personal responsibility; it involved rewards by merit. It did not involve the degree of state control that a policy for equality of outcome would involve. Brown continued that Smith found equality of outcome unacceptable because it assumed that people would eventually have the same outcomes and the same wealth, somehow imposed by a centralised state authority. Brown concluded "I think that this is where the debate has been stuck for the last ten years" (in Stevenson, 1999, p 5). Some observers might wonder both whether Smith's views have been distorted and what debate Brown has been following. However, the importance of responsibility in the form of a 'contract' or 'deal' is central to New Labour. It is most developed in the 'New Deal' or 'welfare to work', but also features in other areas such as housing tenancies, community sentences and parental responsibilities (Dwyer, 2000; Lund, 2002). Both carrots and sticks feature in the deals, and New Labour will not hesitate to apply sanctions to the 'irresponsible' who fail in their obligations. Cohen (1997, p 46, fn) claims the documents associated with the CSJ cite Rawls critically and Nozick positively. Buckler and Dolowitz trace the "shift of emphasis from guaranteed outcomes to procedural fairness as the basis for redistribution" (2000, p 302), and the "commitment to procedural rather than patterned justice" (p 310). However, reciprocity and conditionality feature in both the new communitarian and the old ethical socialist agenda. According to White (1997, 1999), the reciprocity principle has played an important part in the socialist and egalitarian thought of figures such as Laski, Tawney and Crosland, as well as being central to the Beveridge insurance mechanism (but see Driver and Martell, 1998; Lund, 2002 for different views on Crosland).

Intrinsic perspectives: the Annual Reports

One reason for the continuing debate about social justice and equality is its high level of abstraction. The relationship between discourse and policy is not always fully clear. For example, Old Labour's deeds did not always follow from its words. However, while New Labour's deeds are sometimes less than its words, at other times the reverse occurs.

There are some references to social justice and equality in the Annual Reports. The 1998/99 Annual Report aims for "one nation – united in fulfilling the ambitions of all our people" (Prime Minister, 1999, p 4). In the 1999/2000 Annual Report, Blair states that "The central purpose of the Government is to provide opportunity and security in a world of change and to do it in a way that benefits the majority, not just a few. To extend opportunity to all, in return for responsibilities from all" (Prime Minister, 2000, p 3).

At one level, all the Manifesto commitments are concerned with social justice. However, there are few explicit and specific commitments. The few exceptions include: an efficient but fair student maintenance grant scheme (pledge number 22); a fair grant systems for local authorities (142); and a fair deal for fishing in the EU (158). However, these are fairly meaningless, as 'fair' is used merely in the sense of 'good'. Governments would hardly aim for an unfair grant system. Moreover, students, local authorities and fishermen may not agree with the fairness of the pledges.

Nevertheless, it is possible to classify some pledges in terms of their links with New Labour's social justice discourse. Of course, some pledges may be classified under more than one heading:

- *Opportunity:* introduce Individual Savings Accounts (ISAs) (33); stakeholder pensions (97).
- *Opportunity to acquire human capital:* early learning centres (4); national Grid for Learning (7); pilot literacy summer schools (9), and every child leaves school with a reading age of 11+ (10); create University for Industry (23); broaden A-levels/upgrade vocational courses (24); Individual Leaning Accounts (25); any under-18 in work to have the right to study (49); set up National Endowment for Science, Technology and the Arts (120) 'to promote talent, innovation and creativity'.
- *Opportunity and work:* introduce a national minimum wage (46); get 250,000 long-term unemployed people back to work (47); tackle long-term unemployment (48); help single parents back to work (50); national childcare strategy (83).
- *Responsibility:* cut down on benefit fraud (52); introduce parental safety orders (75).
- *Inclusion through services/civic equality:* increase proportion of GDP spent on education (1); guaranteed nursery education for all four year-olds (3); divert £1 billion to health, education and environment (122).
- *Redistribution/targeting (social and spatial):* introduce Education Action Zones (11); no increase in basic and top rates of income tax (26), introduce starting rate of 10p income tax (27); cut VAT on fuel to 5% (28); introduce Employment Action Zones (51); help for the poorest pensioners (95); retain State Earnings Related Pensions (SERPS)/second state pension (96); citizenship pensions for carers (98); improve distribution of lottery funds (123); attack causes of

urban decline (137); shift overseas aid resources towards the poor countries (174).

The success of these pledges is reviewed in each contribution to this volume. However, it may be useful here to provide a brief commentary on the major themes.

There are some clear links between New Labour's pledges and policies and the CSJ Report. According to the CSJ (1994), four propositions run through our policy proposals: we must transform the welfare state from a safety net in times of trouble to a springboard for economic opportunity; we must radically improve access to education and training and invest in the talent of all our people; we must promote real choices across the life-cycle for men and women in the balance of employment, family, education, leisure and retirement; and we must reconstruct the social wealth of our country. There are also similarities in terms of more specific policy recommendations such as: universal pre-school education, basic skills, high achievement for every young person; training investment by employers; learning bank to support lifelong learning; an expansion of university education, with a new and fairer funding system; and an aim to reduce or eliminate health differences that result from factors which are both avoidable and unfair – it is essential that government sets clear goals for reducing health inequalities.

However, there are also some subtle but important differences. "Work is central to our lives. *Paid or unpaid*, it is the way in which we meet needs, create wealth and distribute resources" (CSJ 1994, p 151; my emphasis). The CSJ supports 'fair taxes'. This means that no one should pay 'punitive' levels of taxation – there can be no question of returning to the top tax rates of the 1970s – but a new top tax rate for 'very high earners', for instance, five times average earnings, or designed to affect only, say, 1% or 2% of taxpayers should be considered (pp 397-9). Finally, investors redistribute opportunities rather than *just* redistributing income (p 95; my emphasis).

Lister (2001b, p 65) states that the government has certainly pursued its opportunity agenda with zeal and can point to a range of policies that promote it. However, she argues that "Neither genuine equality of opportunity nor meaningful recognition of equal worth is achievable in our savagely unequal society" (p 66). This has clear parallels with Tawney's (1964) 'tadpole philosophy'. The problem is which inequalities are considered to be the most important, and what degrees of inequality are permitted before they become 'savage'. In terms of income inequality, New Labour has set floors through its paid work strategy. Making work pay is to be achieved through tax credits and the National Minimum Wage. However, there is less concern over ceilings, with little signs of more progressive taxation or a maximum wage. There are many policies to enhance opportunities through increasing human capital. New Labour has criticised the 'forces of conservatism' and the old elites, yet is in danger of being associated with a new elite (for example, Walden, 2001), surrounding itself with the offspring of the famous, friends and former colleagues, partners of insiders, and associated apparatchiks. For Thatcher, the outsider, the 'one of us' question is very different from that of Blair, the insider (cf Rawnsley, 2001). Some evidence from the US suggests that 'attractive' people earn more than 'ugly' people: does this mean that opportunity requires extensive NHS cosmetic surgery?

There are also obvious policy dimensions of responsibilities. They are most developed in the 'New Deal' or 'workfare'. Work for those who can, security for those who cannot implies no security for those who can but do not. The government will make work pay, and provide education and training, but will not hesitate to apply sanctions to the 'irresponsible' who do not take up their opportunities. There are less-developed versions of 'healthfare' (where a maternity grant is conditional on attendance with a health professional), 'crimefare' (where those who fail to carry out their community sentences will have their benefit reduced for a temporary period), and 'childfare' (where there are sanctions against parents whose children fail to attend school or are persistent offenders) (see Lund, 2002). An attack on benefit fraud may also be seen as part of the responsibility agenda (DSS, 1998; Field 2000). Labour phrases about 'hard working families who play by the rules' and the end of the 'something for nothing welfare state' draw on deeply entrenched views about the 'deserving' and 'undeserving' and fit easily into parts of popular discourse (see, for example, Dwyer, 2000). Some of this may be termed authoritarianism by the chattering classes, but perhaps less so by victims of racist graffiti and attacks, who have had the perpetrators evicted.

Commentators (for example, Levitas, 1998; Lister, 1998) have focused on inclusion through paid work, but have tended to neglect inclusion through public services or 'civic equality'. Policies in this area show a mixed picture. On the one hand, there are policies to reduce inequalities in service provision such as 'postcode prescribing' and clinical governance to level up service quality, in a 'one-nation NHS'. There is a policy aim to reduce health inequalities by 2010. On the other hand, devolution may lead to a 'four- (rather than one-) nation strategy' with, for example, moves towards free prescriptions for young people in Wales and towards free continuing care in Scotland. Critics argue that the old left agenda of equality in education by attacking public schools and grammar schools has been diluted. David Blunkett's promise as Secretary of State for Education of 'read my lips, no selection' became interpreted as 'no *more* selection', before being revealed as a 'joke' that many activists found distinctly unfunny. The problem is that as inequalities are addressed, they often reappear in more subtle forms. For example, Hobson states that "Ironically, before Old Labour (and Old Tory) destroyed the grammar schools, entry to Oxbridge was gradually being democratised" (1999, pp 171-2). In the heyday of the grammar schools in the 1950s and 1960s, increasing state school entry to Oxbridge was becoming a 'meritocracy'. However, with the demise of the grammar schools, this proportion has declined. James Callaghan, an elementary school boy, understood this better than Tony Crosland (Highgate School, Oxford student and don). A more recent example is that entrance to 'good' schools may be purchased through buying houses in the relevant catchment areas.

New Labour prefers to redistribute assets and endowments rather than cash. According to David Blunkett, "Too often the centre left has focused on income distribution as the measure of its success or failure without looking behind the statistics as to the real causes of inequality – inequality of skills, education, jobs and assets that people hold" (in Goodman, 2001, p 97). Moreover, linking with opportunity, it has termed saving as the 'four pillars of the welfare state' (Labour Party, 2001), and is considering matching savings for those on low incomes and granting 'babybonds' (see Chapter Ten of this volume; cf Ackerman and Alstott, 1999). This is necessarily a long-term agenda.

Extrinsic perspectives

Goodman (2001) argues that for a party that has had redistribution at its heart for most of its history, this is a government that has had few words to say about income inequality itself. However, as shown in other chapters, although New Labour talks little about fiscal redistribution, it has carried out some 'hidden', 'quiet' or 'backdoor' redistribution or 'redistribution by stealth'. In brief, the impact of New Labour's five budgets has been strongly progressive, and strongly skewed towards those with children. In other words, in the narrow sense, there has been some redistribution. However, while the distribution of net income in Blair's first three years was less regressive than the Thatcher governments, the Major years saw greater progressivity overall (Goodman, 2001). Put another way, while the poor benefited in absolute terms, they did not benefit in relative terms as much as the rich. In the wider sense, income inequality as shown by the Gini coefficient (both before and after housing costs) shows large increases in the 1980s, small dips in the mid-1990s and a rise for three years including the last year of Conservative and the first two years of Labour rule, followed by a slight fall in 1999/2000. "It remains the case that measured inequality was higher in 1999/2000 than before Labour came to power" (Goodman, 2001, p 93). This perhaps suggests the most pessimistic scenario of the early years of New Labour when it was staying within the inherited Conservative spending limits, and before the impact of many new measures can be detected. Nevertheless, it suggests that the efforts of government have to be set within the wider forces of inequality in the labour market.

Conclusion

Lister (2001b) notes that New Labour's redistribution by stealth is not sustainable in the long term, and advocates a 'social justice agenda'. However, one person's social justice agenda may be different from that of another. Answers to questions such as 'What do egalitarians want?' (White, 1997) and 'What kind of equality should the left pursue?' (Miller, 1997) tend to be addressed in negative rather than positive and in abstract rather than concrete terms (cf Kellner, 1999). It is not clear what has to be equalised to achieve 'equal opportunities' or which 'outcomes' should be equalised (see, for example, Hattersley, 1987; Franklin, 1997; Drake, 2001). At one level, commentators are correct that New Labour has sought to redefine social justice and equality. However, this can be overstated. Old Labour's social justice and equality agenda was by no means clear, consistent or coherent, with some gaps between words and deeds (for example, Dell, 2000). Similar claims can be made for New Labour. Just as the right oversimplifies the old left's views on equality (see, for example, Hattersley, 1987; Drake, 2001), critics may oversimplify New Labour's views. Brown (1999) stresses that New Labour's agenda must be credible. One obvious example is New Labour's perception of the practical politics of taxation. Labour pollster Philip Gould (1998, p 287) warned Blair that his focus groups suggested that large numbers think that a higher-rate tax band, even when set at £100,000, is a "tax on success", appearing "punitive rather than fair" (Gould, 1998, p 287). 'Taxation' receives one of the longest index entries in his book. Gould claims that winning the tax war was central: "we lost the 1992 election [when Shadow Chancellor John Smith argued for a tax rate of 50% for incomes of over £40,000] and won the 1997 one in large part because of tax" (p 284).

Leonard (2000) claims that third way politics has not yet decided whether inequality in itself is axiomatically bad; whether the gap in itself matters, or whether an increasing gap within an increasingly fluid social order that is rising in prosperity is acceptable. He writes that we must escape the fruitless opposition between equality of opportunity (a recipe for inequality) and equality of outcome (impossible and anti-aspirational), and begin to define an egalitarian agenda in a more nuanced way that recognises that different rules will apply to different spheres, and that the most pressing questions are access to life chances.

Although there are still debates at the philosophical level, more pressing matters concern policy issues. Contrary to some views, neither Old nor New Labour is a one-club golfer. They may select different clubs and, at times, appear to be playing on different courses. It is also clear that New Labour's scorecard must be viewed in the long term. They may still share beer and sandwiches or Sauvignon Blanc and canapes in the same clubhouse, but it is as yet premature to compare their scores.

Note

[1] I would like to thank Brian Lund and Robert Page for comments on an earlier version of this chapter, although in places I have not changed my position in response to their views.

References

Ackerman, B. and Alstott, A. (1999) *The stakeholder society*, New Haven, CT: Yale University Press.

Blair, T. (1998) *The third way*, London: Fabian Society.

Blair, T. (2001) 'Third way, phase two', *Prospect*, April.

Blair, T. and Schroder, G. (1999) *The third way [Die Neue Mitte]*, London: Labour Party.

Bosanquet, N. and Townsend, P. (eds) (1980) *Labour and equality: A Fabian study of Labour in power, 1974-79*, London: Heinemann.

Brown, G. (1999) 'Equality – then and now', in D. Leonard (ed) *Crosland and New Labour*, Basingstoke: Macmillan, pp 35-48.

Buckler, S. and Dolowitz, D. (2000) 'Theorizing the third way: New Labour and social justice', *Journal of Political Ideologies*, vol 5, no 3, pp 301-20.

Callinicos, A. (2000) *Equality*, Cambridge: Polity Press.

Cohen, G. (1997) 'Back to socialist basics', in J. Franklin (ed) *Equality*, London: IPPR, pp 29-47.

CSJ (Commission on Social Justice) (1994) *Social justice: Strategies for national renewal*, London: Vintage.

Crosland, C.A.R. (1964) *The future of socialism* (abridged edition, first published 1956), London: Jonathan Cape.

Daniel, C. (1997) 'Socialists and equality', in J. Franklin (ed) *Equality*, London: IPPR, pp 11-27.

Dell, E. (2000) *A strange eventful history*, London: HarperCollins.

Drake, R. (2001) *The principles of social policy*, Basingstoke: Palgrave.

Driver, S. and Martell, L (1998) *New Labour*, Cambridge: Polity Press.

Driver, S. and Martell, L. (2000) 'Left, right and third way', *Policy & Politics*, vol 28, no 2, pp 147-61.

DSS (Department for Social Security) (1998) *A new contract for welfare: New ambitions for our country*, London: The Stationery Office.

DSS (1999) *Opportunity for all: Tackling poverty and social exclusion*, London: The Stationery Office.

Durbin, E. (1940) *The politics of democratic socialism*, London: George Routledge & Sons.

Dworkin, R. (2000) *Sovereign virtue: The theory and practice of equality*, Cambridge, MA: Harvard University Press.

Dworkin, R. (2001) 'Does equality matter?', in A. Giddens (ed) *The global third way debate*, Cambridge: Polity Press, pp 172-7.

Dwyer, P. (2000) *Welfare rights and responsibilities: Contesting social citizenship*, Bristol: The Policy Press.

Edwards, J. (1987) *Positive discrimination, social justice and social policy: Moral scrutiny of a policy practice*, London: Tavistock.

Field, F. (2000) *The state of dependency: Welfare under Labour*, London: Social Market Foundation.

Fitzpatrick, T. (2001) *Welfare theory*, Basingstoke: Palgrave.

Franklin, J. (ed) (1997) *Equality*, London: IPPR.

Franklin, J. (ed) (1998) *Social policy and social justice*, Cambridge: Polity Press.

George, V. and Wilding, P. (1985) *Ideology and social welfare*, London: Routledge and Kegan Paul.

Giddens, A. (1998) *The third way*, Cambridge: Polity Press.

Giddens, A. (2000) *The third way and its critics*, Cambridge: Polity Press.

Giddens, A. (ed) (2001) *The global third way debate*, Cambridge: Polity Press.

Goodhart, D. (1999) 'Don't mind the gap', *Prospect*, August/September, p 12.

Goodman, A. (2001) 'Income inequality', *New Economy*, vol 8, no 2, pp 92-7.

Gould, P (1998) *The unfinished revolution*, London: Little, Brown & Company.

Hattersley, R. (1987) *Choose freedom*, Harmondsworth: Penguin.

Hayek, F (1976) *Law, legislation and liberty. Volume 2: The mirage of social justice*, London: Routledge and Kegan Paul.

Hobson, D. (1999) *The national wealth*, London: HarperCollins.

Hodge, M. (2000) 'Equality and New Labour', *Renewal*, vol 8, no 3, pp 34-41.

Howarth, C., Kenway, P. and Palmer, G. (2001) *Responsibility for all: A national strategy for social inclusion*, London: New Policy Institute/Fabian Society.

Jay, D. (1938) *The socialist case*, London: Faber & Faber.

Kaus, M. (1992) *The end of equality*, New York, NY: Basic Books.

Kellner, P. (1999) 'Equality of access', in D. Leonard (ed) *Crosland and New Labour*, Basingstoke: Macmillan, pp 149-66.

Labour Party (2001) *New ambitions for our country* (Election Manifesto), London: Labour Party.

Le Grand, J. (1982) *The strategy of equality*, London: George Unwin and Allen.

Le Grand, J. (1991) *Equity and choice*, London: HarperCollins.

Le Grand, J. (1998) 'The third way begins with Cora', *New Statesman*, 6 March, pp 26-7.

Leonard, D. (ed) (1999) *Crosland and New Labour*, Basingstoke: Macmillan.

Leonard, M. (2000) 'Introduction', in B. Hombach (ed) *The new centre*, Cambridge: Polity Press, pp xi-xxix.

Levitas, R. (1998) *The inclusive society?*, Basingstoke: Macmillan.

Lister, R. (1998) 'From equality to social inclusion: New Labour and the welfare state', *Critical Social Policy*, vol 18, no 2, pp 215-25.

Lister, R. (2001a) 'Not the General Election. Part 2: equality. For true freedom', *New Statesman*, 23 April.

Lister, R. (2001b) 'Doing good by stealth', *New Economy*, vol 8, no 2, pp 65-70.

Lund, B. (2001a) 'New Labour and social justice', Paper presented at SPA Annual Conference, Belfast, July.

Lund, B. (2001b) 'Distributive justice and social policy', in M. Lavalette and A. Pratt (eds) *Social policy* (2nd edn), London: Sage Publications, pp 161-78.

Lund, B. (2002) *State welfare: Social justice or social exclusion*, London: Sage Publications.

Marquand, D. (1998) 'The Blair paradox', *Prospect*, May, pp 19-24.

Marshall, T.H. (1963) *Sociology at the crossroads*, London: Heinemann.

Miller, D. (1976) *Social justice*, Oxford: Clarendon Press.

Miller, D. (1997) 'What kind of equality should the left pursue?', in J. Franklin (ed) *Equality*, London: IPPR, pp 83-99.

Nozick, R. (1974) *Anarchy, state and utopia*, Oxford: Basil Blackwell.

Nozick, R. (1990) *Examined life: Philosophical meditations*, New York, NY: Touchstone Books.

Orwell, G. (1982) *The lion and the unicorn* (first published 1941), Harmondsworth: Penguin.

Phelps Brown, H. (1991) *Egalitarianism and the generation of inequality*, Oxford: Clarendon Press.

Phillips, A. (1999) *Which equalities matter?*, Cambridge: Polity Press.

Plant, R. (1999a) 'Crosland, equality and New Labour', in D. Leonard (ed) *Crosland and New Labour*, Basingstoke: Macmillan, pp 19-34.

Plant, R. (1999b) 'Democratic socialism and equality', in H. Fawcett and R. Lowe (eds) *Welfare policy in Britain*, Basingstoke: Macmillan, pp 94-115.

Plant, R., Lesser, H. and Taylor–Gooby, P. (1980) *Political philosophy and social welfare*, London: Routledge and Kegan Paul.

Powell, M. (1995) 'The strategy of equality revisited', *Journal of Social Policy*, vol 24, no 2, pp 163-85.

Powell, M., Boyne, G. and Ashworth, R. (2001) 'Towards a geography of people poverty and place poverty', *Policy & Politics*, vol 29, no 3, pp 243-58.

Prowse, M. (2000) 'Mind the gap', *Prospect*, January.

Rawls, J. (1972) *A theory of justice*, Oxford: Clarendon Press.

Rawnsley, A. (2001) *Servants of the people*, Harmondsworth: Penguin.

Saunders, P. (1996) *Unequal but fair?*, London: IEA.

Sen, A. (1992) *Inequality re-examined*, Oxford: Clarendon Press.

SEU (Social Exclusion Unit) (1998) *Bringing Britain together*, London: The Stationery Office.

Stevenson, W. (ed) (1999) *Equality and the modern economy. Seminar 4: Why equality? What is equality?*, London: The Smith Institute.

Sullivan, M. (1999) 'Democratic socialism and social policy', in R. Page and R. Silburn (eds) *British social welfare in the twentieth century*, Basingstoke: Palgrave, pp 105-30.

Tawney, R. (1964) *Equality* (first published 1931), London: George Allen & Unwin.

Townsend, P. and Bosanquet, N. (eds) (1972) *Labour and inequality*, London: Fabian Society.

Walzer, M. (1985) *Spheres of justice*, Oxford: Basil Blackwell.

Weale, A. (1978) *Equality and social policy*, London: Routledge and Kegan Paul.

Weale, A. (1983) *Political theory and social policy*, Basingstoke: Macmillan.

White, S. (1997) 'What do egalitarians want?', in J. Franklin (ed) *Equality*, London: IPPR, pp 59-82.

White, S. (1999) 'Rights and responsibilities: a social democratic perspective', in A. Gamble and A. Wright (eds) *The new social democracy*, Oxford: Blackwell, pp 166-79.

Wright, A. (1996) *Socialisms*, London: Routledge.

THREE

Evaluating New Labour's accountability reforms

John Rouse and George Smith

Introduction

In this chapter an evaluation will be made of New Labour's reforms to accountability in the welfare state. These reforms have sought to bring about a new relationship between citizens and the welfare state, creating more accessible opportunities for the public, through representative and participative means, to contribute to the shaping and control of the welfare state. Providers of welfare have been encouraged to innovate and be cooperative, to maintain high standards of performance that are publicly demonstrable, to be efficient in their work and to maintain opportunities for users to be informed and feel satisfied with the services delivered to them. New Labour's reforms have represented an attempt to absorb managerialism within a model of public accountability revived principally through the 'democratic renewal' agenda, with its emphasis upon institutional reform, greater decentralisation and a focus on citizenship and participation. The chapter outlines and evaluates the approach of New Labour to accountability in the welfare state with regard to two key dimensions of its reform programme, democratisation and managerialism through enhanced performance management. It concludes that policy has enhanced the democratic process of the welfare state and that power has been decentralised concurrently with centralisation also being upheld, with the result that there are a number of tensions within the new accountability that have yet to be resolved. The chapter begins with an outline of New Labour's overall approach, followed by an exposition and evaluation of the two key components of increased accountability: democratic renewal and enhanced performance management. After a brief outline of the changes introduced by New Labour in its second term, the final section brings the two strands together and provides a conclusion.

New Labour's approach

When New Labour was elected to office in May 1997, it had revised its thinking considerably about the means by which accountability was best secured within the welfare state. A change of approach had evolved during the long years of absence from national office as an outcome of a multiplicity of factors (Rouse and Smith, 1999). Pivotal to its new approach to accountability was the belief that there was a crisis of confidence in the political system. The system was centralised, inefficient and bureaucratic (Labour Party, 1997). Accordingly, a broad programme for revision of the political system was proposed, the purpose of which was to restore the confidence of the public in the accountability of government and revive social democracy. Democracy was to be enhanced through the creation of new opportunities for citizens to share in decision making. In particular, devolution of power to new assemblies for constituent nations was promised and support was given to the fusion of representative and participative modes of democracy. Collaboration between the state and the informal, voluntary and commercial sectors of welfare was supported. Decentralisation of government was endorsed, together with greater openness and responsiveness to the public. A commitment to new and experimental methods of delivering services was given. Ratification was given also to greater strategic action by the welfare state to minimise fragmented activity. Overall, changes were proposed to dilute the concentration of power at the centre and to enhance the power of all citizens in their relationship with the welfare state.

New Labour's commitment to constitutional change to revive political accountability was matched by enthusiastic support for robust devices to maintain and enhance effective performance management throughout the welfare state. The management revolution brought about by the Conservative government was not to be reversed by New Labour, although there would be a significant number of reforms so as to build a new accountability relationship between citizens and the welfare state. There would be no return to the public administration paradigm, with its emphasis on traditional political accountability bolstered by bureaucratic administration and the dominance of professionals (Rouse and Smith, 1999). While New Labour accepted many of the changes made by its Conservative predecessor to improve performance management, it rejected some and showed an interest in pioneering further innovations that would represent a new approach to the accountability of services for the public.

Both these distinctive strands in New Labour's approach to accountability – democratisation and a new managerialism – were espoused as compatible and complementary. The promise of the 1997 Manifesto was for a programme of change that embraced democratic reforms linked to managerial innovations. Pledges were made in the Manifesto for a parliament for Scotland, an assembly for Wales and the end of voting rights of hereditary peers. A strategic authority and mayor would be created for London. Greater accountability and democratic innovation in local government were promised, together with a fairer grants system, the end of council capping, obligations for local authorities to obtain best value in their services, and to promote economic/social well-being. There would be a shift in governance to the regional level through the creation of Regional Development Agencies and regional chambers and through legislation for referenda on directly elected regional government. Electoral innovation was promised through the introduction of proportional representation for

European elections. Citizenship would be enhanced by the incorporation into British Law of the European Convention on Human Rights and by the introduction of a Freedom of Information Act.

Labour's performance pledges were less specific than those that related to democratisation, but nonetheless they permeated the whole agenda for public services, with the promise of "better schools, better hospitals, better ways of tackling crime, of building a modern welfare state" (Labour Party, 1997, p 97). Of major significance was the pledge to undertake a comprehensive spending review as a means of establishing new spending priorities and performance standards with three-year budgets to promote longer-term planning and new cross-cutting departmental working. This would involve more effective spending, particularly on education and health, by "rooting out waste and inefficiency" (p 13). In education, performance pledges related to raising standards in every school with year-on-year targets for improvement, zero tolerance of underperformance, closer inspection of local education authorities (LEAs) with more devolvement of budgets to heads and governors, and the introduction of Education Action Zones to tackle underachievement through partnership working. For health, pledges related to greater focus on quality and outcomes and holding management accountable for performance levels, and longer-term commissioning in place of the internal market to secure more cooperation and new forms of public–private partnerships. For social services, housing and criminal justice there were fewer specific performance pledges, but those that were made related to improving service standards, particularly through partnership working. Affecting all these services was the pledge that councils would be required to obtain 'Best Value' for the services they delivered, with clear targets for service improvement, an emphasis on working in partnership with others to promote area well-being and, significantly, the pledge to provide additional powers for the Audit Commission and an inspection regime to make sure it happened.

Hence, through the delivery of these pledges, the welfare state would be answerable to the public in a more inclusive sense than it had been before and it would deliver services to the highest performance standards. The next four sections of this chapter outline and evaluate the two strands to New Labour's approach to accountability: first, democratisation and second, managerialism through enhanced performance management, focusing on its achievements during the first term of office.

Accountability through democratic renewal: intrinsic evaluation

During New Labour's first term of office, a succession of reforms was made to the governance of the welfare state to enhance its accountability to the public, as pledged in the Manifesto. Power was devolved to Scotland, Wales and Northern Ireland through the creation of a parliament, two elected assemblies and associated executives. Although there are important differences in the size and composition of the assemblies, in their powers and in their executives, responsibility for matters such as health, housing, education and personal social services was devolved to them. In effect, therefore, the political centre transferred some of its power to make social policy for all of the UK. Instead, three new representative institutions were formed to make decisions for their own jurisdictions. New Labour promised that the new institutions might well take a different path from the UK government on a range of issues. That has been shown most explicitly so far in Scotland's policy for student tuition fees, teachers' pay and long-term care and Wales' policy for a children's commissioner. Meanwhile at Westminster, hereditary peers, in principle, were abolished from the House of Lords. The Wakeham Commission, appointed to review the composition and role of the Lords, recommended a mainly appointed second chamber that the government accepted in principle.

A strategic authority for London with a directly elected mayor was established. The authority has direct responsibility for transport, police, fire service and economic development. Voluntary regional chambers, comprising councillors, business people and trade unionists, were also formed to voice regional interests and they were accompanied by the formation of eight Regional Development Agencies in England outside London. These agencies are mainly concerned with the coordination of economic strategy and consult the voluntary chambers. New Labour has proclaimed the creation of these new regional institutions in England as a first step towards regional government. A new framework for local government was introduced, allowing for directly elected mayors, cabinet-style administrations and improved measures to combat corruption, including a standards committee in every council. Centralised control of finance was relaxed for local authorities, with more relaxation promised. A process of Best Value was introduced into local government.

Referenda were used to establish public support for the introduction of the parliament and assemblies for Scotland, Wales, Northern Ireland and Greater London. Proportional representation was used in the electoral arrangements for these four bodies and for UK members of the European Parliament from 1999. The Jenkins Commission, appointed to review the system for election to the House of Commons, recommended a form of proportional representation to replace the 'first past the post' system. No date has been given for this referendum. Encouragement has been given to public consultation and participation in decision making for services, particularly through the Best Value and modernising government frameworks, and permission given for experimentation with local election procedure to improve turnout.

A Freedom of Information Act was introduced that promised greater openness by the welfare state to the public. A Human Rights Act was passed, incorporating the European Convention on Human Rights into British law. As such, the fairness of policy and practices across the welfare state, in respect of individual rights, will be subject to review.

Democratic renewal: extrinsic evaluation

From its record in office during the first term, New Labour claims to have pursued its project to revive democracy in the welfare state through a variety of measures. It has delivered the most far-reaching reforms for 150 years. Power has been given back to the people. Thus, New Labour's Secretary of State for Scotland, commenting on its programme for constitutional change, has claimed that it is the biggest decentralisation of power in centuries (Walker, 2000). The Prime Minister has also claimed that Labour's programme of constitutional reform is moving Britain away from centralisation "where power flowed top-down, to a devolved and plural state" (White, 2000, p 13).

Nonetheless, although New Labour has implemented a programme for democratic renewal that fulfils many manifesto promises, the programme may be faulted for its lack of cohesion and its half-heartedness in diffusing power to citizens. The definition of democratic renewal that has guided New Labour is that of a set of practical responses to clearly identifiable problems with democracy (Pratchett, 1999). Accordingly, democratic reform has proceeded on a very piecemeal basis. The lack of cohesion in the democratic renewal strategy was acknowledged by the Secretary of State for Scotland. He conceded that the strategy of decentralisation of power was not thought through to a conclusion, for "No one had a route map when we embarked on this journey. There wasn't a text book" (Walker, 2000, p 3). Some examples of incoherence in the strategy are shown by anomalies over devolution for Scotland, by election procedures and by the proliferation of partnerships in the welfare state, discussed later in this chapter.

The devolution of power to Scotland has created the anomaly of Scottish MPs being able to shape some social policy for England, for example health, housing and education, but English MPs being unable to do likewise for Scotland. Moreover, while the Scottish Parliament decides most social policy, abortion policy and social security and taxation are determined by the Westminster Parliament.

The changes made in the methods for election to public office represent an important shift away from the traditional 'first past the post' system. However, there is a lack of consistency in the new approaches. The additional member system is used for elections to assemblies in Scotland, Wales and London. For Northern Ireland, the Single Transferable Vote is employed, while for Mayor of London there is the Supplementary Vote system. Conspicuously absent from the voting systems that have been reformed by proportional representation are the House of Commons and the local government system in England. Yet the mediocre turnout for elections to both fora is surely indicative of a democratic malaise.

The criticism of a half-hearted commitment by New Labour to a diffusion of power to the citizenry can be upheld by consideration of the reforms to government secrecy, the House of Lords, local and regional government and the formation of task forces. As far as government secrecy is concerned, the introduction of legislation for freedom of information was delayed and no date has been announced for it to come into force. While the White Paper was enthusiastically welcomed, its later translation into a draft Bill prompted great disappointment because of the dilution of the original principles. Due to certain conditions and exemptions from the statutory right of access to information held by public authorities, the criticism remains that more open government will materialise as an inferior version of the original promise. The weaknesses of the freedom of information legislation are highlighted by the proposal from the Scottish Executive to introduce its own legislation that promises even greater openness (*An open Scotland* [www.scotland.gov.uk/libraryw/doc07/opsc-00.htm]). While hereditary peers have been removed from the parliamentary arena, there has been no commitment given to a largely elected second chamber.

Local authorities have gained more freedom and are expected to become reinvigorated leaders of their communities, but their independence is still limited by central financial control and largely central sources of funding. Indeed, they may have lost some control through the national standards and regulatory framework for quality and performance under which they must increasingly operate, discussed later in this chapter. As a result, local accountability and autonomy is undermined, shown by poor local election turnout. British local government has a tax base that is both narrower and more meagre as a proportion of local government spending than in most countries (JRF, 1994). Although experimentation with election procedure by several local authorities has succeeded in raising turnout, the lessons have yet to be translated into general practice (Wainwright, 2000). Britain is now the only EU country to maintain the 'first past the post' system for local government (JRF, 2000a). Encouragement to abandon that tradition has been given by the McIntosh Commission, which has recommended the introduction of proportional representation in Scotland. Although streamlining of decision making is the rationale for the new local government framework of elected mayors and cabinets, the demise of the traditional system of service committees has been criticised as a diminution of democracy. For it suggests that power will be concentrated in fewer hands and that the majority of councillors will be merely lobby fodder. Certainly, evidence of councillors' views has shown their opposition to the new local government framework because of fears that power and responsibility will be removed from the majority of councillors (Rao, 2000).

Steps towards democratic regional governance have been a separate and rudimentary development. Both the strategic authority created for London and the elected mayor have limited direct responsibilities. No legislation has been passed for referenda for directly elected regional assemblies and research into Regional Development Agencies and voluntary regional chambers suggests little progress has been made in the development of regional governance. Indeed, ambiguity and confusion appear to characterise the current stage of regional governance (JRF, 2000b; Tomaney and Hetherington, 2000). Regional Development Agencies lack clear lines of demarcation from Government Offices in the Regions and have limited autonomy from central government. The regional chambers do not yet represent much of a political force. Further enhancement of regional governance may be impeded by the local government changes made as a separate development.

New Labour has sought to open up government through the inclusion of outsiders with expertise into the corridors of power. Many review groups and task forces have been established over most aspects of government policy with the aim of enhancing policy making. However, three criticisms have been made of this development. There is procedural inconsistency and meagre openness about the task forces and a lack of representation to the groups, with producer interests being dominant (*Democratic findings 4: Ruling by Task Force* [www.fhit.org/democratic_audit/taskforce/sumtaskpdf]).

Whatever the virtues of the emergent approach to accountability that New Labour has developed in office, it has disappointed proponents of constitutional reform who seek a more systematic and emphatic diffusion of power away from the centre in Westminster and Whitehall (Weir and Beetham, 1999; Charter 88 [www.unlockingdemocracy.org.uk/info/ud_short.html]; *The Guardian*, 2000). For these critics, the constitutional reforms of New Labour are valued positively for the repair of assorted democratic deficiencies they make, but they are regarded as insufficient for failing to develop a comprehensive and robust strategy of constitutional reform. A democratic deficit remains, with confusion and contradiction from the piecemeal process of reform. The reforms abandon traditional constitutional principles without replacing them with new ones. While some power has been shifted away from Whitehall and Westminster, much is still concentrated there. Furthermore, the strict performance management of the welfare state exercised by Downing Street undermines the reforms, as we explain later. Moreover, the fusion of the majority party in government with the civil service creates an executive that dominates parliament and all institutions of the state including local government. There are few checks and balances on the conduct of public affairs by the executive, for it operates largely in an informal, discretionary and secret manner. These critics conjecture that, in the long run, the reforms may generate further reforms that lead to a much more open and accountable welfare state.

The limited extent to which decentralisation of power has occurred during New Labour's period of office can be attributed to the ambivalence of opinion within the ranks of New Labour and indeed among the public at large. For two contradictory perspectives on democracy have been identified (Marquand, 2000). One of these philosophies upholds the retention of power at the centre, with the consent or acquiescence of the public to decisions made in their name. The other supports the dispersal of power to the public so that they can actively participate in decision making. The centralised conception of democracy has dominated the governance of the welfare state from its very beginnings. It is buttressed by public opinion that expects geographical uniformity of provision in welfare for fairness to all, before local democratic control and the diversity that might involve (Walker, 2000). Because of competition between the two divergent philosophies of democracy, "New Labour's democratic renewal is mired in paradox" (Marquand, 2000, p 268). Consequently, the outcome of New Labour's revision of political accountability has been the creation of a more complex and ambiguous system for the scrutiny and control of the welfare state. It seems that New Labour's strategy for democratic renewal has contributed to the enhancement of democracy, albeit with some confusion over the distribution of power resulting from the diverse initiatives. Decentralisation of power from the centre has occurred, but it has been accompanied by the maintenance of centralised power.

Accountability through performance management: intrinsic evaluation

New Labour's increasing emphasis on the delivery of more performance-orientated public services as a means of enhancing accountability of the welfare state illustrates all too well the divergent philosophies of democracy and, in particular, the tensions between decentralisation and centralisation. The 1997 Manifesto's commitment was to enhancing accountability through raising the standards of public services. This commitment to absorb managerialism within a model of public accountability was seen by New Labour as compatible with, and complementary to, the democratic renewal agenda. During New Labour's first term, however, the performance management agenda grew beyond the significance assigned to it in 1997, and it assumes even greater prominence in New Labour's second term.

There have been many strands to New Labour's vision of accountable public services, although there was no clear statement of this vision in the 1997 Manifesto or in the pledges made. The government's core belief has been, and remains, that by being specific about *what* outcomes it wants but flexible about *how* they should be achieved, it could free up public services to innovate and improve continuously (Blair, 2000). What counts is what works and the government's apparent post-ideological approach to public service processes and systems has been to express no preference for delivery mechanisms. Accountability is in terms of results rather than processes, with emphasis on improved standards rather than new structures. However, although there has been an apparent indifference to delivery structures, at the centre of the government's approach has been an insistence on a fundamental change of thinking as the key to better public services. Public servants must be outward-looking, challenge purposes and design innovative approaches to quality delivery, which could involve markets, networks and hierarchies cutting across the boundaries of public/private/voluntary sectors to deliver joined-up services. Intolerance of low standards and the delivery of a step-change improvement in public service performance have been key issues, with performance defined in terms of the outcomes desired by more inclusive reference groups, actively canvassed for their views via participative democratic processes, albeit in the context of clear national standards and an inspection/regulatory regime. Hence, the government has seen its agenda as involving a step-change in the enhancement of performance in the context of the renewal of democracy to secure a genuinely accountable welfare state (HM Treasury, 1998).

Here is, it would appear, a government that has been attempting to build a more developmental approach to performance management, one that is broader than the technocratic and managerialist approach with its restricted notion of accountability that characterised the previous Conservative government (Clarke and Newman, 1997; Rouse, 1999; Rouse and Smith 1999; Newman, 2000). Whereas the developmental approach is concerned with the effective performance of the system as a whole in an essentially political environment that embraces public service values, the technocratic concentrates on detailed issues around the delivery of public services, seeing performance as 'unpolitical', a question of good management (Rouse, 1999). New Labour's approach of "modern management" (Newman, 2000, p 47) has been designed to eradicate past problems, recognising public service values and the challenge of managing the new fragmented structure of governance, the 'differentiated polity' (Rhodes, 1997), in the context of a modernisation agenda to update public services.

Critical to New Labour's approach has been an attempt to broaden the performance accountability framework. Performance targets are now expressed as outcomes – either as the end results that taxpayers' money is intended to deliver or service standards, with a focus on effectiveness and efficiency, on quality outcomes and specific improvement, and not merely inputs and economy. Related to this outcome focus is what Cutler and Waine (2000, p 325) call "the implicit stakeholder approach to performance". In the Performance Assessment Frameworks (PAFs) for the health service, social services and education, for example, good measurement is seen more inclusively, not only in terms of the interests of the managers/taxpayers, but also for patients, clients and customers. To implement inclusiveness requires knowledge of, and trade-off between, the broad range of stakeholder preferences if consistent sets of performance plans and measures are to result. The government has advocated a more consultative frame, with participation of the range of stakeholders in determining priorities and as a means of reflecting the aspirations of 'citizens' and to strengthen the legitimacy of political decisions (Brooks, 2000), particularly for local services. Performance and quality management have been seen as a dialogue between stakeholders, essentially political and process driven, with consultation providing the potential to widen the membership of policy communities eliciting a range of stakeholder views to build into more inclusive performance plans (Rouse, 1999).

Alongside inclusiveness and participation has been the importance of collaboration and networking within the government's approach to performance. A partnership model of governance has emerged, determined to overcome the many problems resulting from the 'design deficit' of confusing complexity left by market fragmentation (Jervis and Richards, 1997; Clarence and Painter, 1998; Painter and Clarence, 2000). The ending of the NHS internal market and its replacement with more collaborative longer-term service agreements, a key pledge, is a case in point. The Social Exclusion Unit, established in the Cabinet Office in December 1997 under the personal guidance of the Prime Minister, has been given the task of promoting more holistic and preventative approaches to social policy problems by encouraging greater cooperation across central government as well as between the different levels of government to improve coordination. Going beyond collaboration within government has been the desire for more innovative structures that join up the delivery experience for citizens. This is one of the key themes of the 1999 *Modernising government* White Paper (Cabinet Office, 1999) and the Cabinet Office has been at the helm in this area, with recognition that there are a number of 'cross–cutting' issues that require coordination both within government and between government and 'external' agencies. The 'mixed economy of provision' recognises that service departments cannot deliver any of their responsibilities unless they act in partnership with other parts of the public sector, and the private and voluntary sectors too. Area Based Initiatives (ABIs) are an example of the approach used to tackle wider policy aims of social exclusion and inequalities in health and education by ensuring greater coordination and integration of what is delivered so as to achieve better outcomes for local people. Examples have included the New Deal for Communities, Sure Start, Health and Education Action Zones. Their focus has been on community and capacity building. Others include the reinvigorated Private Finance Initiative and the promotion of the public–private partnership to enhance service delivery.

Those aspects of the performance management approach that have involved challenging thinking, inclusiveness, participation and stakeholder dialogue, together with more flexible collaborative interagency provision, have offered the opportunity for innovative solutions, entrepreneurialism and local variation in both definitions and delivery of performance and a paradigm of continuous improvement. This has provided a performance architecture different from that of the previous government, one dependent on, and consistent with, the democratic renewal agenda. It has offered public service agencies more freedom to determine the approach they take to seemingly intractable social problems such as social exclusion, employability, low educational attainment and health inequalities (Painter and Clarence, 2000).

However, there has been another dimension to the performance framework. The government's vision for performance has been essentially driven from the centre and the need to demonstrate accountability for the use of public funds. The key players have been the Prime Minister himself, the Cabinet Office and the Treasury, with the latter assuming increasing importance – although the second term shows signs of this trend being tempered slightly. The promised Comprehensive Spending Review (CSR) took place in 1998 and introduced a fundamental review of government priorities with every department required to reassess its budget from a zero base, with a resulting change of spending priorities both within and between departments. There was also a move towards three-year spending agreements to replace annuity and a key feature was the introduction of conditionality contracting – the 'something for something' approach that has increasingly characterised policy, whereby additional public funds were made conditional on the delivery of quality public services. Moreover, much of the extra money was ring-fenced, earmarked for specific purposes rather than left to the discretion of, for example, local spending bodies such as health authorities or LEAs. Some of the additional spending was allocated centrally to local spending bodies, bypassing the usual bureaucratic structures. The December 1998 White Paper (HM Treasury, 1998) introduced Public Service Agreements (PSAs) for all central departments and agencies, and by implication local delivery agencies, as the means for compliance. PSAs set out each department's aims and objectives, with targets set in terms of specific improvements in services or in the results those services would achieve.

At the level of local government, the Best Value (BV) performance regime promised in the Manifesto was introduced to provide a framework for the delivery of enhanced performance (DETR 1998). Technically a replacement for Compulsory Competitive Tendering in local government, BV is much more, since, like the CSR/PSA framework, it has required a fundamental questioning of current approaches in terms of priorities, values, objectives and delivery systems designed to challenge thinking and achieve commitment to continuous improvement. BV has placed a statutory duty on local government to achieve effective services, balancing quality and cost, by the most effective and efficient means available. Fundamental performance reviews have been required of all local services over a five-year period, applying the four Cs of challenge, compare, consult and compete (DETR, 1998). Clear performance targets have been set and published in Local Performance Plans for both the authority and for individual services that become the basis of the performance contract with both local communities and central government. Although local consultation and preference is a key to BV, including the determination of relevant performance measures, central government has continued to set the context for services provision through the PSA framework, providing a battery of performance indicators, standards and targets and a BV Inspectorate to ensure compliance.

The CSR/PSA and BV frameworks have centralised the importance of performance in the government's modernisation programme by requiring accountable contracts for performance from public service agencies. The PSA, for example, is a contract between the relevant department, the Treasury and the public, articulating departmental priorities and setting clear targets for improvement over a three-year cycle, with the requirement to report annually on progress. The White Paper proclaims the approach as an "important step in improving democracy and accountability [since] by publishing clear, measurable targets, we are making it possible for everyone to judge whether we meet them ... [this representing] a fundamental change in the accountability of government to Parliament and the public [since] PSAs show the public what they can expect for their money" (HM Treasury, 1998, p 2). New Labour's approach, like the previous Conservative government's, is a target-driven one, with the explicit evaluation of target achievement via performance indicators as a critical part of the accountability framework.

Another essential feature of the performance framework in general, and the CSR/PSA framework in particular, has been the importance of explicit national quality standards and the outlawing of 'unacceptable' variations in standards. This has particularly been the case with regard to hospitals, schools and social services departments, although it has been true across much of the sector. A number of new agencies have been established both to monitor and pronounce on national standards, and old ones have been 'beefed up'. For example, the National Institute for Clinical Excellence (NICE) has been set up to provide a single focus for clear, consistent guidance for clinicians about which treatments work best for which patients, with both clinical effectiveness and cost-effectiveness influencing its judgements.

Incentivising performance – rewarding success, not tolerating mediocrity and sanctioning failure – has been another critical and related component for promoting excellence and quality in public services and a key issue in the accountability framework. Comparing and sharing good practice through benchmarking policy making and service standards has been the positive side of this approach. Of even greater importance, however, has been the rise of an enhanced regulatory framework and strong monitoring mechanisms. This has become an essential part of the accountability framework for performance, required to challenge cosy collegiality and ensure delivery or results. Hood et al (1999, 2000) have identified the continuation, even acceleration, in the growth of regulation since 1997, with the most notable category of growth being the new special purpose Inspectorates alongside established ones such as OFSTED, the Audit Commission and the Social Services Inspectorate (SSI). For example, there are two new BV Inspectorates, the new Housing Inspectorate, the Quality Assurance Agency, NICE and the Commission for Health Improvement (CHI), to name but a few. These bodies have been given responsibility for checking conformity with an organisation's performance approach and plan, including national standards, which it might have had a role in setting. They have used a range of national and local performance indicators, often in the form of published league tables, to establish internal and comparative performance through benchmarking, with poor performance identified through a process of 'naming and shaming'. Some check has been made on user satisfaction through public consultation. Finally, there has been 'earned autonomy', a particular theme developed in the *Modernising government* White Paper (Cabinet Office, 1999), which rationalises intervention in inverse proportion to an organisation's success, with more formal and external regulation for poor performers while treating successful organisations with 'a light touch' and giving them the freedom to manage. Being tough on non-performers was stressed in the Manifesto and has been implemented, although there has been little 'lightness', at least in the first term.

Hence, on the one hand, New Labour's approach for the delivery of excellence and quality in public services has been an attempt to provide a more open, inclusive, participative and accountable framework for performance, one that complements the democratic renewal agenda, including constitutional reform. On the other hand, the drive from the centre via national PAFs, national quality standards and the array of regulatory and monitoring agencies, suggests a number of tensions both within the approach itself and between the performance approach and that of democratic renewal. It is to these that we now turn.

New Labour's managerial accountability: extrinsic evaluation

Since the government decided to remove the fiscal constraints of the previous government that it had accepted for the first two years of its first term in office, public services' funding increased considerably, particularly for education and health. However, long periods of underinvestment in public service infrastructure, particularly the training of relevant specialists such as doctors, nurses and teachers, led to immense problems for the delivery of ambitious government targets on such things as waiting lists and class sizes. There has been a lack of coordination between political aspirations and the resource planning process, with central targets via PSAs not always consistent with the capacity of local delivery systems. Further frustration has resulted from policy overload and initiative fatigue. Even the government itself recognised that the pace of change within the performance management agenda has been too fast for most to absorb. A report from the Cabinet's Performance and Innovation Unit (February 2000) concluded that "there are too many government initiatives causing confusion, not enough coordination, and too much time spent on negotiating the system rather than delivering" (Cabinet Office, 2000). The report concluded that this had slowed down delivery of the government's agenda and led to considerable confusion over accountability.

Talbot (2000), in pursuit of this theme, has identified a number of confusions in what he calls 'the performance of performance'. He says there has been little conceptual clarity about the meaning of performance, citing structural complexity and confusion at the centre, particularly between the Treasury and the Cabinet Office. Although the central framework is tight, Talbot claims that it has not been clear within government who is responsible for setting performance targets, with consequential confusion over accountability. He also cites similar obscurity over the delivery of PSAs, with confusion over accountability and responsibility between ministers and departments comparable to that under the previous government. Further complexity and confusion has been added by the "army of auditors, inspectors, regulators and standard setters [who] play a part in determining performance targets" (2000, p 65). All have a vision of how public services should perform, but a different one, reinforcing the confusion.

This last point emphasises another major issue of concern in the performance accountability framework – the tension between central oversight, even surveillance, and autonomous self-regulation. The whole PSA system, for example, has put immense power in the hands of the Treasury since, in effect, the Treasury has negotiated policy objectives for departments through the spending process and decided what is worthy of funding, insisting on productivity increases through annual efficiency targets, intervening far more directly and openly in the policy processes of departments, with the Cabinet Office and individual departments losing some control. The performance framework, as a result, has not been as wide and inclusive as the government claims since central domination, national standards and universalism have driven out local autonomy, flexibility, diversity and innovation. The framework has increasingly become a strait-jacket dictating both outcomes and, more and more, delivery mechanisms – the *how* as well as the *what*. The consequence is the same 'centralised-decentralisation' (Hoggett, 1996, p 18) that occurred under the previous government, with operations devolved to business units such as trusts, schools or agencies but control over policy kept centrally in Whitehall. If anything, given the enhanced power of the Treasury via the CSR/PSA framework, the simultaneous moves to centralise policy strategy and decentralise policy delivery have been even stronger. Indeed, as Deakin and Parry (2000) have argued, there has been an increase in the trend for the Treasury to further its long-term ambitions to control not only the expenditure totals but also the substance of policy, a trend in tension with local democratic renewal.

Targets and performance indicators have played a critical part in maintaining control and incentivising performance and in the accountability framework. For example, for local government, the Audit Commission has had over 100 Best Value Performance Indicators (BVPIs) and has expected local authorities to have a similar number of locally derived ones. These BVPIs have been on top of the performance indicators already expected by the Audit Commission, the so-called Audit Commission on Performance Indicators (ACPI). The Local Government Association has claimed that the large number of nationally prescribed performance indicators inhibited the ability of local authorities to respond to local needs through the setting and monitoring of local indicators, thereby compromising one of the government's key objectives associated with democratic renewal. Moreover, tension has developed in using performance indicators for performance accountability to the public. At one level, the increasingly large, disparate and complex performance indicators and league tables have not provided the public with clear performance information on which to base their performance judgements. On another level, crude league tables of waiting times, for example, have hidden more than they reveal, both distorting the public's perceptions and creating unfortunate incentives among practitioners and managers to focus on the wrong things, neglecting real priorities.

A further problem has been that the obsession with targets and performance indicators, centrally driven, is likely to contradict with holistic, joined-up government, a key characteristic of New Labour's espoused approach. Where there is non-alignment between an organisation's boundaries and service delivery – as in the case of 'cross-cutting' programme areas like crime reduction that are influenced by a number of disparate organisations, public, private and voluntary – accounting for performance through measurement becomes more challenging. Where efficiency or success is calculated at the level of the organisational unit through, for example, a series of Key Performance Indicators (KPIs), organisations will have an incentive to improve their own rather than overall service performance (Clarke et al, 2000, p 258). The result has been that an emphasis on specific targets or standards, the essence of the government's approach, particularly in the context of departmental budgetary conventions, has frustrated the pursuit of joined-up government and distorted managerial behaviour away from more creative solutions (Lovell and Hand, 1999).

To implement the performance framework, regulation, audit and monitoring through a range of evaluative agencies have been playing an increasing role in New Labour's approach. There is considerable evidence to suggest that the balance has swung towards even more managerial surveillance than in the previous government, with checking replacing trust as the dominant approach. Indeed, Cope and Goodship see regulation under New Labour as "a manifesto of mistrust by the centre of those agencies providing public services locally" (1999, p 11). National standards, the need to deliver election promises and an army of regulatory bodies have been leading to compliance, at a considerable cost, rather than ownership and the development of innovative ideas and new ways of working (Pollitt et al, 1999; Clarke et al, 2000; Cope and Goodship, 1999; Painter and Clarence 2000; Newman et al, 2001). Excessive checking is likely to be demotivating, and may not encourage the innovation and learning so necessary for continuous improvement and dealing with increasing complexity, the so-called 'wicked problems'. Evidence-based policy is desirable, but too much checking can be dysfunctional. Indeed, Rhodes (1997) has argued that the traditional command operating code has become increasingly inappropriate in the differentiated polity, producing outcomes contrary to policy makers' goals. To manage networks in the differentiated polity requires an "operating code which steers through indirect management and builds trust" (Rhodes, 1997, p 196). The need is for interorganisational negotiation and compromise, since at the heart of networks and partnerships is the idea of working collaboratively at the local level, and top-down steering is likely to be counterproductive (Skelcher, 2000). Managerial prescription from central government is in danger of driving out the very structures so necessary for managing the differentiated polity, and which are such a distinctive part of New Labour's performance architecture.

The problem to resolve is the tension between inclusiveness and the diversity it inevitably must embrace, and the role of regulation that promotes national agendas and uniformity. There is a real issue not only of *what* counts but also *who* counts. To illustrate this, Powell and Boyne (2001) identify an increasing tension in the government's performance agenda between its desire for territorial justice, essentially defined by the centre to secure national provision to guarantee horizontal equity, and local autonomy. Regulatory and audit bodies, with their emphasis on comparative performance through, for example, benchmarking, have increasingly categorised the local diversity resulting from local autonomy as deviations from centrally decided norms and a cause for concern. As Powell and Boyne say: "far from being evidence of failure, geographical variations *may* be regarded as evidence of the success of responsiveness to the local population" (2001, p 8), a key component of the democratic renewal and accountability agenda.

Of course, the very discourse of joining up, collaboration, partnership and networking, inclusiveness and diversity is not without its problems and political constraints. Inevitably, divergences of interest and conflicting goals between potentially collaborating partners, together with inequalities of power and resource, will constrain such developments and inhibit the achievement of the more diffuse goals and outcomes involved in tackling 'cross-cutting' issues. Skelcher has referred to a number of issues arising from the emergence of 'the congested state', which he defines as "a complex of networked relationships between public, private, voluntary and community actors creating a dense, multi-layered and largely impenetrable structure for public action" (2000, p 4). There is much in common between this and Rhodes' 'differentiated polity', although Skelcher stresses that self-organising, interorganisational networks are being superseded by more structured partnerships that are closely linked to, and regulated by, government at the centre. There is the emergence of plural modes of governance to negotiate the development and delivery of public programmes, reflecting the shift from primary government bodies, which operate directly to elected politicians, to secondary appointed agencies, such as 'quangos', and, increasingly, to numerous partnerships bringing together two or more agencies in pursuit of a public policy objective, referred to as tertiary-level organisations. He argues that the transfer of responsibility and power to tertiary bodies poses major issues, since it removes centres of decision making further from elected political structures, increasing their distance from citizens and often becoming invisible to public view, challenging traditional notions of public sector accountability just as quangos did in the mid-1990s (Skelcher, 2000, p 13). He notes, too, that New Labour's democratic renewal agenda has concentrated on the processes and institutions of elected government rather than the multitude of partnership bodies. The result is that there may be "even more democratic imbalance [with] revitalised elected bodies with a reduced role in public policy set against partnership boards detached from democratic processes and having an increasingly important function in the development, management and delivery of public objectives" (Skelcher, 2000, p 18).

The consultative and participative frame of the government's performance approach is essential to its reinvention and an important departure from the former government's approach. However, participation throws up its own problems for both accountability and excellence in service delivery. Participatory forms of democracy have "the potential to promote democracy and provide a practical demonstration of civic behaviour without the corrosive effects of party politics" (Brooks, 2000, p 608). However, there are questions about whether such approaches can be genuinely inclusive and representative of community diversity, and there are dangers that "consultation risks merely framing questions that reflect the dominant discourse" (Brooks, 2000, p 609; see also Newman, 2000). With regard to local authorities, consultation will be within the context of existing policy and assumptions, and may be also used by politicians as a method to legitimise their actions, only partially accepting the opinions they are offered. Consultation may also result in producing unrealistic expectations, thus leading to even greater dissatisfaction. And at the end of the day, consultation will be unable to resolve genuine differences of interest, of identity and of social or economic position, within the politics of diversity (Newman, 2000, p 57).

Hence, there appears to be considerable potential in the government's new managerialism for a more developmental approach to the delivery of excellence and quality in public services as the basis for an expanded approach to managerial accountability. The discourse of modernisation, public consultation, citizen participation, collaboration, Best Value and democratic renewal go beyond the narrow technocratic approach to performance of the former government and offer an expanded and developmental perspective for managing in a political environment, one fully compatible with democratic renewal. However, there are real tensions, even contradictions, between this developmental approach to performance accountability and the restrictive managerialist one that seems to have emerged as a result of an unduly controlling and centralising tendency. Centralisation is in danger of driving out inclusiveness, innovation, diversity, organisational learning and imaginative approaches to continuous improvement in public services. It is also in danger of driving out joined-up and participative approaches to policy development, collaboration and partnership in service delivery. It certainly seems in tension with the democratic renewal agenda.

Policy developments since the 2001 General Election

There are limited signs that some of these tensions, both within and between the democratisation and performance management components of the accountability framework, have been recognised. It is apparent that the enhancement of standards for our welfare services is to dominate the second term as it did the first, with 'modernisation and reform' remaining primary objectives for accountability and effective public services (Labour Party, 2001). Indeed, there is a reinforcement of the message of control and intolerance of poor standards, with implications that the centre will continue to exercise tight control. There is an increased acceptance of the discourse of the market and the role of private sector providers, often working in public–private partnerships, to deliver the higher standards of welfare provision promised by New Labour. There are new league tables to enhance public accountability: for example, for hospitals and consultants. Areas previously excluded from the full rigours of performance scrutiny, such as the police, are to be included. However, there are indications that the government is reviewing its approach to managing performance with an emphasis on 'new freedoms' to deliver better public services, at least for those who can demonstrate that they deserve a less interventionist approach. For example, the December 2001 White Paper on local government enhances the democratic basis of local government by reducing some central control (DTLR, 2001). There is a retreat from the number of plans and strategies that have been required under Best Value, a scaling down of ABIs and a promise to move away from local administration to local government. Under the banner of 'earned autonomy', further freedoms will be granted to high-performing councils, but decisive intervention is threatened where performance is poor, including an enhanced role for private contractors. The simultaneous freeing and tightening of the performance accountability framework characterises the current approach. Inspection is to be more proportionate and integrated, but will still remain central to accountability.

New Labour may not have explicitly accepted the criticisms made by supporters of a comprehensive reform strategy, but it has, nonetheless, modestly recognised that there is unfinished business in respect of democratic renewal. For its second term, it reiterated support for a strong and accountable local government, a regional system of government, a review of the voting system for the House of Commons and completion of reform of the House of Lords (Labour Party, 2001). Yet the Queen's Speech was conspicuous for the omission of constitutional reform proposals (Wintour, 2001), although there is public support for greater decentralisation of power. For example, with regard to devolution to Scotland and Wales, the public has acquired an appetite for democracy that has not yet been satisfied (Hazell, 2000). So far, the continuation of New Labour's modest and piecemeal approach to democratic renewal has been exemplified by proposed reforms to the House of Lords and local government. The White Paper on the House of Lords reform of November 2001 maintains support for the Wakeham Commission for a mainly appointed second chamber, thus causing considerable disappointment across the political spectrum.

Conclusion

New Labour's strategy for enhancing accountability in public services in general and the welfare state in particular appears to have been built on the synergistic development of democratic renewal and a new managerialism necessary in a more complex and diverse society. Here is a new focus on institutional reform, greater decentralisation, citizenship and the widest participation, and the delivery of performance-orientated public services as a means to increased accountability. Legitimacy is to be seen as a matter of consent, mutual commitment and effective service delivery to a citizen body.

A pattern of governance of the welfare state is emerging that indicates that a start has been made on redefining accountability within a differentiated polity, making the welfare state more answerable to the public it serves. It seems that New Labour's strategy for democratic renewal has contributed to the enhancement of democracy, albeit with some confusion over the distribution of power resulting from the diverse initiatives. Decentralisation of power has occurred, but it has also been accompanied by the maintenance of centralised power. Given the piecemeal nature of the reform agenda, the outcome of New Labour's revision of political accountability has been the creation of a more complex and ambiguous system for the scrutiny and control of the welfare state. In addition, although there appears to be much potential in the government's expanded approach to managerial accountability with its emphasis on public consultation, citizen participation, collaboration and networking, there remains too much emphasis on excessive centralisation, uniformity and bureaucracy.

A more comprehensive approach to democratic renewal than that pursued by New Labour suggests that further evolution in the governance of the welfare state is necessary if the inconsistencies and ambiguity that now prevails are to be removed and if a more complete democratic transformation is to be secured. Thus some critics maintain that the guarantee of democracy in Britain requires a written constitution or constitutional framework of rules for the conduct of government (Weir and Beetham, 1999; Charter 88, 2000; *The Guardian*, 2000). Other favoured constituents of a fully open and accountable welfare state include: a separation of the executive from the legislature; a fully elected second chamber; a House of Commons much reformed in its methods of working and in its mode of election; greater devolution of power to the new parliament and assemblies; and a transfer of power in England from Whitehall and Westminster to either local or regional government.

Unless a Citizens' Constitution is introduced, accompanied by a matching philosophical justification, the critics contend that democratic order is at great risk of dispute, disengagement and disintegration. Indeed, if there is to be a coherent approach to accountability, then there needs to be a real synergy between the democratisation and managerialist agendas. The adoption of a genuinely developmental approach to performance management would enable this to happen. The government must release more control to local decision makers so that inclusiveness, innovation, diversity, organisational learning and imaginative approaches to continuous improvement become real possibilities in public services. Genuine collaboration and partnership, so necessary for managing the differentiated polity of complex social problems, will only emerge if the potential partners are given greater freedom. This will require central government to devise a performance monitoring system fully compatible with respecting, even encouraging, legitimate difference in approaches and outcomes. It will require the whole performance measurement and regulatory system to be overhauled, with less obsessive attention to short-term targets and performance indicators focused on narrow organisational boundaries. Above all, it will require a move away from the punitive culture that has increasingly characterised the system. The distinctive purposes, values and conditions of the public services must be fully appreciated and celebrated if there is to be genuine compatibility between the performance and democratisation agenda, and a coherent and new approach to accountability is to emerge. Although there are encouraging signs of change for the second term, there are also a number of signals that indicate the continuation, even enhancement, of control.

New Labour can be credited with fulfilling, to a considerable extent, its promises for democratic renewal and for raising the importance of quality public services fully accountable to citizens. However, there are various anomalies and democratic gaps in the evolving pattern of governance. There is further scope for New Labour to pursue democratic renewal in a second term by consolidating the measures that have already been taken and by promoting the politics of trust rather than those of control.

References

Blair, T. (1998) *The third way*, London: Fabian Society.

Blair, T. (2000) 'Foreword' to Citizens First, *Modernising government Annual Report*, London: The Stationery Office.

Brooks, J. (2000) 'Labour's modernisation of local government', *Public Administration*, vol 78, no 3, pp 593-612.

Cabinet Office. (1999) *Modernising government*, Cm 4310, London: The Stationery Office.

Cabinet Office (2000) *Reaching out – The role of central government at regional and local level*, Performance and Innovation Unit Report, London: The Stationery Office.

Clarence, E. and Painter, C. (1998) 'Public services under New Labour: collaborative discourses and local networking', *Public Policy and Administration*, vol 13, no 3, pp 8-22.

Clarke, J. and Newman, J. (1997) *The managerial state*, London: Sage Publications.

Clarke, J., Gerwirtz, S. and McLaughlin, E. (2000) 'Reinventing the welfare state', in J. Clarke, S. Gerwitz and E. McLaughlin (eds) *New managerialism new welfare?*, Milton Keynes/London: Open University/Sage Publications, pp 1-26.

Clarke, J., Gerwirtz, S., Hughes, G. and Humphreys, J. (2000) 'Guarding the public interest? Auditing in public services', in J. Clarke, S. Gerwitz and E. McLaughlin (eds) *New managerialism new welfare?*, Milton Keynes/London: Open University/Sage Publications.

Cope, S. and Goodship, J. (1999) 'Regulating collaborative government: towards joined-up government?', *Public Policy and Administration*, vol 14, no 2, pp 3-16.

Cutler, T. and Waine, B. (2000) 'Managerialism reformed? New Labour and public sector management', *Social Policy and Administration*, vol 34, no 3, pp 318-32.

Deakin, N. and Parry, R. (2000) *The Treasury and social policy: The contest for control of welfare strategy*, London: Macmillan Press.

DETR (Department of the Environment, Transport and the Regions) (1998) *Modern local government: In touch with the people*, Cm 4014, London: The Stationery Office.

DETR (2000) *Regional government in England*, London: DETR.

DTLR (Department for Transport, Local Government and the Regions) (2001) *Strong local leadership – Quality public services*, Cm 5237, London: The Stationery Office.

Hazell, R. (ed) (2000) *The state and the nations: The first year of devolution in the UK*, Exeter: Imprint Academic.

Hoggett, P. (1996) 'New modes of control in the public service', *Public Administration*, vol 74, pp 3-32.

Hood, C., James, O. and Scott, C. (2000) 'Regulation of government: has it increased, is it decreasing, should it be diminished?', *Public Administration*, vol 78, no 2, pp 283-304.

Hood, C., James, O., Jones, G.W. and Travers, A. (1999) *Regulation inside government*, Oxford: Oxford University Press.

Jervis, P. and Richards, S. (1997) 'Public management: raising the game', *Public Money and Management*, vol 17, no 2, pp 9-16.

JRF (Joseph Rowntree Foundation) (1994) 'Local and central government relations research', Findings, 29 July, York: Joseph Rowntree Foundation.

JRF (2000a) 'Electoral reform in local government: lessons from the rest of Europe,' Findings 940, September, York: Joseph Rowntree Foundation.

JRF (2000b) 'Regional Development Agencies and local regeneration', Findings 550, May, York: Joseph Rowntree Foundation.

Labour Party (1997) *New Labour because Britain deserves better* (Election Manifesto), London: Labour Party.

Labour Party (2001) *Ambitions for Britain* (Election Manifesto), London: Labour Party.

Lovell, A. and Hand, L. (1999) 'Expanding the notion of organisational performance measurement to support joined-up government', *Public Policy and Administration*, vol 14, no 2, pp 17-29.

Marquand, D. (2000) 'Democracy in Britain', *Political Quarterly*, vol 71, no 3, pp 268-76.

Newman, J. (2000) 'Beyond the new public management? Modernizing public services', in J. Clarke, S. Gerwitz and E. McLaughlin (eds) *New managerialism, new welfare?*, Milton Keynes/London: Open University/Sage Publications, pp 45-61.

Newman, J., Raine, J. and Skelcher, C. (2001) 'Transforming local government: innovation and modernisation', *Public Money and Management*, vol 21, no 2, pp 61-8.

Painter, C. and Clarence, E. (2000) 'New Labour and inter-governmental management: flexible networks or performance control?', *Public Management*, vol 2, no 4, pp 477-98.

Pollitt, C., Girre, X., Lonsdale, J., Mul, R., Summa, H. and Waeress, M. (1999) *Performance or compliance?*, Oxford: Oxford University Press.

Powell, M. and Boyne, G. (2001) 'The spatial strategy of equality and the spatial division of welfare', *Social Policy and Administration*, vol 35, no 2, pp 181-94.

Pratchett, L. (1999) 'Defining democratic renewal', *Local Government Studies*, vol 25, no 4, pp 1-18.

Rao, N. (2000) *Reviving local democracy: New Labour, new politics?*, Bristol: The Policy Press.

Rhodes, R.A.W. (1997) *Understanding governance: Policy networks, governance, reflexivity and accountability*, Buckingham: Open University Press.

Rouse, J. (1999) 'Performance management, quality management and contracts', in S. Horton and D. Farnham (eds) *Public management in Britain*, Basingstoke: Macmillan, pp 76-93.

Rouse, J. and Smith, G. (1999) 'Accountability', in M. Powell (ed) *New Labour, new welfare state? The 'third way' in British social policy*, Bristol: The Policy Press, pp 235-55.

Skelcher, C. (2000) 'Changing images of the State: overloaded, hollowed-out, congested', *Public Policy and Administration*, vol 15, no 3, pp 3-19.

Talbot, C. (2000) 'Performing "Performance" – a comedy in five acts', *Public Money and Management*, vol 20, no 4, pp 63-8.

The Guardian (2000) *Manifesto*, 25 September.

Tomaney, J. and Hetherington, P. (2000) *Monitoring the English regions*, Report No 1, Newcastle Upon Tyne: Centre for Urban and Regional Development Studies.

Treasury (1998) *Public services for the future: Modernisation, reform, accountability*, Cm 4181, London: The Stationery Office.

Wainwright, M. (2000) 'Making it easy', *The Guardian*, 15 May, p 17.

Walker, D. (2000) *Analysis an altered state?*, Transcript of a recorded documentary (news.bbc.co.uk/hi/english/static/audio_video/programmes/analysis/transcripts/state.txt).

Weir, S. and Beetham, D. (1999) *Political power and democratic control in Britain*, London: Routledge.

White, M. (2000) 'Blair admits case for regional governments', *The Guardian*, 29 March, p 13.

Wintour, P. (2001) 'Ministers braced for confrontation', *The Guardian*, 21 June, p 6.

FOUR

Evaluating New Labour's approach to independent welfare provision

Edward Brunsdon and Margaret May

Introduction

One of the key features distinguishing the first Blair administration from its Labour predecessors was its espousal of non-statutory welfare. Shunned or marginalised by postwar Labour policies, Blair's government sought to encompass voluntary and community organisations (VCOs)[1] and commercial service providers[2] within its emergent vision of the future welfare edifice. This vision was initially conveyed through a somewhat disparate set of election commitments in which the Party (HMG, 2000) set out to:

- introduce Individual Savings Accounts (33);
- reinvigorate the Private Finance Initiative (PFI) (37);
- overcome NHS PFI problems (63);
- establish a Royal Commission on Long Term Care (100);
- introduce a Long-Term Care Charter (101);
- introduce Independent Inspection of Nursing Homes and Domiciliary Care (102);
- develop a National Citizens Service Programme (124).

But it was also embedded in a broader and more imposing list of proposals that included: its pledge to cut NHS waiting lists (5); the Manifesto commitments to improve the NHS, strengthen communities and modernise welfare (6 and 7): and the more detailed assurances addressing issues ranging from pre-school provision to urban regeneration. In these instances, however, the significance of independent providers, particularly from the commercial sector, only surfaced gradually during the government's first term.

This chapter addresses the nature and translation of New Labour's vision for independent welfare, and looks at governmental and non-governmental evaluations of its success and the broader policy issues it poses[3]. It is as much about the vision as its instigation, primarily because the approach to independent providers was uneven and evaluations were sparse. Translations into practical agendas differed in timescale and in approach to the different types of provider, and, in terms of commercial welfare per se, varied from market to market. Encased in the language of 'partnership', the translation for voluntary providers was more fully developed from the outset and centred on establishing cross-agency mechanisms to further the reconfiguration of Britain's welfare mix. By comparison, those for commercial providers spoke of market 'harnessing' and sought, either through enhanced regulation or particular types of partnerships, to respond to market-specific, often exigency-driven, issues.

Building strong communities: New Labour's aspirations for VCOs

In its own eyes, and indeed those of many VCOs, New Labour entered office with the aim of recasting voluntary provision. It sought to enhance VCOs' policy-making role, extend their service-delivery capacity and accord them a central set of responsibilities. This contrasts quite markedly with the precepts of earlier governments. While less statist than some commentators have indicated, postwar Labour governments upheld public services as the guarantors of consistent, comprehensive and universal provision, relegating voluntary organisations and volunteering to an auxiliary role. Working in the shadow of state services, however, enabled VCOs to develop more specialist provision, pioneering care programmes for a range of client groups and developing advocacy and advisory services. It also facilitated their focus on user awareness and their continued operation as watchdogs and lobbyists, exposing unmet need, monitoring government policies and campaigning for improved statutory provision.

The 1970s saw the beginning of a challenge to this auxiliary role as Conservative and neoliberal critics of state welfare sought to reconceptualise VCOs as alternative rather than subsidiary suppliers of welfare. The Conservative governments of the 1980s and 1990s also embraced this notion, implementing policies to increase voluntary (and commercial) provision on a competitive, contract-driven basis. Faced with this change in conception and the related revamping of state welfare, Labour, in opposition, shifted its approach to voluntary endeavour, giving it a broader, more central, place in its new welfare order (Labour Party, 1989).

The rewording of the Party's constitution to include working not only with unions (and other affiliated organisations) but with voluntary agencies, consumer groups and other representative bodies signalled this change. The nature of the alliance, sketched out in consultations with VCO representatives in the build-up to the 1997 election (Labour Party, 1995; Blunkett and Kilfoyle, 1996), was explicated in the Manifesto and related documents. These addressed the widespread unease among VCOs generated by the advent of the contract culture, the downgrading of their non-service activities, and a parallel decline in both volunteering and charitable giving. New Labour's proposals were powered, however, by a more fundamental anxiety over the state of civil society and the need to rebuild social capital (Putnam, 1993; Giddens, 1998). This was seen as a prerequisite not only for economic regeneration in deprived areas but also for the reconstruction of responsible citizenship (CSJ, 1994; Blair, 1996).

The Manifesto set voluntary activity firmly within this dual project for democratic renewal and welfare modernisation, declaring:

> An independent and creative voluntary sector, committed to voluntary activity as an expression of citizenship, is central to our vision of a stakeholder society.
> (Labour Party, 1997a, p 31)

Similarly, its policy document on the sector held:

> Partnership with the voluntary sector is central to Labour's policy of achieving cohesion in a one-nation society. Voluntary action and the act of volunteering are both essential to citizenship and to re-establishing a sense of community.
> (Labour Party, 1997b, p 1)

More specifically, its seventh electoral commitment pledged New Labour to building 'strong communities'. Drawing on earlier proposals (CSJ, 1994), it promised to develop a 'National Citizens Service Programme', to "tap the enthusiasm of the young" and "harness the imagination of all those people who have so much to offer for the benefit of the community". This was to be an inductive process "devised and developed by people within their own communities" (Labour Party, 1997a, p 31). To facilitate this, VCOs were to receive extra funding and infrastructural support. As importantly, New Labour maintained that it would introduce a 'compact' along the lines envisaged by the Deakin Commission (1996) that would recognise the autonomy and lobbying activities of voluntary agencies and offer a partnership approach to replace the contract culture (Labour Party, 1997b).

VCO policy developments 1997-2001

In office, New Labour's proposals were elaborated through extensive consultation with VCOs in a succession of working groups and ministerial task forces. The promised compact for England was launched in November 1998, with parallel documents for the other UK nations (Home Office, 1998). It set out a framework for governing relations between central government and voluntary and community groups based on a 'shared vision' of their 'complementary functions' and the latter's 'fundamental' role in developing a 'democratic, socially inclusive society'. The government reaffirmed that it wanted to work in partnership with VCOs while recognising their 'independence' and campaigning rights. In consultation with the sector, it also undertook to develop local compacts underwritten by five codes of good practice (for funding, consultation and policy appraisal, volunteering, community groups and ethnic minority organisations). Responsibility for furthering the compacts was incorporated into the Home Office Public Service Agreement (PSA) published in December

1998 and amplified by separate Action Plans (Home Office, 2000a). Future growth in demand for voluntary activity also emerged in a stream of other policies, ranging from those aimed at modernising government, urban regeneration, community safety, Action Zones and the New Deal to those of the Social Exclusion Unit (SEU) and its policy action teams. The anticipated increase, however, also reinforced concerns about the sector's capacity and its funding. The government responded to these with two further initiatives in 1999: a 10-year rolling programme to increase volunteering (launched by the Prime Minister) and a second scheme to 'get Britain giving' (heralded in the Chancellor's pre-Budget statement).

By the second half of its first term, the government had translated its communitarian vision (Blair, 1996, p 209) into an array of measures for expanding voluntary action and the sector's capacity to deliver the required growth in services. The twin aims were to create a "a step change in public involvement in community life" and develop a "strong voluntary and community sector to provide services and reduce social exclusion" (Home Office, 1999a, p 1). These necessitated the reconstruction of the framework in which voluntary agencies operated and, equally fundamentally, 'changes in attitude' towards community involvement such that "every person in every community knows that they count and that they can make a difference" (Home Office, 1999b, vol 1, p 47). Labour pursued these aims through a five-point strategy that involved:

• boosting volunteering and widening its social base;
• increasing charitable giving;
• enhancing VCOs capacity and effectiveness;
• engaging VCOs in policy making;
• establishing a partnership approach to service delivery.

Translating these strategic goals into measurable targets commensurate with the Treasury's SMART (specific, measurable, achievable, relevant, timed) requirements, however, proved problematic. Indeed, the government was warned that "an elaborate apparatus of targets and performance indicators [would] not work" since the state could only "facilitate and encourage" and not "direct" voluntary effort (Home Office, 1999a, para 22). In spite of this, targets were set for some goals, although with schedules that went way beyond the government's first term of office. Meeting these featured in the remit of several departments, but primary responsibility was vested in the Home Office and, more specifically, its Voluntary and Community Unit. From January 1999, this was reassigned to a new and larger Active Community Unit (ACU). Modelled on the SEU and reporting to both the Cabinet and the Home Office, it was charged with developing integrated cross-departmental measures that involved consultation with VCOs and avoided a 'top-down' approach.

Intrinsic evaluation: a citizens' service for a new millennium?

From the government's perspective, the framework for realising its goals was thus in place by the end of its first term of office and 'real progress' was being made on a number of fronts (Home Office, 2000b, p 56). Meaningful assessments of its claims, however, were limited by the schedules the government set itself and were largely based on VCOs' viewpoints. In consequence, most evaluations focused on two issues: the effectiveness of the mechanisms adopted by the government to meet its strategic goals, and their possible implications for voluntary agencies.

In terms of its first goal, the government claimed that it had instituted a programme designed to reverse the decline in volunteering experienced during the 1990s and increase participation by underrepresented groups. Initially, this was couched in general terms, with the Home Office being asked to "increase the quantity and quality of voluntary and community activity" (Home Office, 2000b, p 57). From 2000, however, the Chancellor set more specific targets, pledging the government to increase the numbers 'actively involved in their communities' by one million by 2004 (HM Treasury, 2000b). Subsequently, he proposed that this target be extended so that two thirds of adults undertook at least two hours of voluntary activity per week by 2005, with the proportion rising to three quarters by 2010 (Brown, 2001). His expectation, reiterated by the Prime Minister, was that the government's recruitment drive would also secure a socially and ethnically more diverse volunteer force.

According to the Home Office, the mechanisms to facilitate this expansion were either in place or 'on course' by the end of its first term (Home Office, 2001, p 57). In line with its PSA, it had established five demonstration projects to heighten public awareness of the value of volunteering. A long-term media campaign to update the image of volunteering and highlight its 'two-way benefits' was under way, supported by the BBC, One2One and the Community Channel. More direct mechanisms for stimulating the volunteer labour market were also on target. The Home Office had developed a time-bank scheme enabling VCOs to 'advertise' the openings available and potential recruits both to pursue these and to indicate their interests. In conjunction with Business in the Community (BiTC), the ACU had also launched an employee-volunteer scheme. Indicating a rather different agenda, all public services had been charged with expanding opportunities for voluntary service.

Pump-priming measures to widen participation were also on schedule. Young volunteers had been recruited through the Department for Education and Employment's £48 million three-year Millennium Volunteers scheme with its inducements of accreditation and youth-oriented activities. By 2001, the Home Office could also point to other initiatives designed to regularise volunteering. The promised National Experience Corps promoting voluntary work among retirees was on stream, with a recruitment target of 250,000 55- to 64-year-olds between 2001 and 2003 and a further one million in 2004 (HM Treasury,

2000a). Inducements to boost volunteering by members of Britain's different ethnic communities was built into this and, in line with the government's objectives, complemented by extra funding. This included diverting £20 million from the New Opportunities Fund to the Millennium Commission to fund ethnic minority projects and injecting a further £180 million from the Treasury in January 2001 to support volunteering generally. More fundamentally, the government had also instituted a longer-term initiative to foster community involvement through its inclusion in the 'citizenship' component of the national curriculum from 2002 and its incorporation into higher education by 2010.

Despite its significance, only a few observers questioned either the grounds or the implications of this wide-ranging attempt to normalise volunteering. The mainly VCO-driven research that was undertaken focused on assessing the short-term impact of the government's measures. Reassuringly for New Labour, they pointed to an upturn in volunteering. But, although the earlier decline had been halted, there was little sign of a surge in altruism among individuals or widespread release of staff by employers. Volunteering also remained a predominantly white and middle-aged activity (Obaze, 2000). Some analysts suggested this limited progress reflected a slow and patchy response among VCOs, particularly to the government's 'diversity challenge'. Others queried the feasibility of government-led drives to generate an inherently volitional activity and, more particularly, its focus on service-based forms of voluntarism. They also wondered whether, as in the case of some unions, increased voluntary activity had been perceived as a threat to public provision and had led to the less than enthusiastic response (Wintour, 2001). Most analysts, however, attributed the low take-up to the inadequacies of the government's promotional measures. These were widely perceived by VCOs as poorly coordinated and based on inappropriate competitive bidding systems, with little allowance for the needs of small local groups or the many hidden costs entailed in managing and training new recruits and ensuring their suitability (Unwin, 2001).

Similar issues surfaced, albeit in a more indirect sense, in surveys of the impact of the government's attempt to arrest the decline in charitable giving. After extensive consultation with VCOs, its target became one of boosting donations by £1 billion a year by 2002. This was to be achieved through a new fiscal regime and a state-sponsored media campaign designed to promote what the Chancellor termed 'civic patriotism' and, more particularly, American-style corporate citizenship. To stimulate individual giving, the 2000 Budget simplified the Gift Aid scheme, increased tax relief and extended it to gifts of shares including those from companies. More radically, it enabled businesses to make donations from pre-tax profits and offered new incentives to employee giving by lifting the cap on such schemes and introducing a three-year bonus relief system. To enable charities to benefit from this enhanced income, the Budget released £400 million during 2000/01 by reducing the compliance costs associated with Gift Aid and extending exemptions and VAT relief on fund-raising events and related activities. To promote increased levels of philanthropy, the Chancellor also sought to stem the widespread public disquiet over the regulation and internal management of charities disclosed, for example, by the 1998 Public Accounts Committee. To this end, the Charity Commission's remit was tightened and subjected to a highly specific PSA.

As with the government's recruitment drive, interim studies of charitable giving revealed a rather mixed picture. By mid-2001, there was considerable evidence of widespread public awareness and support for the revised Gift Aid scheme. It also appeared that individual donations were creeping back to the levels of the early 1990s (Walker, 2001). There was little indication, however, of any major escalation in generosity and there were also signs of deep-seated resistance to conventional forms of giving among the young (Bentham, 2001). It may be premature to question whether the revamped scheme will generate the £350 million projected by the National Council for Voluntary Organisations (NCVO) (HM Treasury, 2000a). But by the end of the government's first term, it was clear that the increase in corporate donations had not materialised. Charities were still dependent on gifts from a few large companies and, despite the Chancellor's exhortations, corporate giving still averaged only 0.2% of overall pre-tax profits (Murphy, 2001).

In accounting for these findings, most studies again focused on the limitations of the government's approach. Raising corporate giving to the American levels anticipated by the Chancellor, it was argued, required more effective mechanisms. These included setting targets for the proportion of profits to be donated by companies and the use of contract compliance to force adherence among those bidding for or gaining government contracts (NCVO, 2001). In similar vein, it was suggested that the government should ensure that financial services advisers included employee and charitable giving in their advice to clients. A few studies, however, highlighted the failure of charities themselves, especially smaller ones, to encourage tax-efficient giving (Hill, 2001) and emphasised the impact of continuing public concern over their efficiency. This concern remained unalloyed despite the government's attempts to tighten the scrutiny exercised by the Charity Commission.

The commission's 1999 PSA required it to "ensure that charities are able to operate for their proper purposes within an effective legal, accounting and governance framework" (Home Office, 2001, p 166). To this end, it was given quantifiable targets for its monitoring activities, including the proportion of charities placed on the register to which it gave advice, the number and length of investigations it undertook, its rectification of problems, the substantive guidance it provided and the accuracy of its database. Although these were met (Home Office, 2001), the commission faced continued concern over the effectiveness of charitable governance fuelled by media coverage of what was presented as charities' disproportionate administrative costs. The potential damage to the government's wider plans for VCOs posed by such reports was heightened by a succession of well-publicised studies charting the many anomalies of charitable registration, their lack of accountability and the tax privileges accruing to enterprises such as private hospitals and schools. Like the Deakin Commission, these advocated a single 'public benefit' test as the basis for registration as well as closer external scrutiny of charities' effectiveness.

The government's initial response was to strengthen the Charity Commission's remit by expanding its budget (an increase of 40%) and setting it more rigorous PSA targets (Home Office, 2001). From April 2002, it is scheduled to expand its inquiries by over a quarter, double the number of visits it undertakes and publish three annual 'cross-cutting' reports. Relevant charities will be expected to comply with the resulting recommendations. The limited impact of government measures to restore public confidence and generate higher giving also led to two further developments. First, following the 2001 election, the Cabinet Office Performance and Innovation Unit (PIU) was asked to review the legal and regulatory framework of charities and, more generally, the voluntary sector as a whole. Second, the Treasury charged one of the reviews set up as part of the 2002 CSR to consider "the role of the voluntary sector in providing services" and, in particular, "the necessary instruments to improve this contribution" (HM Treasury, 2001).

In establishing these two studies, the government not only reasserted the central role it had assigned to voluntary provision in its remodelling of welfare, but tacitly acknowledged the limited headway it had made in meeting another of its goals, that of enhancing VCO's overall capability. This was to have been achieved through more systematic funding by government departments coordinated by the ACU, and used for infrastructural investment to facilitate innovation, interagency working, the pooling of resources and, in particular, the development of ethnic minority agencies. On the surface, the ACU appeared to have met its brief (Home Office, 2000b). Regional Voluntary Sector Networks were either established or 'on course' by 2000. It was distributing £12 million in 'strategic grants' to some 55 key agencies and applications from minority-led VCOs were being 'actively encouraged' and their development supported by specific funding schemes such as the Connecting Communities Race Equality Support Programme (Home Office, 2001).

Other departments were also providing extensive pump-priming monies for new projects, particularly community building, through initiatives that ranged from Sure Start, Neighbourhood Renewal and Action Zone programmes to the Children's Millennium Commission and Community Resource Funds. As the government became increasingly aware, however, the disparate nature of voluntary endeavour made for slow progress. At local level, organisations with varying agendas were often reluctant to engage in collaborative ventures. 'Capacity building' was also impeded by the difficulties faced by the ACU in coordinating the flow of initiatives emerging from other departments. Despite its cross-cutting remit, it did not have the SEU's single power base or tight focus and appears to have had insufficient resources for effective interdepartmental liaison. The government's bid to enhance infrastructural support for VCOs was, in consequence, widely seen as ill conceived and poorly coordinated and the ACU as ineffective (Plowden et al, 2001). Nor was the government as munificent as it claimed it was. New funding was announced and then often repackaged as part of other, ostensibly, different and more generous schemes. It was typically short-term, tied to specific activities rather than an agency's overall needs and made only minimal allowances for core costs (Unwin, 2001).

The ubiquity of these long-standing concerns in VCO studies also raises questions about the government's success in meeting its fourth goal of involving VCOs in policy formation. Here it promised a new partnership with voluntary groups playing a key role in the enhancement of community governance and the bid to counter social exclusion. At national level, New Labour's main vehicle for engaging VCOs in policy making was the national compact. The lengthy discussions involved in developing its related codes of practice meant, however, that the compact remained an icon rather than a realisation of the government's intentions. The process of developing local compacts proved even more protracted, with some local authorities and voluntary groups negotiating compacts ahead of the local guidelines while others waited until their publication (WGGRS, 2000). Their development, moreover, was often overtaken by the obligation to establish other collaborative structures. To secure New Labour's community governance commitments, local authority consultation with VCOs was made a statutory duty in many policy areas, notably through the Local Government Acts of 1999 and 2000 and the requirements of the Best Value regime. In addition, central subventions for regeneration, anti-social exclusion and other local initiatives were increasingly tied to public–voluntary partnership bidding.

According to the government, these measures gave VCOs a pivotal role in policy design, enabling them to pursue a proactive, strategic approach and initiate as well as develop new projects. This applied both to schemes such as Sure Start and the broader processes of democratic renewal and community building (Labour Party, 2001). Here they were upheld as empowering agents, involving those traditionally outside or disinterested in the policy process, facilitating 'bottom-up' approaches and acting as the locus of community activity (Home Office, 1999b). Whether the resultant array of emergent compacts, joint ventures, partnership boards, action teams and civic forums had begun to deliver 'real' partnerships or more participatory forms of decision making was open to question. While acknowledging the increased role of VCOs in local planning and bidding structures, most studies found that this was outweighed by the constraints on VCOs' ability to participate effectively (Craig and Warburton, 2001; Powell et al, 2001). This applied particularly to smaller, black and ethnic minority groupings that were not only overstretched but also underrepresented in the development of local compacts and other consultative bodies (Craig et al, 2002). More generally, the nature, timing and sheer proliferation of many new initiatives, combined with their control of planning cycles, meant local authorities invariably took the lead in policy formation and, with their larger resource base, tended to dominate partnership activities (Pahroah et al, 1998; Craig et al, 1999; Taylor, 2001). Many VCOs consequently felt they were simply 'playing the partnership game' (Powell et al, 2001).

Table 4.1: Progress against Manifesto/Annual Report targets for the voluntary sector

Pledge	New Labour's assessment	Score/10
124: Develop a National Citizens Service Programme	On course	7

In response to such findings, Dahrendorf (2001) maintained that, far from opening up policy making, New Labour's partnership schemes amounted to a form of nationalisation. While this perception was widely challenged by voluntary providers, it did draw attention to the extent to which New Labour's varied schemes were intended to expand VCOs' regulated role in service delivery as well as policy formation. In order to avoid controversy, perhaps, the government did not directly document its success in achieving this, its fifth strategic goal. Nevertheless, it presided over an accelerated expansion of voluntary welfare services. Consistent with the Manifesto's proposal, it extended the state's use of voluntary provision in areas such as adult social care and children's services where it was already a key player. More fundamentally, New Labour also limited the expansion of public services in favour of using voluntary agencies to deliver many of its new area- and issue-based policies.

Yet this aspect of the government's elevation of voluntary endeavour, as distinct from the assessments of particular programmes, attracted little attention. As has been seen, most non-governmental evaluations were VCO-driven. Operating within an expansionary climate they focused, not surprisingly, on the government's benchmarks and their implications for VCOs. With regard to the latter, opinion diverged between those who saw VCOs' increasing service provision and dependence on public funds as a threat to their autonomy and those who argued that the two were not incompatible.

Despite such differences, there was widespread consensus that New Labour had raised the profile of voluntary endeavour, bringing it back into the mainstream of policy making (Kendall, 2000). While it had met with mixed success in achieving its five-part strategy (Home Office, 1996b), it had taken many of the steps necessary to establish its National Citizens Service Programme and could justifiably claim to have realised its Manifesto target.

Extrinsic evaluation

From a wider perspective, however, the government's attempt to rehabilitate voluntary welfare and inculcate a new civic culture poses a different set of questions. These relate both to its perception of voluntary provision and the place of volunteering in its wider welfare agenda. New Labour undoubtedly saw widespread civic engagement as the basis of a healthy democracy and a corrective to earlier over-statist welfarism. But its conception of volunteering in practice was narrower and more passive than its rhetoric implied and based on an essentially unproblematised and consensual approach. As pledge 124 signified, active citizens were construed as those involved in various forms of personal or community services, mentoring, befriending, training and supporting others, providing transport or domestic assistance and contributing to the management of schools and other agencies including VCOs. Such participation combined with VCOs' consultative activities in turn fed into a democratic decision-making process based on the representation of a plurality of local interests.

The assumption that political resources were widely diffused and could be covered by giving a voice to self-constituted voluntary groupings is highly questionable. Not only did it equate participation and consultation with power, it credited VCOs with a public mandate and representation that few possessed (Ross and Osborne, 1999; Skelcher, 2000; IPPR, 2001) and in the process threatened to dilute their campaigning/scrutinising roles. New Labour's adoption of new modes of governance based on networking and partnership (Rhodes, 1996), moreover, seems to have shifted decision making further from the public gaze towards a plethora of unelected and only indirectly accountable bodies.

Equally critically, it promoted a version of voluntarism embedded in and serving cohesive communities that masked the contested nature of local identities and the disciplinary overtones of much capacity building. It also hid the extent to which the presentation of volunteering as a citizen's duty was driven by the need to supplement underresourced public provision and enable VCOs to deliver substitute services. As with earlier Conservative governments, this rested on a number of largely untested assumptions derived primarily from VCO publicity (Brenton, 1985) about the relative merits of voluntary provision over other types of service provider. Compared to public agencies, VCOs were depicted as less rule-bound, more responsive, flexible and innovative and, above all, resource-effective. They also had the added value of operating without a profit-making taint. There were few studies of the extent to which VCOs matched this image or, indeed, the transaction costs entailed in partnership working (Knapp et al, 1999). The empirical work that had been undertaken indicated that their niche areas of provision made it difficult to compare voluntary providers with state or commercial agencies in terms of either the '3Es' (economy, effectiveness and efficiency) or broader 'quality' and 'outcome' measures (see Chapter One of this volume).

A new deal for business: New Labour's aspirations for commercial welfare

As with VCOs, the government's approach to commercial welfare providers was partly framed by its perception of the limitations of earlier Labour policies. However, unlike the voluntary sector where it attempted to build a national framework based on a clear conception of the role of voluntary endeavour, its interventions in commercial practice were more cautious and only exceptionally supra-market. This was in part a consequence of the organisational complexity of commercial welfare, with products and services being traded in markets of different composition, size and levels of competitiveness, and subject to different regulatory conditions. But it was also the outcome of the absence of detailed forward planning for the welfare business contribution to the mixed economy. What in retrospect might seem features of an holistic conception, for example, the increase in self-funding, the strengthening of consumer protection and the promotion of public–private partnerships, were, at least in the first instance, simply cases of reactive policy making.

This pragmatic approach is evidenced in the administration's pre-electoral positioning where commercial welfare services were variously subsumed within the general terms that related to 'business', addressed indirectly through proposals for statutory or voluntary providers, or considered selectively in terms of particular problems in specific markets. In the case of the latter, it was typically responding to issues that its Conservative predecessor also confronted or created. New Labour documented this perceived legacy in the Manifesto. With pensions and long-term care, for instance, it shared the Conservatives' concern about the potential costs of an ageing population and pledged to encourage and support self-provisioning against life-cycle contingencies. It proposed achieving this through a "partnership between public and private provision" and "a balance between income sourced from tax and invested savings" (Labour Party, 1997a, p 13). To promote the latter, a new tax-discounted individual savings account was planned alongside a revamped pension system. However, in the light of the financial scandals of the late 1980s and early 1990s, New Labour felt it necessary to restore consumer confidence by tightening the regulation of the insurance and savings markets.

The decision to introduce or strengthen consumer protection was also a response to issues in other markets. In the case of housing, for example, it was part of a package to address "the needs of homeowners and tenants alike" (Labour Party, 1997a, p 26). Mortgage holders were offered more protection and flexibility and leaseholders greater purchasing options. A new 'communal tenure' was promised, along with a 'revived private rented sector, subject to stronger controls' and a 'three-way public partnership' to promote 'good social housing' (see Chapter Six of this volume). In adult social services, tighter regulation was part of a conception that sought to reduce the incidence of poor-quality services in all sectors while freeing up local authorities to develop their mix of providers. While promising a long-term care charter, New Labour sidestepped the contentious issue of long-term care funding by proposing to establish a Royal Commission. This also enabled it to deflect attention away from the self-financing element implicit in its pensions and savings proposals.

The Party took a different, and contrasting, position in the Manifesto when it came to questions concerning commercial healthcare and education. Unlike other services, these forms of provision were not identified as sources of problems. Neither were they initially seen as contributing to the solutions to those problems located in statutory provision. New Labour had taken a pre-electoral decision to abolish income tax relief on private medical insurance for the over-65s, but for the most part avoided any mention of direct intervention in the healthcare markets. Rather, it maintained the stance of previous Labour governments in seeking state-funded, state-delivered healthcare. It spoke of a health service 'based on need alone – not the ability to pay,' and openly avowed its opposition 'to the privatisation of clinical services'. It said nothing, however, about existing commercial acute care hospitals, their primary care counterparts, the opthalmics market or private dental practice.

The Party took a more positive stance towards private education. Although it vowed to abolish the assisted places and nursery voucher schemes, it countered these with a commitment to create a nationwide system of quality nursery education (involving non-statutory agencies) and proposed new links with private schools. It clearly anticipated a mixed economy of educational provision when it undertook "never [to] force the abolition" of good private schools and, more generally, offered "to build bridges" across the "educational apartheid created by the public/private divide" (p 7). At the time of the Manifesto, this vision of partnership with private education providers was the most overt indication of its *rapprochement* with commercial welfare and, although not explicitly linked at the time, was later used to illustrate New Labour's broader vision of a 'new deal for business'. What the Party saw in this vision was a reconciliation of business calculation and social justice to be achieved by 'harnessing markets' so that they could 'serve the public interest' (Blair, 1996, 1998).

Harnessing the market? Policy developments and intrinsic evaluations 1997-2001

The Manifesto proposals for the different commercial welfare services were generally elaborated in consultative papers and then subjected to the varied requirements placed on government departments by their PSAs. Implementation often involved time-consuming primary legislation and progress tended to be gauged in terms of changing service structures rather than measurable transformations in delivery. The consequent evaluations therefore either focused on inputs and process management, or involved more conjectural assessments of the policy outcomes. Adding to the complexity of these appraisals was the fact that, in some instances, the government changed tack. This was in part a response to an increased awareness of the depth of problems confronting it, but it was also the product of the emergence of new issues and shifts in New Labour's understanding of policy-making procedures.

Its immediate priority was dealing with the Conservative legacy, and this largely meant resetting the regulatory limits of commercial practice and restoring consumer confidence. Both were prerequisites for its plans for a modernised pension and benefit system and for maintaining a mixed economy in housing and social care. In its bid to rebuild trust in financial services markets, the government adopted a number of tactics. Its first was to institute an extensive compensation scheme, backed by a 'naming and shaming' campaign, to spur companies into retraining staff, eradicating bad practices and implementing higher standards of customer care. In line with its electoral commitments, New Labour also strengthened the regulation of financial and other welfare products, establishing a new umbrella body – the Financial Services Agency (FSA) – in 1999 to oversee the pensions, insurance and long-term savings markets. Its powers were gradually extended to other products, most notably mortgages, health and long-term care insurance. New Labour also gave the FSA an extensive consumer education remit, including a requirement specified in the 1999 Budget to publish comparative data and league tables on savings and insurance products. The promotion of Charges, Access, Terms (CAT) standards and kite-marking schemes complemented this increase in advice and consumer protection. This was further enhanced by the increasingly proactive investigations of the Office of Fair Trading (OFT) and the extension of its powers under the 1998 Competition Act.

The regulatory developments in financial services were mirrored in the health and social care markets. The National Care Standards Commission (NCSC) was established in April 2001 under the 2000 Care Standards Act. As with the FSA, it was construed as both a 'standards inspector' and a 'standards promoter' with responsibility for a wide-ranging set of service providers. These included residential, nursing and children's homes, nursing agencies and the hitherto unregulated domiciliary care providers, independent fostering agencies and small children's homes. Also drawn within its province were non-NHS hospitals and clinics previously regulated under the 1984 Registered Homes Act and the many small clinics that had operated outside this legislation. From becoming fully operational in April 2002, the NCSC will set national minimum standards for each service and support consumers by providing information and investigating complaints. Its remit was reinforced by other information and regulatory initiatives. True to its Manifesto commitments, the government instituted a Long-Term Care Charter, which, with its associated local charters, set out the range of provisions for consumers. To secure its early years and childcare strategy, it also introduced a new regulatory regime, subjecting registered childminders and pre-school providers to a national standards scheme monitored (in England) by OFSTED inspections.

In evaluating these regulatory structures, most studies followed the government's line and focused on their efficacy in redressing the problems left by the Conservatives. Not unexpectedly, consumer groups, while supporting the emphasis on standard setting as well as physical facilities, were drawn to gaps in legislation and the limited character of enforcement procedures. In social care, for example, user groups questioned the extent to which the NCSC would 'police' the health and care industry as distinct from benchmarking good practice, whereas in childcare they contested the appropriateness of OFSTED acting as the regulatory authority. In financial services, consumer comments and criticism were directed at the FSA for its failure to stem the widespread use of misleading promotional and marketing techniques and its overreliance on the provision of consumer advice and information. Much of this was seen as poorly targeted (SSC, 2000) and when coupled with revelations about endowment mortgage mis-selling and the near collapse of Equitable Life, did little to contribute to confidence in the FSA's authority and procedures.

As might be expected, industry analysts took a somewhat different direction in their assessments. In the case of the financial services market, for instance, the revival in sales of pension and long-term savings products was seen as a vindication of New Labour's policies. In adult social care, the new regulatory regime combined with Best Value requirements was held to have established a 'more even playing field' between commercial and state providers as well as increasing confidence in the future viability of the commercial delivery of domiciliary care. Such positive responses were balanced, however, by concerns about the impact of the compliance costs faced by financial and care service providers. This was particularly visible in the residential care market where the requirements presaged by the Care Standards Act contributed to both increased corporatisation and a sharp contraction in the quantity of commercial provision, adding to pressure on the NHS and, ironically, to a shift in New Labour's approach to private hospitals (Laing, 2000).

Other evaluations focused less on the merits and demerits of the new regulatory frameworks than on New Labour's concomitant attempt to reconfigure the balance between personal and collective forms of income protection. As successive policy documents made clear, pre-empting 'overreliance on state benefits' by encouraging saving against life-cycle contingencies was central to New Labour's new welfare contract (DSS, 2000, para 4). In terms of long-term savings and pensions, its Green Paper (DSS, 1998) maintained that fiscal and demographic pressures necessitated a switch from predominantly public to predominantly privately funded schemes. The 60/40 balance in favour of the former was to give way to a 60/40 balance in favour of the latter by 2050. Similar concerns underlay New Labour's approach to long-term care funding and other forms of social protection. While it kept its promise to establish a Royal Commission on the question of funding, New Labour's response made it clear that individuals were expected to contribute to the costs of personal care and maintained this line despite contrary developments in Scotland and Wales.

This emphasis on self-provisioning formed part of a broader campaign to foster a culture of contingency saving (see Chapter Ten of this volume). To kick-start the requisite shift in savings habits, the Chancellor launched the promised Individual Savings Account (ISA) scheme in 1999. In a bid to attract investors as well as savers, the National Savings system was contracted out for reengineering and subsequently rebranded (in early 2002) as National Savings and Investments. Like the pension changes (see Chapter Ten of this volume), the immediate outcomes were mixed. Some observers remained unconvinced both by the government's case and the effectiveness of its campaign to increase personal savings. Others felt the government's policies recognised the efficacy of the pensions and savings markets and the way, appropriately regulated, they could be shaped for social purposes (Glennerster, 1999).

At first sight, this latter view seemed to be confirmed by the financial services industry's heavy promotion of ISAs and their high initial take-up. As with stakeholder pensions, however, market surveys suggested that this reflected a switch of funds or extra saving by existing savers rather than a widening consumer base. New Labour's attempt to stimulate other forms of saving also made little headway. Despite a stream of ministerial exhortations on the need for greater prudence, most citizens remained oblivious to the scale of private savings that New Labour's policies required (Evason et al, 2001). Indeed, the government itself admitted the majority were not "saving enough for their old age", nor were they making adequate contingency savings (HMG, 2000, p 17). In 2000, one third of adults had no savings, while half of those with savings had less than £1,500 (ONS, 2001, p 110). On the other hand, borrowing had escalated, with household debt standing at 110% of disposable income in mid-2001, compared to 94% in early 1998 (Stuart and Denny, 2001).

Seeing the limited impact of its savings policies, New Labour developed a number of new measures towards the end of its first term (see Chapter Ten of this volume). Personal finance was added to the school curriculum (as part of the conception of 'citizenship'), while the 2001 Manifesto presented another attempt to promote personal saving through the 'baby-bond' scheme. Somewhat belatedly, the government also became aware of the need to counter financial exclusion and convince people of the need to save. It met, however, with minimal success due in no small part to low interest rates and the financial uncertainties associated with underachieving endowment mortgages and falling annuity rates. Stock market volatility also led to low take-up of the 'third round' of equity ISAs, adding weight to the case made by analysts who saw systemic limitations in commercially funded forms of income protection. Their concerted view was that the government's mixed-provision approach to long- and short-term savings was unlikely to deliver either the standard of living or the equities expected of traditional social insurance schemes (Ginn, 2001). In particular, it failed to address the constraints faced by those, particularly women, in low-paid, irregular or part-time employment (Ginn and Arber, 2000). Self-funding based on equity returns was similarly unlikely to meet the financial needs of individuals especially the elderly, requiring long-term care.

In contrast, self-provisioning was not an issue in the spheres of health and education. As previously stated, in health New Labour's initial concern was to maintain a universal needs-led service, free at the point of consumption. To that end, it sought to upgrade the quality and effectiveness of state provision. Apart from revoking the medical insurance tax relief for the over-65s, it said very little about the role of commercial services, and the then Secretary of State for Health, Frank Dobson, remained committed to a publicly funded and delivered system. New Labour's failure to reduce NHS waiting lists, however, particularly during the winter crises, prompted a significant change in policy. In July 2000, under a new Secretary of State (Alan Milburn), the government published its NHS Plan, which included the first attempt by any postwar government to incorporate commercial health providers into its general health strategy. While maintaining its commitment to healthcare based on 'need and not the ability to pay,' the Plan outlined a 'national framework for partnership' in the form of a concordat between the government and private providers. This was designed to end the postwar 'stand-off' between the two and 'harness the capacity' of the latter in the development of a seamless service untrammelled by 'ideological boundaries'. Cooperative working under the concordat was to centre on elective, critical and intermediate care, providing for NHS use or purchase of private facilities for elective surgery, two-way transfers of patients with critical conditions and, more radically, private development of new rehabilitative facilities. Commercial providers were also to be involved for the first time in local health planning (DoH, 2000, pp 96-8).

While the commercial healthcare markets had been buoyant in the latter half of the 1990s (Fitzhugh, 2001), the concordat gave private providers a range of additional opportunities. It allowed them to trade on the government's confirmation of their quality, gave them an answer to the long-standing problem of over-capacity and the chance to diversify into post-operative and intermediate care services (Laing, 2001). Not all of New Labour's actions, however, contributed positively to this partnership. The proposed cooperation between the sectors was tempered by the government's attempt to introduce new contracts limiting the private work undertaken by full-time NHS consultants and its continued support for NHS trusts offering pay beds. The concordat then was far from a carte blanche for commercial hospitals; while giving them opportunities for increased profitability, it did so on terms and conditions determined by the needs of the NHS.

New Labour's less ambiguous stance towards private education and training enabled a more straightforward response from commercial suppliers. Both Sure Start and the broader policy of generating nursery school places for all four-year-olds led to an upsurge in commercial provision (Toynbee and Walker, 2001). Meanwhile, the New Deal and related training initiatives led to the expansion of private recruitment agencies offering counselling and placement services. Growth was most visible, however, in fee-charging schools whose intakes reached a postwar peak of 492,000 students in 2000 and were predicted to grow throughout the decade (Clare, 2001). Although this was a product of a number of factors, industry analysts highlighted what the Secretary of State for Education, Estelle Morris, termed a 'major cultural change' in New Labour's approach to private schools. In deference to past policies, it abolished the 'unfair' Assisted Places Scheme, but otherwise did little to counter their privileged position. Conscious of the barriers to limiting parental choice, particularly in the light of its own human rights legislation, New Labour adhered to its 'bridge-building' manifesto with another concordat.

This confirmed parents' rights to send their child to a school of their choice and paved the way for trans-school activities. In a further shift away from the past, ministers also upheld private schools as a benchmark for state education and private management as the solution for failing state provision. In practice, this antidote was rarely implemented and did not involve direct service provision

Table 4.2: Progress against Manifesto/Annual Report targets for commercial welfare

Pledge		New Labour's assessment	Score/10
33:	Introduce ISAs	Done	7
37:	Reinvigorate the PFI	On course	5
63:	Overcome NHS/PFI problems	Done	5
100:	Establish a Royal Commission on Long Term Care	Done	4
101:	Introduce a Long-Term Care Charter	On course	9
102:	Introduce Independent Inspection of Nursing Homes and Domicilary Care	On course	8

by existing providers. By mid-2001, only three schools were being run by private agencies and some 20 local authorities had contracted management services. The prospect of more extensive use of commercial enterprise in schools, as elsewhere, however, attracted intense scrutiny, particularly as the government's plans for rejuvenating and improving the Private Finance Initiative (PFI) in the NHS unfolded. To its adherents in the Treasury and elsewhere, this offered an efficient mechanism for funding the construction, refurbishment and facilities management of public services. To its critics, building and refurbishment through the PFI would be more costly than traditional forms of public procurement, while private management would only make efficiency gains at the expense of workforce salaries and conditions of employment (Ruane, 2001). No clear-cut findings emerged from these conflicting studies, making it difficult to form any firm conclusion about the government's success in meeting its stated aims (Ball et al, 2000).

While controversy over the PFI, particularly in regard to the NHS, dominated analyses of New Labour's policies for commercial welfare, it does seem clear that the government had met its headline commitments, establishing both new regulatory structures and its proposed savings scheme. Most importantly, by the 2001 General Election commercial provision had been brought within the ambit of governmental welfare planning.

Extrinsic evaluation

It was the attempt to incorporate commercial welfare as part of its vision that contributed to the distinctive welfare approach taken by the first Blair administration. Through the promotion of market harnessing, it sought to utilise the skills and expertise of private enterprises in an agenda in which the goal of effective and responsive services was of far greater significance than the means and mode of delivery (Blair, 1998). Some analysts took a similar 'pragmatic' view, arguing that users were more concerned with service quality than whether it was delivered by state or independent providers (IPPR, 2001). This viewpoint has, however, met with forceful counter arguments. The Fabian Society stance (Jacobs, 2001), for example, maintains that the distinction between means and ends is a false division; means, he argues, 'embody values too'. Further, those imparted by publicly provided services are intrinsically different to the values conveyed by commercial and VCO contractors. Like Titmuss, he suggests that public services embody an ideal of collective provision defined by the need of the service user not his or her market power (Jacobs, 2001, p 74). This argument can be extended further to raise doubt about New Labour's approach to service management. Here it has singularly failed to take on board recent reevaluations of the effectiveness of public bureaucracies (Jackson, 2001). It has also neglected the limitations of the few studies directly comparing public service management with its independent sector counterparts, which have tended to rely on narrow economistic criteria rather than considering the broader social purposes served by public welfare agencies and the direct accountabilities they offer.

Furthering partnership: independent welfare after the 2001 General Election

The government clearly perceived itself as developing its welfare narrative on strong grounds. The 2001 Manifesto offered an extension of policies already in place, promising increased use of independent providers 'to support public endeavour' (Labour Party, 2001, p 17). This was to apply both to core services and newer areas such as nurseries and childcare. The NHS was to be supported by increased use of commercial capacity, education by further partnership arrangements and the benefit system by new incentives to personal saving. "More far-reaching partnerships" with VCOs for service delivery and community renewal were also promised, along with further investment in an "effective infrastructure" for volunteering (Labour Party, 2001, pp 33-4).

To secure VCOs' expanding service role, the government established two reviews, one by the PIU and the other a wider Treasury study. At the time of writing neither had reported. The PIU was, however, under heavy pressure to recommend a single public benefit test for charities, although there were mixed views as to whether this should apply to private schools, hospitals and other bodies 'sheltered' by existing law. Equally radical changes were being urged on the Treasury, with the NCVO arguing that for VCOs to fulfil the enlarged role envisaged by the government, they should get further fiscal relief and core funding. For some, this meant funding along lines similar to local authorities' revenue support grant (Brindle, 2001).

The implications of this use of public resources were lost in the wider debate over public–private partnerships, particularly in healthcare. In line with the NHS Plan, the government commissioned the first tranche of Direct Treatment Centres, including one to be run by BUPA, and extended its use of private hospitals in the UK and Europe. Early in 2002, it proposed to contract managers from private firms and hospitals to rescue 'failing' NHS hospitals. But then, in the face of questions over their managerial experience, it backtracked in favour of 'takeovers' by 'successful' NHS hospital managers. By spring 2002, Blair had recommitted New Labour to a universal tax-funded health system and to achieving European levels of care (see Chapter Seven of this volume). While this still left scope for commercial provision, growth remained contingent on the fortunes of the NHS. A similar scenario applied to schooling. Here, too, New Labour's plans for 'failing' schools and authorities were constrained by the limited capacities of management service firms. With private schools averse to extending their responsibilities, the government was forced to contrive (as in Hackney) a different form of partnership – specially constituted mutual trusts – a mode of governance also under consideration for the NHS.

Outside the core areas of health and schools, however, New Labour maintained the quiet growth of voluntary and commercial welfare, particularly through the expansion of its many area-based and specialist programmes to which were added new initiatives such as ConneXions. The government also extended its campaign to increase self-provisioning through the financial services markets. The Savings Gateway and the Child Trust Fund, for instance, herald a more comprehensive drive to promote both asset-based welfare and financial literacy. To support these developments, the FSA's educational role is being expanded, while the 2001 Enterprise Bill presages a broader consumer protection role for the OFT.

Whether these measures will counter the uncertainties and inequities of market-based income protection schemes is, as yet, unclear. What is clear is that New Labour is overseeing a 'strategic shift' away from the balance of responsibilities between state and individual created in the 1940s (Glennerster, 1999). While retaining government responsibility for the key services of health and schools, it is promoting a greater role elsewhere both for newly responsible citizens and independent welfare providers.

Notes

[1] VCOs encompass a diverse range of groupings that are notoriously difficult to define. Here the term refers to non-profit-making, self-governing bodies that are institutionally separate from government, may or may not be registered as charities and are engaged in activities for community benefit.

[2] Space pre-empts a consideration of related developments in employer-based welfare discussed elsewhere (Brunsdon and May, 2003: forthcoming).

[3] Although much of the discussion applies across the UK, the focus here is primarily on developments in England.

References

Ball, R., Heafey, M. and King, D. (2001) 'Private Finance Initiative: a good deal for the public purse or a drain on future generations?', *Policy & Politics*, vol 29, no 1, pp 95-108.

Bentham, M. (2001) 'Young refuse to support charity collections', *The Sunday Telegraph*, 9 September.

Blair, T. (1996) *New Britain: My vision of a young country*, London: Fourth Estate.

Blair, T. (1998) *The third way*, London: Fabian Society.

Blunkett, D. and Kilfoyle, P. (1996) *Millennium volunteers: Labour's proposals for Citizens' Service*, London: Labour Party.

Brenton, M. (1985) 'Privatisation and voluntary sector services', *The Year Book of social policy in Britain 1984-5*, London: Routledge & Keegan Paul.

Brindle, D. (2001) 'Cutting to the core', *The Guardian*, 21 March.

Brown, G. (2001) 'Let the people look after themselves', *The Times*, 11 January.

Brunsdon, E. and May, M. (2003: forthcoming) Milton Keynes: Open University Press.

Clare, J. (2001) 'Pupil numbers at private schools', *Daily Telegraph*, 25 April.

Craig, G., Taylor, M., Sczanto, C. and Wilkinson, M. (1999) *Developing local compacts: Relationships between local public sector bodies and the voluntary and community sectors*, York: York Publishing Services.

Craig, G. and Warburton, D. (2001) 'Willing partners: voluntary and community associations in the democratic process', Paper presented to the Social Policy Association Conference, Belfast, July.

Craig, G., Taylor, M., Wilkinson, M. and Bloor, K. with Monro, S. and Syed, A. (2002) *Contract or trust? The role of compacts in local governance*, Bristol/York: The Policy Press/Joseph Rowntree Foundation.

CSJ (Commission on Social Justice) (1994) *Social justice strategies for national renewal*, London: Vintage.

Dahrendorf, R. (2001) *The 18th Annual Arnold Goodman Charity Lecture*, London: Charities Aid Foundation.

Deakin Commission (1996) *The Commission on the future of the voluntary sector in England: Meeting the challenge of change: Voluntary action into the twenty first century*, London: NCVO.

DoH (Department of Health) (2000) *The NHS Plan*, London: The Stationery Office.

DSS (Department for Social Security) (1998) *A new contract for welfare: Partnership in pensions*, Cm 4179, London: The Stationery Office.

DSS (2000) *Report on the contributory principle*, Cm 4867, London: The Stationery Office.

Evason, E., Dowds, L. and Devine, P. (2001) 'Pensions: provisions, perception and preferences amongst persons under pensionable age', *Benefits*, issue 31, pp 14-18.

Fitzhugh, W. (2001) *The Fitzhugh Directory of independent healthcare and long-term care 2001-2002*, London: Health Care Information Services.

Giddens, A. (1998) *The third way*, London: Polity Press.

Ginn, J. (2001) 'Gordon's guys and Darling's dolls', Paper presented to the SPA 'Gender and New Labour' Conference, 20 September.

Ginn, J. and Arber, S. (2000) 'Personal pension take up in the 1990s', *Journal of Social Policy*, vol 29, no 2, pp 205-29.

Glennerster, H. (1999) 'A third way', in H. Dean and R. Woods (eds) *Social Policy Review 11*, Luton: Social Policy Association, pp 28-44.

Hill, N. (2001) 'Push and pull', *The Guardian*, 7 November.

HM Government (2000) *The Government's Annual Report 1999-2000*, London: The Stationery Office.

HM Treasury (2000a) *Final Regulatory Impact Statement: Getting Britain giving in the twenty first century*, London: HM Treasury.

HM Treasury (2000b) *Prudent for a purpose: Building opportunity and security for all the government's public spending plans 2001-2004*, London: The Stationery Office.

HM Treasury (2001) 'Andrew Smith sets out priorities for 2002 Spending Review', Press Release, 25 June.

Home Office (1998) *Compact getting it right together*, Cm 4100, London: Home Office.

Home Office (1999a) *Giving time, getting involved. A strategy report by the Working Group on the Active Community*, London: Home Office.

Home Office (1999b) *Annual Report 1998-1999*, vol 1, Cm 4205, London: The Stationery Office.

Home Office (2000a) *Action Plan for implementing the compact on relations between the government and the voluntary and community sector in England 2000-2001*, Home Office (gov.uk.acu.actionplan.htm).

Home Office (2000b) *Annual Report 1999-2000*, Cm 516, London: The Stationery Office.

Home Office (2001) *Connecting communities*, London: The Home Office.

IPPR (2001) *Building better partnerships*, London: IPPR.

Jacobs, M. (2000) 'Narrative', in A. Harvey (ed) *Transforming Britain: Labour's second term*, London: Fabian Society.

Jackson, P.M. (2001) 'Public sector added value: can bureaucracy deliver?', *Public Administration*, vol 79, no 1, pp 5-28.

Kendall, J. (2000) 'The mainstreaming of the third sector into public policy in England in the 1990s: whys and wherefores', *Policy & Politics*, vol 24, no 4, pp 541-61.

Knapp, M., Hallam, A., Beecham, J. and Barnes, B. (1999) 'Private, voluntary or public? Comparative cost effectiveness in community mental health care', *Policy & Politics*, vol 27, no 1, pp 35-9.

Labour Party (1989) *Meeting the challenge: Make the change: A new agenda for Britain. Final Report of Labour's policy review for the 1990s*, London: Labour Party.

Labour Party (1995) *Renewing democracy: Rebuilding communities*, London: Labour Party.

Labour Party (1997a) *New Labour because Britain deserves better*, London: Labour Party.

Labour Party (1997b) *Building the future together: Labour's policies for partnership between government and the voluntary sector*, London: Labour Party.

Labour Party (2001) *Ambitions for Britain Labour's Manifesto for 2001*, London: Labour Party.

Laing, W. (2000) *Care of elderly people market survey*, London: Laing & Buisson.

Laing, W. (2001) *Laing's Health Care Market Review*, London: Laing & Buisson.

Murphy, P. (2001) 'Top companies leave charities in the cold', *The Guardian*, 5 November.

NCVO (2001) 'NCVO: A ten point plan for action', Press Release, 12 February.

Obaze, D. (2000) *Noticeable by their absence: Black volunteers in charities*, London: National Coalition for Black Volunteering.

ONS (Office for National Statistics) (2001) *Social Trends 31*, London: ONS.

Paharoah, C. (1998) *Achieving the double bottom line*, London: Charities Aid Foundation.

Plowden, W. Kearney, J., Williamson, A., Burt, E., Taylor, J., Green, C. and Drakeford, M. (2001) *Next steps in voluntary action*, London: Joseph Rowntree Foundation.

Powell, M., Exworthy, M. and Berney, L. (2001) 'Playing the game of partnership', in R. Sykes, C. Bochel and N. Ellison (eds) *Social Policy Review 13*, Bristol: The Policy Press, pp 39-61.

Propper, C. and Green, K. (2001) 'A larger role for the private sector in financing UK health care: the arguments and the evidence', *Journal of Social Policy*, vol 30, no 4, pp 685-704.

Putnam, R. (1993) *Making democracy work*, NJ: Princeton University Press.

Rhodes, R.A.W. (1996) 'The new governance: governing without government', *Political Studies*, vol 44, no 4, pp 652-67.

Ross, K. and Osborne, S.P. (1999) 'Making a reality of community governance', *Public Policy &Administration*, vol 14, no 2, pp 49-61.

Ruane, S. (2001) 'A clear public mission? Public–private partnerships and the recommodification of the NHS', *Capital & Class*, vol 73, pp 1-6.

Skelcher, C. (2000) 'Changing images of the state: overloaded, hollowed out, congested', *Public Policy & Administration*, vol 15, no 3, pp 3-19.

Social Security Select Committee (2000) *Fifth Special Report*, London: The Stationery Office.

Stuart, H. and Denny, C. (2001) 'Personal debt hits record high', *The Guardian*, 31 August.

Taylor, M. (2001) 'Partnership', in M. Harris and C. Rochester (eds) *Voluntary organisations and social policy in Britain*, London: Palgrave, pp 94-107.

Toynbee, P. and Walker, D. (2001) *Did things get better?*, Harmondsworth: Penguin.

Unwin, J. (2001) *Who pays for care costs?*, London: Acevo.

Walker, C. (2001) 'The British culture of giving: generous, motivated and responsible?', *Proceedings of the 7th Researching the Voluntary Sector Conference*, London: NVCO.

Wintour, P. (2001) 'Volunteers plan stirs up unions', *The Guardian*, 1 January.

WGGRS (Working Group on Government Relations Secretariat) (2000) *Local compact guidelines*, London: NCVO.

FIVE

Parents, children, families and New Labour: developing family policy?

Jane Millar and Tess Ridge

Introduction

New Labour's 1997 election manifesto included the pledge to "help build strong families and strong communities" (Labour Party, 1997). In October 1998 the Home Office published a discussion document, *Supporting families*, which, as the foreword pointed out, "was the first time any [British] government had published a consultation paper on the family" (Home Office, 1998). This chapter examines New Labour's family policy, particularly as it affects families with children. However, examining 'family policy' is not a straightforward task. This is partly a reflection of the difficulties of definition. Family policy can be defined in various ways. At one extreme it can be argued that all government policies, across all areas of activity, have an impact on families and that we should therefore consider policy across the range. Thus within the 177 Manifesto pledges there are many that affect children and parents, directly and indirectly, especially those concerned with education. The indicators that have been developed to monitor outcomes likewise include many that seek to measure the impact of policy on families. But none of these identify specific areas of policy as 'family policy', and family policy issues are found across the range of government departments.

Here we do three things. First, we briefly discuss the government's approach to families with children, examining the policy goals that have been identified and the main policy measures proposed and/or introduced. We then go on to examine three specific policy areas in more detail. These are: the pledge to end child poverty in 20 years; the target of 70% set for employment among lone parents; and the pledge to provide good-quality and affordable childcare for all children aged under 14. We choose to focus on these because they are all important areas of policy innovation. No previous government has set these goals, and these policies are redrawing the line between state and family responsibilities. Issues of childcare, for example, have always been seen in Britain as part of the private duties of the family, and not as an area for state intervention. These measures also represent a shift towards a more explicit focus on the needs and circumstances of children, again reflecting a greater role for government in family life. And finally, these measures are particularly important for women. Women are at greater risk than men of living in poverty, especially women with sole caring responsibilities, and it has long been argued that women's needs are not adequately addressed in British social policy. For each of these three policy areas, we examine the policy pledges made and summarise what we know about outcomes so far. In the final section we critically examine progress so far, both in relation to the government's overall assessment of progress and in respect of the nature of the policy goals that have been set.

Policy developments: families, rights and responsibilities

As noted above, there is no single place where we can find a clear statement of family policy and we need to look across various different government departments for policy initiatives in this area. The two main documents we need to consider are the 1997 Labour Party Manifesto and the 1998 *Supporting families* Home Office discussion document.

The Manifesto noted that there have been fundamental changes in attitudes to race, sex and sexuality, and argued that New Labour's task in government would be to combine change and social stability: "The clock should not be turned back" (Labour Party, 1997, p 25). However, apart from the pledge to strengthen families, the 1997 Manifesto contained few direct references to families. The five pledges most directly concerned with family policy issues were:

- helping single parents back to work (50);
- the National Childcare Strategy (83);
- 48-hour week, holiday rights and parental leave (84);
- retaining universal child benefit (85);
- introducing parental responsibilities orders (75).

(Labour Party Manifesto, 1997)

These five pledges reflect three important underlying themes. First, they show the early focus on the importance of paid work as a route out of poverty and social exclusion and thus the need to encourage and support parents to work through specific measures and the promotion of family-friendly employment practices (50, 84 and to some extent also 83). Second, there is a commitment to the maintenance of financial support for children (85). This was later strengthened into promise to increase support for children and to end child poverty, an issue I will discuss later. Third, there is an emphasis on ensuring that families recognise and meet their responsibilities and obligations to each other. This appears here in the form of parental responsibility orders (75), under which parents of young offenders must comply with certain conditions laid down by the courts[1].

These themes were further developed in the 1998 Green Paper *Supporting families* (Home Office, 1998), which set out New Labour's future vision for strengthening family life. While acknowledging the 'new realities' of family

Table 5.1: Supporting families (1998)

General area	Proposed measures
Better financial support for families	• Higher Child Benefit • Working Families' Tax Credit, including a Childcare Tax Credit • The New Deal for Lone Parents • Education Maintenance Allowances • Reform Child Support
Helping families balance work and home	• Setting a framework for family-friendly employment rights • Promoting family-friendly employment practices
Better services and support for parents	• National Family and Parenting Institute • National helpline for parents • Enhanced role for health visitors • The Sure Start programme
Strengthening marriage	• Measures to strengthen the institution of marriage • Support for all families including advice on adult relationships • Reducing conflict on relationship breakdown
Better support for serious family problems	• Reduce truancy/school exclusions • Tackle youth offending • Reduce teenage pregnancy rates • Tackle domestic violence

Source: Home Office (1998)

life, including rapid demographic change and considerable diversity in family structure, the paper goes on to privilege marriage as the surest foundation for raising children. Five main areas were identified as priorities for action, as shown in Table 5.1. These show both the general policy areas to be addressed and propose specific measures for each. They include some very specific proposals relating to the work–life balance and to the financial support of families. The personal responsibility agenda appears in particular in the proposals for "better services and support for parents" and in the proposals to "strengthen marriage" (Home Office, 1998).

These were the early statements of New Labour's intentions. How far have these been realised in practice?

Ending child poverty

The promise to end child poverty did not appear in the Manifesto or in *Supporting families*, or indeed in any of the Green Papers dealing with welfare reform. This promise was first made by Tony Blair in 1999 (Blair, 1999). The situation facing the incoming Labour government in respect of child poverty was indeed grim. It had inherited one of the poorest records on child poverty in the developed world (Bradbury and Jäntti, 1999), and the 1980s and 1990s had seen a three-fold increase in the numbers of children in poverty, as children had borne the brunt of changes in economic conditions, demographic structures and

Conservative government free market economic policies (Oppenheim and Harker, 1996; Walker and Walker, 1997; Millar, 2001). In 1998/99 about 4.5 million children (35% of all children) were living below 50% of mean household income after housing costs (DSS, 2000a). But New Labour's concern for poor children was not immediately apparent after the 1997 election. In fact one of its first acts in power had been to cut benefits to lone-parent families by removing One Parent Benefit and the Lone Parent Premium in Income Support. This, coupled with the pledge to hold to the previous government's spending plans for two years, had not augured well for low-income families.

However, in a lecture on the future of the welfare state in March 1999, the Prime Minister stated that "our historic aim is that ours is the first generation to end child poverty forever, and it will take a generation. It is a 20-year mission but I believe that it can be done" (Blair, 1999, p 7). Transitional targets were also set, first to reduce the number of children living in poverty by half within 10 years, and later in a Public Service Agreement (PSA) to reduce by at least a quarter, by 2004, the number of children living in households with an income of less than 60 per cent of the median (DSS, 2000a).

This new, and to many rather unexpected, promise was justified mainly in respect of the impact of poverty on children's life chances and opportunities. For example, the Treasury pointed to research that showed that "disadvantages in childhood frequently leads to disadvantage in adult life and that increasing numbers of children are growing up in disadvantaged families" (HM Treasury, 1999, p 26). The policy was also promoted as a common goal for all: "abolishing child poverty should not just be the aim of the Government – it should be the aim of everyone. That is why this has to be a partnership between all of us. We all want to tackle child poverty" (Brown, 1999, p 8).

Two main sorts of policies were introduced to achieve this aim – additional financial support for families, and targeted programmes of various sorts. The additional financial support has been substantial (see Chapter Ten of this volume for a discussion of these in the context of other changes to social security and tax policy). The main measures for children have been:

- Increases in Child Benefit (the universal payment for all children), which was worth £11.05 per week for the first child in 1997 and £15 by 2000.
- Increases in Income Support rates for children, which for younger children amount to an 80% rise in real terms between 1997 and 2001 (Lister, 2001).
- The introduction of the Working Families' Tax Credit in October 1999 to replace the previous benefit (Family Credit). It is payable to families where a parent is in employment for more than 16 hours per week, with earnings below a certain level, based on family size. It includes a 'Childcare Tax Credit' that contributes towards the costs of registered childcare (70% of costs up to a ceiling).
- The introduction of a new Children's Tax Credit from April 2001, initially worth £10 per family per week for standard rate taxpayers with, from April 2002, an extra £10 per week in the year of a child's birth (HM Treasury, 2001a).

In addition, there have been a number of new programmes targeted at children, and especially at poor children. These include:

- *Sure Start:* initially in 250 disadvantaged areas, with a budget of £450 million per annum, to equip pre-school children for starting school.
- *Educational Maintenance Allowances:* in 15 pilot areas, means-tested support for children aged 16+ who attend full-time courses at school or college.
- *On Track:* aimed at reducing the risk factors that link young people with future criminal behaviour, with a budget of £27 million for 20-30 pilot projects.
- *ConneXions:* to provide information, advice, guidance and access to personal advisers for all young people aged 13-19.
- *The Children's Fund:* with a budget of £450 million over three years, mainly targeted on preventive work with children in the 5-13 age group.

These programmes are being delivered at the local level, through partnerships with voluntary organisations, and with a special emphasis on poor children, but not necessarily exclusive to children in poverty.

A new employment strategy for lone parents

The 1997 Manifesto promised to 'help single parents back to work' but the specific target of having 70% of lone parents in employment by the next decade did not appear until the pre-Budget report of 2000 (HM Treasury, 2000) and was repeated in the 2001 Employment Green Paper, *Towards full employment in a modern society* (DfEE/DSS/HM Treasury, 2001). The Manifesto points to the New Deal for Lone Parents as the main means of fulfilling this pledge, but in fact there have been a substantial number of policy initiatives in this area, as summarised in Table 5.2. This shows that the New Deal for Lone Parents is part of a wider range of measures intended to encourage lone parents into paid work. These include the in-work benefits measures, the increased provision of childcare, and provisions intended to ease the transition into work. One important policy change has been the phased introduction of compulsory work-focused interviews as part of the claim process for Income Support. Participation in the New Deal itself remains voluntary but all lone parents claiming Income Support will be required to attend these interviews, regardless of the age of their children. The New Deal for Lone Parents is mainly an advice and information service, available on a voluntary basis to lone parents in receipt of Income Support (Millar, 2000; Grey, 2001). It is less structured than the other New Deal programmes and has a relatively small budget, especially compared with the 'flagship' New Deal for Young People (see Chapter Ten of this volume).

The National Childcare Strategy

As discussed above, commitments to 'family-friendly' employment and to helping parents balance employment and family responsibilities were part of New

Table 5.2: Lone parents and employment: New Labour government policy measures, 1997 onwards

Date	Measure
July 1997	• Phase 1: New Deal for Lone Parents in eight 'prototype' areas – voluntary interviews, target group of those with youngest child aged 5 years and 3 months
May 1998	• Phase 2: New Deal for Lone Parents, national for new and repeat Income Support claimants • National Childcare Strategy announced
Oct 1998	• Phase 3: New Deal for Lone Parents, national for all claimants
June 1999	• ONE Service pilot in four areas – voluntary work-focused interviews for claimants of various benefits, including lone parents
Oct 1999	• Introduction of Working Families' Tax Credit, includes Childcare Tax Credit • Benefits 'run-on' for lone parents who have been on Income Support for at least 12 months, benefit payments continue for first two weeks of job of 16 hours per week plus • Ten 'innovative' pilots of variations within the New Deal run for 12 months
Nov 1999	• ONE service pilots extended to a further eight areas
April 2000	• ONE work-focused interviews compulsory for all new and repeat claimants in the pilot areas • In-work training grants pilots, employers who recruit lone parents can claim up to £750 towards the cost of training
June 2000	• New Deal for Lone Parents – target group for voluntary interviews extended to lone parents with youngest child aged 3 years
Oct 2000	• Compulsory work-focused interviews for lone parents with youngest child aged 5 years and 3 months plus in three 'pathfinder' areas • Pilot of 'Choices' scheme for lone parents receiving Income Support – gives access to £15 per week Training Premium, £20 per week earnings disregard, help with childcare costs for first year in employment (less than 16 hours per week)
Nov 2000	• Target of 70% of lone parents in employment 'by the end of the decade'
April 2001	• A compulsory work-focused interview for lone parents with children of school-age making a new or repeat claim for Income Support, and for current recipients with children aged 13-15. Includes six-monthly and then annual reviews • Choices scheme introduced nationally • Jobseeker's Grant (which pays a lump sum to those entering work) extended to lone parents receiving Income Support for six months or more
June 2001	• Childcare Tax Credit in Working Families' Tax Credit increased
Oct 2001	• Annual compulsory work-focused interviews for all lone parents on Income Support (phased in by Oct 2004) • New Deal for Lone Parents extended to all non-working lone parents (not just those receiving Income Support)
April 2002	• Disregard of £10 of child support payments for Income Support recipients
April 2003	• Integrated Child Tax Credit to replace children's rates of Income Support and Working Families' Tax Credit • Maternity leave and pay to be extended, and two weeks' paid paternity leave introduced
March 2004	• Guaranteed childcare place in the 'most disadvantaged' areas available for every lone parent entering employment

Labour's early pledges. Specific measures have included the Working Time Directive, which limits working hours for many people to 48 hours a week and the implementation of the European Parental Leave Directive, giving parents the right to three months' unpaid leave after the birth or adoption of a child. This brought the UK into line with the rest of the EU, but still at the lowest level of provision. The government has also initiated a £1.5 million Work–Life Balance Challenge Fund in 2000 to help employers develop work–life balance practices. The Department of Trade and Industry Green Paper, *Work and parents: Competitiveness and choice* (DTI, 2000) includes proposals for extending maternity pay and for the introduction of parental leave.

The National Childcare Strategy is an integral part of this family-friendly employment agenda and is also crucial to the success of New Labour's child poverty measures and the New Deal for Lone Parents. The 1997 Manifesto promised that the New Labour government would provide guaranteed free nursery places for all four-year-olds, and places for all three-year-olds whose parents wanted it. The National Childcare Strategy was launched a year later (DfEE, 1998). This set out the government's intentions to provide good quality, affordable childcare for children aged 0 to 14 in every neighbourhood. Funding in England was £470 million over the lifetime of the first parliament. This included £170 million from the New Opportunities Fund (NOF) for out-of-school provision (DWP, 2001). Delivery would be through the Early Years Development and Childcare Partnerships (EYDCPs), to be set up at local level and to include all childcare stakeholders. In 2000 an extra £255 million was allocated to the 'most disadvantaged' areas, to be spent between 2001 and 2004, for the creation of new daycare places and to close the gap in provision between the best and worst-off areas.

Intrinsic evaluation

The New Labour government has committed itself, as in other policy areas, to monitoring and evaluating the impact of these policy measures. There have also been some independent assessments of the extent to which these policy goals have been met. Here we look again at each area in turn.

Ending child poverty

To monitor the outcomes of its anti-poverty policies New Labour committed itself to an annual poverty audit report under the title *Opportunity for All* (DSS, 2000b), which has set out specific and measurable indicators relating to the well-being of children (see Table 5.3). This was an innovatory step towards establishing a set of indictors that go beyond the income poverty lines that have tended to dominate in the past. But there are, perhaps inevitably, some gaps and problems. First, there are other indicators that are not included but which would have given a greater awareness of poor children's lives. For example, Bradshaw (2001) lists 17 additional outcome measures for children that are

Table 5.3: *Opportunity for all*: **indicator trends by third report**

Goal	Indicators	Official assessment of trends
Improving family incomes by tackling worklessness and increasing financial support for families	1. Number of children in workless families 2. Number of children in low-income households • relative • absolute • persistent	 Improving Improving Improving Constant
Investing in the crucial early years and education to break the cycle of disadvantage	3. Key Stage 1 attainment in Sure Start areas 4. Key Stage 2 attainment 5. 16-year-olds with at least one GCSE 6. 19-year-olds with at least level 2 qualifications 7. Truancies 8. School exclusions 9. Educational attainment of children looked after by local authorities	Not available Improving Improving Improving Constant Improving n/a
Improving the quality of lives of children and young people	10. Housing below decency standard 11. Infant mortality rates 12. Smoking rates for • pregnant women • children aged 11-15 13. Serious unintentional injury 14. Reregistration on child protection register	n/a n/a n/a Constant Improving Improving
Supporting young people in the transition to adult life	15. Teenage pregnancy • teenage conceptions • teenage parents not in education, employment or training 16. 16- to 18-year-olds in learning	 Improving Improving Improving

Source: DWP (2001)

known to have an association with child poverty. These include low birth weight, child death rates and children living in temporary accommodation. In addition, he highlights other indicators that, while not poverty outcomes, would nevertheless provide a valuable insight into the circumstances of poor children. These include the numbers of children living in families receiving Income Support and the percentage of children living in households lacking three or more socially perceived necessities (see Middleton et al, 1997 and Gordon et al, 2000). The list of indicators presented in *Opportunity for all* has a pick-and-mix quality about it, and appears to reflect different departmental initiatives rather than a coherent anti-poverty strategy.

Second, some of the government's indicators are not poverty outcomes. For example, a reduction in the proportion of truancies and school exclusions is a worthy intention, but there is little evidence for an association between school exclusions and poverty, and school exclusions affect only a small proportion of pupils. Arguably, it is exclusions *within* school, through inadequate participation and lack of opportunities, that may pose a far greater threat to poor children (Ridge, 2002). Third, there is also concern that many of the indicators were not based on up-to-date data, and that there will be a considerable time lag between policies taking effect and a measurable impact in statistical terms. For example, the Integrated Child Credit was announced in March 2000, is to be implemented in 2003, but statistical data showing the impact of this measure will not be available until 2005 (Hills, 2000).

Some of the concerns about the indicators chosen have been addressed by the Department of Social Security/Department for Work and Pensions (DSS, 2000; DWP, 2001) and the subsequent reports have made a number of changes, dropping some of the Sure Start ones, refining other ones and including some new ones. This appears to be an ongoing process and it remains to be seen how many indicators, and which ones, survive for any length of time. Table 5.3 shows the indicators that appear in the third report (DWP, 2001) and the government's assessment of outcomes at that point. In general, these suggest that the situation on most indicators has been 'improving', although the report points out that it is not always possible to assess this because of lack of data.

Further evidence of the government's progress can be gauged from looking at trends in children's benefit receipt and through simulations of the impact of the measures introduced on the incomes of poor families (Piachaud and Sutherland, 2000, 2001). Between February 1997 and February 2001 there was a 50% increase in the numbers of families in receipt of in-work benefits, from about 730,000 Family Credit claimants in 1997 to about 1,180,000 Working Families' Tax Credit claimants in 2001. This includes nearly two-and-a-half million children living in families receiving Working Families' Tax Credit, with families receiving, on average, about £80 per week, about £40 per week more than under its predecessor (Inland Revenue 2001). About 137,000 of these families also receive the Childcare Tax Credit, gaining on average £35 per week towards childcare costs (Inland Revenue, 2001). The proportion of children in workless households fell from 17.9% in spring 1997 to 15.8% in spring 2000, and there are 300,000 fewer children living in families receiving out-of-work benefits (DSS, 2000a). Taking the measures up to 2000, the Treasury estimated that the average household with children had gained by £850 per year, with the highest gains (about £1,500 to £1,560) at the lowest two deciles (HM Treasury, 2000). Hills (2000) compares the impact of the budget measures introduced since 1997 with what would have happened if benefits and taxes had simply been uprated for inflation, and finds that low-income couples with children gained between £1,300 and £3,000 per year by 2000.

Both government and independent assessments agreed that over one million children would be lifted out of poverty by these measures (HM Treasury, 2000; Piachaud and Sutherland, 2000). Piachaud and Sutherland (2001) estimated the likely impact of these tax and benefit changes to be even greater. Using a 60% of median income threshold[2], they found that 1.33 million children could have been taken out of poverty – a reduction of 39%. These findings indicated that New Labour was on target to fulfil its PSA of one quarter reduction in child poverty by 2004. However, the actual figures for 2000/01 showed that these expected reductions had not been achieved, and that child poverty had fallen by only about 500,000 (DWP, 2002). Brewer et al (2002) suggest that three factors explain this shortfall. First, the poverty line has risen because of increases in average incomes[3]. Second, the full effects of increased benefits and tax credits has yet to show in official figures. Third, some families are not taking up their full entitlements.

Lone parents and employment

There are various different ways we can look at outcomes of the policy measures intended to increase employment among lone parents. There was an extensive evaluation of the prototype New Deal for Lone Parents and there is an ongoing evaluation of the national programme. There are also regular statistics published from the New Deal Database, as well as statistics on overall trends in benefit receipt and employment. Table 5.4 shows the summary statistics for the national programme up to October 2001. By then about 330,000 lone parents had attended an initial interview (it is after this interview that participants formally join the programme or not), many of these being drawn from outside the target group (initially those with children aged under five, later including those with children aged under three). Most (89%) agreed to participate; around four in 10 participants have found work and around one in 10 have taken part in some education or training. Those who find work may continue to be part of the New Deal programme (there is provision for in-work mentoring and support) and around one in three current participants are in employment. It is

Table 5.4: New Deal for Lone Parents: summary statistics, up to October 2001

	Number	%
Initial interview	329,490	100
Agreed to participate	293,770	89 (100)
Has taken part in education/training[a]	24,950	7.5 (8.5)
Has found employment	132,810	40 (45)
Current participants in the New Deal	105,960	41 (100)
• receiving advice and guidance	67,814	(64)
• in education/training	5,930	(6)
Receiving in-work support	32,480	(31)
Left the New Deal programme[b]	187,820	(100)
• for employment	100,320	(53)
• transfer to other benefits	1,730	(1)
• withdrew, still on Income Support	74,630	(40)
• no longer eligible	4,170	(2)
• left for unknown destinations	6,960	(4)

[a] These are not exclusive categories (ie, those who took part in education may have gone on to find jobs).

[b] This includes some people who left after an initial interview, who are not counted in the participant total.

Source: New Deal Evaluation Database, Statistical First Release, July 2001.

not known, however, how much support they actually receive in practice. Among those who have left the New Deal for Lone Parents, around 40% have returned to Income Support.

There are two important statistics that are not available from the database: the take-up rate (how many eligible lone parents are coming forward) and the employment additionality (how many of the lone parents who find jobs would have done so anyway, without participating in the programme). Neither is easy to measure. Estimating take-up is complicated because there are many participants who come from non-target groups or who come forward early, so the 'eligible' population is hard to define. The phased introduction of compulsory interviews also complicates things. Estimating employment additionality depends on making various more or less robust assumptions about employment outcomes for lone parents not on the New Deal for Lone Parents programme (non-NDLP lone parents) with specified characteristics (for example, ages and number of children) and about labour demand in particular labour markets. The evaluation of the prototype did provide estimates of both take-up and employment additionality (Hales et al, 2000). About a quarter of lone parents in the prototype samples participated in the programme, giving this as a maximum estimate of take-up at that time. Lone parents in the prototype areas had slightly higher exit rates from Income Support than those in comparison areas (about 3.3% higher), and employment additionality was estimated to be in the range of 20-28%. Hales et al (2000, p 9), in their synthesis of the prototype evaluation as whole, thus conclude that the programme had a 'small but appreciable effect' at a modest net cost.

Looking at overall trends, the number of lone parents receiving Income Support fell from about 1,020,000 in February 1997 to about 893,000 in August 2001. Over the same period, the number receiving in-work benefits (Family Credit/Working Families' Tax Credit) rose from around 335,000 to around 653,000, with the number of lone parents receiving help with childcare costs rising from around 28,000 to around 134,000 (all figures from Quarterly Benefit statistics). Employment rates for lone mothers have risen from 45% in 1997 to 51.5% in 2001 (HM Treasury, 2001a). This is greater than the increase for married mothers over the same period. It is difficult, of course, to attribute these sorts of changes directly to specific policy measures. Falling numbers receiving Income Support and increasing employment participation rates may be more the result of general economic conditions than of any specific policy measures. Nevertheless, these trends are clearly heading in the right direction for meeting the employment target for lone parents, although there is still a long way to go.

The National Childcare Strategy

By 1998/99, there were 60,000 new childcare places and a free nursery school education for every four-year-old whose parents wanted it. The government estimates that between April 1997 and June 2001 new childcare places were created for 773,000 children and that by March 2004 there will be an extra million childcare places in England alone (HM Treasury, 2001b). However, although provision has increased, there are still shortfalls. For example, in 1997 there was one place for every nine children under the age of eight, and by 2001 there was still only one place for every seven (Daycare Trust, 2001a; Land, 2001). Moreover, 51% of EYDCPs reported difficulties with sustainability of places (DfEE, 2000) and in dealing with extremely complex funding arrangements. A snapshot survey of funding in April 2001 found that there were over 55 different sources of funding available, all with separate bidding processes, criteria, payment schemes and timescales (Daycare Trust, 2001b).

The new Childcare Tax Credit has been received by an increasing number of families and, along with other measures such as the New Opportunities Fund (for childcare outside of school hours), represents a significant injection of money into the demand side of childcare. For example, Harker (2001) estimates that funding has increased six-fold since the Childcare Tax Credit was introduced. But the support the Childcare Tax Credit offers is restricted in several ways. It is only available to families who are receiving Working Families' Tax Credit and among couples it is only those with two earners who are eligible. It is available only for registered childcare places and many parents use more informal systems of childcare. A typical full-time nursery place for a two-year-old now costs over £110 per week, which is equivalent to more than £5,700 a year. This makes it more than an average two-parent household with children spends on housing each year (about £4,520) or on food (about £4,400) (Daycare Trust, 2001b). In some regions like London and the South East, childcare costs can be as much as £135 per child per week (Daycare Trust, 2001b). This means that for many families childcare may still be unaffordable, even with the Childcare Tax Credit meeting some of the costs. It may also be that the Childcare Tax Credit has contributed to some increase in costs, with some providers taking advantage of the subsidy to charge higher prices.

A recent MORI survey for the Daycare Trust revealed that parents wanted more affordable provision, more childcare places and more employer support for childcare (Daycare Trust, 2001c). But, apart from stating that employers were the key to the success of the National Childcare Strategy, the government has not engaged with employers to produce improvements in the number of workplace crèches or reserved nursery places. Only 5% of companies currently provide a workplace nursery and only 2% have a reserved nursery places scheme (Daycare Trust, 2001d). Thus it seems that the childcare strategy is not yet delivering the level and type of childcare that parents want.

Annual Reports

Table 5.5 shows how the government assessed its performance in respect of these policy areas in the 1998/99 and 1999/2000 Annual Reports. In 1998/99 the original five pledges were directly addressed and were all assessed as either 'done' or 'on course'. There was no similar list of pledges in the 1999/2000

Table 5.5: Manifesto/Annual Report progress on pledges on family policy

Pledge	New Labour's assessment	Score/10
50: Help single parents back to work	Kept: the New Deal for Lone Parents launched as a national programme in October 1998	6
83: National Childcare Strategy	On course: strategy launched in May 1998, with 666,000 extra places created in the first year	6
84: 48-hour week, holiday rights and parental leave	On course: 48-hour week and holiday rights introduced from Oct 1998. Plan to introduce three months' parental leave by Dec 1999	8
85: Retain universal child benefit	Done: with increased levels	10
75: Introduce parental responsibilities orders	Done: pilot schemes in nine areas	5
Annual Report 1999/2000: 'Extra help for families with children'		
More support for children	Increased Child Benefit, introduced Working Families' Tax Credit, the Sure Start programme – by 2001 spending an extra £7 billion per year	7
Support for parents too	Set up the National Family and Parenting Institute, set up the parents' helpline, extended the role of health visitors	7
Family life and work	The 48-hour working week, parental leave, leave to deal with family crisis, longer maternity leave, right to four weeks' paid holiday per year, National Childcare Strategy, creating an extra 200,000 places	7

report; instead there was an overall look at three policy areas (support for children, support for parents and work–life balance). However, in both years, the report lists the measures introduced but does not assess their effectiveness. In our discussion above, we highlighted both the radical and innovatory nature of some of these family policy developments, but also pointed to some gaps and shortcomings. The final column of Table 5.5 provides an overall score out of 10 for the position in 2001. This is, of course, impressionistic rather than precise. For example, we have scored the employment pledge for lone parents and the National Childcare Strategy at 6/10, reflecting the fact there is still a long way to go in respect of both of these. The 70% target for lone parents in employment will be very challenging, particularly if there is a downturn in the economy and employment more generally. The pledge to retain child benefit is scored at 10/10, since this has not only been retained but also increased. Concerns have been expressed about the future of child benefit in the context of the Integrated Child Credit, due to be introduced in 2003 (Millar, 2001), but at the moment Child Benefit is still a significant part of state support for all families with children. There is very little information to assess how the parenting orders are operating in practice, although the government reports that feedback 'has been positive' (HM Treasury, 2001a, p 49). We therefore offer a neutral score there. As an overall assessment, in the lower part of the table, we would suggest that the government has made some very significant changes in policy and provision and so an overall score of seven out of 10 is given.

We also need to assess the government's record in respect of the specific targets discussed in this chapter and, notwithstanding the many new measures introduced, these still look very difficult to achieve in practice. Reducing child poverty is already proving to be problematic. Employment rates for lone parent are increasing but are still a long way from the 70% target. The same is true for childcare – the supply has increased but remains far below demand.

Extrinsic evaluation

Finally, we should look beyond the effectiveness of policy in achieving the goals as set by government and assess the nature of these goals themselves. At the start of this chapter, we identified three key features of New Labour's policies towards families with children – the importance of paid employment for parents, the need for additional support for children and the importance of responsibilities being attached to rights – and in this section we take a wider look at these goals.

Towards 'family-friendly' employment?

The 'work for all' aspect of New Labour's social policy has received a great deal of attention (see Chapter Ten of this volume), including questions about the extent to which local labour markets can actually absorb large increases in employment. Here we want to draw attention to the concerns that have been raised with respect to families, and particularly women. One source of criticism is that these policies simply do not go far enough – they offer too little and on too limited a basis and still leave the UK far behind many of our fellow EU member states in respect of measures such as parental leave, childcare provision and financial support for meeting childcare costs (Land, 1999).

These policies also assume that all individuals can participate in paid work on the same basis and fail to take account of how women's labour market participation is constrained by their caring and domestic responsibilities. Lewis (2001) points out that there has been little acknowledgement of the fundamental tension between welfare-to-work policies founded on an 'adult citizen worker' model and women's responsibilities for the bulk of caring within families. Rake argues that the New Labour government has failed to tackle gender-based labour market inequalities and that "the emphasis on entering employment needs to be balanced with strategies for improving the quality and conditions of employment" (2001, p 227).

There have also been various specific criticisms of the New Deal for Lone Parents (Land, 1999; Barlow and Duncan, 2000a; Millar, 2000; Gray, 2001). There has been concern that compulsion, although currently limited to attending interviews, reduces women's choice to decide about the best way to care for their children. There has also been criticism of the 'work-first' approach, which focuses on getting people into work rather than in improving skills so that people can find better jobs. Barlow and Duncan (2000b) suggest that the whole New Deal approach is flawed because it is based on misleading assumptions about how people make decisions about employment and parenting.

Overall, the focus on paid employment can be seen as problematic from a gendered perspective because of the way in which it values paid work in the labour market above unpaid caring work in the home. As Hilary Land (1999, p 143) argues:

> Overall genuinely family-friendly employment policies will only flourish in a culture which values the time, effort and skills spent on caring for the family as much as it values the activities associated with paid work.

Supporting children?

There is no doubt that the goal to end child poverty is one of the most radical of the government's promises and few would disagree with the importance of this goal. This promise clearly sets New Labour's approach to issues of poverty apart from that of the Conservative government, which involved either denying the existence of 'real' poverty or arguing that the poor could only be helped by a strong free-market economy, and not by government redistribution. But there are a number of issues relating to how the government has set about achieving this goal. First, the main mechanism associated with the goal is increased parental employment. However, as we noted earlier, not everyone can get access to paid employment, either because they cannot find suitable jobs or because they are not currently able to work for various reasons, including health problems and caring responsibilities. Many people, including many lone parents, face very significant and complex barriers to taking up paid work (Millar and Ridge, 2001). The employment strategy can only go so far in meeting the anti-child poverty target.

Second, this pledge can be described as one of the most 'old' Labour of current policy goals in that it cannot be achieved without a significant redistribution of resources, including – perhaps especially – to non-working families. Children lifted by the poverty measures will tend to have been children in families closer to the poverty line (Piachaud and Sutherland, 2000), and those well below the poverty line will be harder to reach. They are also more likely to be suffering multiple disadvantages. The focus on paid work as a means to boost income does little for children living in workless households. Although benefit levels for children have been significantly uprated, there has been no increase for adults, and basic levels of Income Support are substantially below the 60% of median income poverty line used by the government; a couple with two children receive only 72% of the poverty level (Piachaud and Sutherland, 2001). Future success at meeting poverty reduction targets may well depend on how willing New Labour is to develop greater redistributive policies towards children in the poorest, non-working families.

New Labour's ongoing commitment to eradicate child poverty may also be weakened by its apparent inability to seek and develop a strong social consensus and cross-party support for these measures. Much of the redistribution of income through progressive Budgets has brought significant gains for the poorest families, as we summarised earlier. However, these measures have been played down by New Labour, which appears to be 'doing good by stealth' (Lister, 2001, p 66). As a result many people remain unaware (or unconvinced) of the real improvements in many children's lives. This is not helped by the statistical time-lag between policies taking effect and demonstrable statistical results. Without cross-party support, the 20-year pledge the future of child anti-poverty measures looks vulnerable to a possible change in administration.

Family responsibilities?

The aspect of *Supporting families* that was most controversial was the 'strengthening marriage' agenda (Land, 1999; Barlow and Duncan, 2000b). These proposals – which included ideas such as the recognition of 'pre-nuptial' agreements, giving registrars a wider role in helping people prepare for marriage, and more counselling services for both married and cohabiting couples – generated the most critical reactions, as noted in the summary of responses:

> Many of the responses welcome the Government's commitment to address an extremely sensitive issue, but some feel that the proposals will not strengthen marriage sufficiently. A similar number feel that the Government has focused too heavily on marriage at the expense of other relationships. (Home Office, 1999)

The diversity of family life today, and the decline in marriage and rise in cohabitation, makes this a difficult area of policy and it is perhaps not surprising that the government has tended to retreat from very strong statements and measures. In January 2001, the government announced that it intends to repeal Part II of the 1996 Family Law Act. This would have made it compulsory for couples wishing to divorce to attend 'information meetings'. Pilot schemes were found to be unsuccessful and hence the repeal of the requirements to attend them. However, voluntary measures continue, and the Lord Chancellor's Department has announced a new grant programme, the 'marriage and relationship support grant', which will start in 2002, and has allocated a budget of about £5 million to support services (Lord Chancellor's Office, 2001). The family responsibilities agenda is also apparent in other areas, for example in the targets to reduce teenage conceptions and in the introduction of parenting orders.

Barlow and Duncan suggest that this approach depends on the use of "legislation to promote what it sees as desirable family forms and to discourage other, less-favoured, forms" (2000b, p 129). This, they argue, is both inefficient (it cannot succeed because it fails to take account of how people actually approach these decisions) and morally wrong (insofar as people are compelled into particular types of behaviour). Similarly, others have suggested that the social exclusion policy agenda includes very strong normative assumptions about shared values and ways of living – it is about including people in a particular construction of society and not about valuing diversity (Lister, 2000).

The tension between social support and social control is, of course, far from new, but arguably it is particularly relevant to family policy, which is more directly normative than many other policy areas. It is difficult to have neutral policy goals in this area, but explicit family policy statements are likely to generate controversy and disagreement. Thus the government seems to have stepped back from the concept of 'family policy' as a specific and separate area of activity. *Supporting families* has not made many further appearances in New Labour's policy discourse since 1999, when the summary of responses was published (Home Office, 1999). There has been no follow-up paper, and while New Labour politicians continue to talk about supporting families, about helping parents balance work and home and about child poverty, they do not often do so in the context of 'family policy'. They do, however, increasingly talk about support for 'parenting'. Thus the pre-2001 Budget paper from the Treasury on child poverty (HM Treasury, 2001a) lists a range of measures under the heading 'parenting for life'. The list includes the National Family and Parenting Institute, the Family Support Grant Programmes, the increases in maternity and paternity leave, the child support reforms, measures to tackle teenage pregnancy and adoption reform.

Developments since the 2001 General Election

New Labour's first term of office was thus a period of intense activity in respect of family policy and this looks set to continue into the second period of government since the 2001 Election. Two pre-Budget reports published in November 2001, one on 'tackling child poverty' (HM Treasury, 2001a) and one on 'employment opportunity for all', confirm this (HM Treasury, 2001b). These papers do not propose many new measures, but they do commit the government to continued investment in these areas, and implementation of policies already announced. These include, for example, the proposed introduction of a Child Tax Credit in 2003, a major reform in the way in which children are supported through the tax and benefits system (Millar, 2001). The 'work-first' agenda is supported by the introduction of JobCentre Plus (merging the Benefits Agency and the Employment Service) and the 'Action Teams for Jobs' are introducing transitional employment schemes to help people in areas of high unemployment into work. Child Support reform is coming into effect from April 2002. There is an increased interest in the issue of savings and asset building, and another pre-Budget paper (HM Treasury, 2001c) discusses the proposed introduction of a 'savings gateway' (targeted at low-income people) and a 'child trust fund'. The child trust funds would be set up for all children at birth and the government would make further financial contributions at ages 5, 11 and 16. This is still under consultation so the exact shape of the policy is not yet known, but this potentially offers a new way of providing financial support to families with children.

Conclusion

Is there a New Labour family policy? A number of clear policy goals have been set, programmes have been established to deliver these, and resources set aside to pay for the new initiatives. There have been some significant new developments and innovations in Britain's family policy, which seem to represent a break with the past and, as noted at the start of this chapter, a redrawing of the boundaries between state and family responsibilities.

The increased focus on children has been a major element in this. Given the very disadvantaged circumstances of many children in the UK, this has been generally welcomed as a positive development. But much more could be done to include children themselves in policy developments. There have been a series of consultations with children and young people across the country, including the Policy Action Team 12 report on Young People, and the setting up of a Children and Young People's Unit, with a brief to administer the Children's Fund and involve children in its development. These are important, although still limited, steps towards a more 'child-centred' approach to policy making and policy evaluation. Overall, children and young people have become much more visible in the policy process, and this is itself a significant development. But how far children can continue to be separated out from their families and selectively targeted by policies remains to be seen.

Similarly, the positive measures to support employment and help parents combine work and family life start to bring the UK more into line with other European countries, but the real tensions between supporting paid work and supporting care work are difficult to reconcile. Thus, for example, policy in respect of childcare has focused on childcare as a measure needed to support parental employment, rather than as a measure intended to support children's needs and child development. And the work-for-all approach has targeted particular groups of women, such as lone mothers, but family-friendly employment policies have still made only a limited attack on gender inequalities in the labour market. There is a long way still to go.

Notes

[1] These are now called 'parenting orders', perhaps to avoid confusion with the 'parental responsibility orders' under the 1989 Children Act. The parenting orders give unmarried fathers rights to make decisions concerning their children.

[2] Increased by 4% to allow for a rise in the 60% median income line caused by policy changes.

[3] Child poverty measured against the 1996/97 poverty line fell by 1.3 million.

References

Barlow, A. and Duncan, S. (2000a) 'Supporting families? New Labour's communitarianism and the "rationality mistake": part I', *Journal of Social Welfare Law and the Family*, vol 22, no 1, pp 23-42.

Barlow, A. and Duncan, S. (2000b) 'Supporting families? New Labour's communitarianism and the "rationality mistake": part II', *Journal of Social Welfare Law and the Family*, vol 22, no 2, pp 129-43.

Blair, T. (1999) 'Beveridge revisited: a welfare state for the 21st century', reproduced in R. Walker (ed) *Ending child poverty: Popular welfare for the 21st century*, Bristol: The Policy Press, pp 7-18.

Bradbury, B. and Jäntti, M. (1999) *Child poverty across industrialised nations*, Innocenti Occasional Papers, Economic and Social Policy Series No 71, Florence: UNICEF.

Bradshaw, J. (ed) (2001) *Poverty: The outcomes for children*, London: The Family Policy Studies Centre.

Brewer, M., Clark, T. and Goodman, A. (2002) *The government's child poverty target: How much progress has been made?*, London: Institute for Fiscal Studies.

Brown, G. (1999) 'A scar on the nation's soul', *Poverty*, no 104, pp 8-10.

Cm 5050 (2000) *Schools – Building on success*, London: The Stationery Office.

Cm 5084 (2001) *Towards full employment in a modern society*, London: The Stationery Office.

Daycare Trust (2001a) 'Making children's places real for all', *Childcare Now*, issue 15, pp 1-14.

Daycare Trust (2001b) *The price parents pay*, London: The Daycare Trust.

Daycare Trust (2001c) *Childcare voices, childcare choices*, London: The Daycare Trust.

Daycare Trust (2001d) *All our futures: Putting childcare at the centre of every neighbourhood*, London: Daycare Trust.

DfEE (Department for Education and Employment) (1998) *Meeting the childcare challenge*, Cmnd 3959, London: The Stationery Office.

DfEE (2000) *A survey of early years development and childcare partnerships*, London: The Stationery Office.

DfEE/DSS/HM Treasury (2001) *Towards full employment in a modern society*, London: The Stationery Office.

DSS (Department of Social Security) (2000a) *Public service agreement*, London: The Stationery Office.

DSS (2000b) *Opportunity for all: One year on – Making a difference*, London: The Stationery Office.

DTI (Department of Trade and Industry) (2000) *Work and parents: Competitiveness and choice*, London: The Stationery Office.

DWP (Department for Work and Pensions) (2001) *Opportunity for all: The third annual report*, London: The Stationery Office.

DWP (2002) *Households Below Average Income 2000/01*, London: The Stationery Office.

Gordon, D., Adelman, L., Ashworth, K., Bradshaw, J., Levitas, R., Middleton, S., Pantazis, C., Patsios, D., Payne, S., Townsend, P. and Williams, J. (2000) *Poverty and social exclusion in Britain*, York: York Publishing Services for the Joseph Rowntree Foundation.

Gray, A. (2001) '"Making work pay" – devising the best strategy for lone parents in Britain', *Journal of Social Policy*, vol 30, part 2, pp 209-32.

Hales, J., Lessof, C., Roth, W., Gloyer, M., Shaw, A., Millar, J., Barnes, M., Elias, P., Hasluck, C., McKnight, A. and Green, A. (2000) *Evaluation of the New Deal for Lone Parents: Early lessons from the Phase One Prototype – synthesis report*, DSS Research Report no 108. Leeds: Corporate Document Service.

Harker, L. (2001) 'The poverty time lag', *New Economy*, June, pp 116-17.

HM Treasury (1999) *Supporting children through the tax and benefit system*, London: HM Treasury.

HM Treasury (2000) *Building long-term prosperity for all*, Cmnd 4917, London: The Stationery Office.

HM Treasury (2001a) *Tackling child poverty: Giving every child the best possible start in life*, London: HM Treasury.

HM Treasury (2001b) *The changing welfare state: Employment opportunity for all*, London: HM Treasury and DWP.

HM Treasury (2001c) *Delivering savings and assets: The modernisation of Britain's tax and benefits system*, no 9, London: HM Treasury.

Hills, J. (2000) *Taxation for the enabling state*, CASE Paper 41, London: Science Centre for the Analysis of Social Exclusion, London School of Economics and Political Science.

Home Office (1998) *Supporting families*, London: The Stationery Office.

Home Office (1999) *Supporting families: Summary of responses to the consultation document*, London: The Stationery Office.

Inland Revenue (2001) *Working Families' Tax Credit Statistics, Quarterly Enquiry, February*, London: Inland Revenue.

Land, H. (1999) 'New Labour, new families?', in H. Dean and R. Woods (eds) *Social Policy Review 11*, London: Social Policy Association, pp 127-44.

Land, H. (2001) 'Lone mothers, employment and childcare', in J. Millar and K. Rowlingson (eds) *Lone parents, employment and social policy: Cross-national comparisons*, Bristol: The Policy Press, pp 233-52.

Lewis, J. (2001) 'Orientations to work and the issue of care', in J. Millar and K. Rowlingson (eds) *Lone parents, employment and social policy: Cross-national comparisons*, Bristol: The Policy Press, pp 153-68.

Lister, R. (2000) 'Strategies for social inclusion: promoting social cohesion or social justice', in P. Askonas and A. Stewart (eds) *Social inclusion: Possibilities and tensions*, Basingstoke: Macmillan, pp 37-54.

Lister, R. (2001) 'Doing good by stealth', *New Economy*, vol 8, no 2, pp 65-70.

Lord Chancellor's Office (2001) Press releases (www.lcd.gov.uk/family/famfr.htm).

Micklewright, J. and Stewart, K. (2000) 'Child well-being and social cohesion', *New Economy*, vol 7, no 1, pp 18-23.

Middleton, S., Ashworth, K. and Braithwaite, I. (1997) *Small fortunes. Spending on children, childhood poverty and parental sacrifice*, York: York Publishing Services for the Joseph Rowntree Foundation.

Millar, J. (1998) 'Family policy', in P. Alcock (ed) *The students' companion to social policy*, Oxford: Blackwells.

Millar, J. (2000) 'Lone parents and the New Deal', *Policy Studies*, vol 21, no 4, pp 333-45.

Millar, J. (2001) 'Benefits for children in the UK', in K. Battle and M. Mendelson (eds) *Benefits for children – A four country study*, Ottawa, Canada: The Caledon Institute, pp 187-25.

Millar, J. and Ridge T. (2001) *Families, poverty, work and care: A review of the literature on lone parents and low-income couples with children*, DWP Research Report 153, Leeds: Corporate Document Services.

ONS (Office for National Statistics) (2001) *Labour Market Trends: Women in the labour market results from the Spring 2000 LFS*, London: ONS.

Oppenheim, C. and Harker, L. (1996) *Poverty: The facts*, London: Child Poverty Action Group.

Piachaud, D. and Sutherland, H. (2000) *How effective is the British government's attempt to reduce child poverty?*, CASE Paper 38, London: London School of Economics and Political Science.

Piachaud, D. and Sutherland, H. (2001) 'Child poverty: aims, achievements and prospects for the future', *New Economy*, vol 8, no 2, pp 71-6.

Rake, K. (2001) 'Gender and New Labour's social policies', *Journal of Social Policy*, vol 30, part 2, pp 209-32.

Ridge, T. (2002) *Childhood poverty and social exclusion: From a child's perspective*, Bristol: The Policy Press.

Walker, A. and Walker, C. (1997) *Britain divided: The growth of social exclusion in the 1980s and 1990s*, London: Child Poverty Action Group.

Safe as h

Housing policy under New La

Brian Lund

Introduction

Compared to the problems bequeathed to John Major in the early 1990s, New Labour's housing inheritance was benign. House prices fell in real terms by 10% between 1988 and 1993, creating 'negative equity' (ownership of a dwelling worth less than the amount paid for it) for 1.7 million households. However, house price inflation after 1994 eliminated much of this problem and, aided by a sharp fall in interest rates, mortgage foreclosures fell from a peak of 75,500 in 1991 to 33,000 in 1997 (Wilcox, 1999, p 154). Michael Heseltine's 'rough sleepers' initiative, launched in 1991, reduced the number of people sleeping rough in London by 700 and the Department of the Environment had started to extend the scheme to other areas. The number of households in temporary accommodation arranged by local authorities fell from 68,000 in 1992 to 48,000 in 1997. In England, the percentage of dwellings below the fitness standard declined from 8.8 in 1986 to 7.6 in 1996 and, in Wales, from 8.8 to 7.2. In the same period, the percentage of dwellings below Scotland's 'tolerable' standard declined from 4.7 to 1.0 (Revell and Leather, 2000, p 14).

The Conservative's White Paper, *Our future homes: Opportunity, choice, responsibility* (DoE, 1995a), indicated a disengagement from the strident market philosophy of the late 1980s. Under the 1988 Housing Act, rents had been pushed towards 'market' levels, with Housing Benefit 'taking the strain' (Ridley, 1991, p 86). In contrast, the 1995 White Paper anticipated a reduction in the rate of increase, to be achieved by imposing grant penalties on local authorities and registered social landlords (a new name for housing associations plus other not-for-profit housing organisations) if they set rents above national guidelines. The White Paper also attempted to repair some bridges with local government. It emphasised local authorities as 'strategic enablers' and promoted 'local housing companies', with local government representatives on their controlling boards, as extra agencies for managing stock transferred from direct local authority control. 'Mixed communities', where a "balanced mix of households, young and old, low income and better off, home owners and renters, live alongside each other" (DoE, 1995a, p 35), were encouraged.

Promises

Evaluating the housing outputs and outcomes according to the objectives set by New Labour encounters a number of problems. First, there is the paucity and vagueness of New Labour's housing promises. Prior to the 1997 General Election, Gordon Brown's iron grip on spending pledges and the subordination of New Labour's National Executive in the Party's policy formation process led to a dearth of policy documents illuminating New Labour's thinking on housing issues. New Labour's Manifesto (Labour Party, 1997) was terse on housing, and housing featured neither on Blair's list of 10 'covenants', nor on the flashcard of five specific pledges distributed during the election campaign. Indeed, New Labour formulated its core housing policy in office with the help of the Civil Service. This, in part, explains its technocratic, managerial, incremental ambience and its close links with the Conservative programme of the mid-1990s.

The second problem concerns the definition of 'housing policy'. The placing of housing under the heading 'We will strengthen family life' in New Labour's Manifesto intensified speculation that "the end of the millennium may be an appropriate time to accept that talk of a distinctive housing policy is no longer meaningful" (Cowan and Marsh, 2001, p 6). In office, New Labour incorporated housing into its social inclusion agenda. Its housing policy statement, *Quality and choice: A decent home for all: The way forward for housing*, announced the government's objective as to offer "everyone the opportunity of a decent home and so promote social cohesion, well-being and self-dependence" (DETR/DSS, 2000a, para 2.15). This fusion of housing into social inclusion sidelined particular housing outcomes as performance indicators and made it difficult to identify specific housing inputs. Should the resources allocated to New Deal for Communities and the Neighbourhood Renewal Fund be classified as 'housing' expenditure when a large share was devoted to community development and promoting 'joined-up' thinking and action? Moreover, the idea of social inclusion contains a contradiction of particular importance for housing policy. Does social inclusion embrace people who are difficult to live alongside, and are these people 'included' when allocated 'social housing'? If so, given the 'residualisation' and spatial concentration of 'social housing', then does their neighbourhood become more socially excluded? In other words, are people excluded *from* housing or *through* the housing system (Cameron and Field, 2000)?

The third difficulty relates to the performance criteria set by New Labour when in office. Some 'high-level' performance targets have emerged, mainly through the binding of the spending departments to the Treasury's will through Public Service Agreements (HM Treasury, 2001). However, they are moving targets, frequently imprecise, often expressed in outputs not outcomes, and with fulfilment dates sometimes set for the distant future. The reduction by one third in the number of local authority dwellings below a 'decent' standard, set for 2004, was accompanied by a definition of a 'decent home' as one that must "be above the current statutory minimum standard for housing (the fitness standard); be in a reasonable state of repair; have modern facilities and services; and provide a reasonable degree of thermal comfort" (House of Commons, Written Answers, 2 July 2, 2001). The 60% target for the share of new development on 'brownfield' sites is set for 2008 and, although the housing statement, *The way forward for housing*, refers to 'affordable' rents, it gives no definition of affordability.

Fourth, there is the issue of where accountability lies for the achievement of the 'low-level' objectives set by New Labour. One of New Labour's manifesto pledges was to replace the compulsory competitive tendering of local government services, including housing management, with a duty to provide 'Best Value' (see Chapter Three). From April 2000, local authorities were required to set Best Value targets and their attainments are subject to scrutiny of a Housing Inspectorate located in the Audit Commission. Performance criteria are also identifiable in the Audit Commission's performance measures, in the DETR's Housing Strategy documents and in the Housing Corporation's National Housing Investment Strategy plus its Best Value regime for registered social landlords. But, given the tight central control over 'social' housing providers, is failure or success in meeting these goals to be attributed to the government or to the numerous agencies directly responsible for delivering housing outcomes? There is also the problem of assessing the 'housing' stewardship of the Scottish Parliament and Welsh Assembly in the context of economic, fiscal and benefit policies – especially Housing Benefit policy – set at Westminster. Finally, of course, housing policy has a long chrysalis time; inputs such as the release of local authority capital receipts produces outputs of new or improved dwellings some three years down the line.

In its 1997 Manifesto, *New Labour because Britain deserves better*, New Labour promised (pp 25-7):

- there would be no return to the "boom and bust policies which caused the collapse of the housing market";
- to work with mortgage providers to encourage greater provision of more flexible mortgages to protect families in a world of increasing job insecurity;
- stronger consumer protection for mortgage buyers "for example by extension of the Financial Services Act, against the sale of disadvantageous mortgage packages";
- to ensure that those 'who break their bargains' are "liable to pay the costs inflicted on others, in particular legal and survey costs";
- reinvestment of "capital receipts from the sale of council houses, received but not spent by local councils", to build new houses and rehabilitate old ones;
- to provide "protection where it is most needed for tenants in houses in multiple-occupation" by "a proper system of licensing by local authorities which will benefit tenants and responsible landlords alike";
- simplification of "the current rules restricting the purchase of freeholds by leaseholders";

- the introduction of 'commonhold', "a new form of tenure enabling people living in flats to own their homes individually and own the whole property collectively";
- to "place a new duty on local authorities to protect those who are homeless through no fault of their own and are in priority need";
- to attack the problem of homeless young people by "the phased release of capital receipts from council house sales to increase the stock of housing for rent" and by leading "the young unemployed into work and financial independence".

Policy developments

Homelessness

New Labour's 1997 Manifesto declared that "There is no more powerful symbol of Tory neglect in our society today than young people living rough on the streets" (Labour Party, 1997, p 27). It promised to tackle the problem through the welfare-to-work programme and the release of right-to-buy capital receipts. Rough sleeping received early consideration from the Prime Minister's Social Exclusion Unit (SEU), set up in late 1997 (SEU, 1998a), and this attention led to the production of a rough-sleeping strategy. Homelessness 'tsars' were to be appointed with a target to reduce rough sleeping in England by one quarter by December 2000, one third by June 2001 and at least two thirds by 2002 (DETR, 1999). This target was to be achieved by appointing additional outreach workers organised into assessment teams, reviewing the processes involved in leaving care, prison and the armed forces, discouraging the 'homelessness street culture' and supporting rough sleepers to 'come in out of the cold' into night shelters and hostels where they would be helped to 'move on' to a job and settled accommodation. Material aid to rough sleepers from the public was frowned on and, accompanying the launch of the SEU's report on rough sleeping, was a sharp reminder that neglected obligations would be enforced. "Should the 'Tsars' fail", Blair announced, then "rough sleeping would be criminalized and the police called in to clear the rough sleepers off the streets" (in Hall, 1998). In 1999, the Department of the Environment, Transport and the Regions repeated this warning:

> ... rough sleepers themselves have a responsibility to come in. Once we are satisfied that realistic alternatives are readily available we – and the public at large – are entitled to expect those working on the streets to seek to persuade people to take advantage of them. This includes the police who sometimes have not been able to use their powers because of a lack of options to move rough sleepers on to. (DETR, Rough Sleepers Unit, 1999, p 10)

In November 2001, despite the deep concerns expressed about the validity of its rough-sleeper count (White, 2001), New Labour claimed that the number of rough sleepers in England had declined from 1,850 in 1998 to 532 in 2001 (DTLR, 2001a).

Rough sleeping should not be equated with homelessness. Leaving aside people living in squats, staying unwillingly with friends, sleeping in hostels, and so on, there is the issue of incidence of 'statutory' homelessness – people covered by the provisions of the 1996 Housing Act. The Conservatives devised the 1996 Housing Act to eliminate the alleged 'perverse effects' of the 1977 Housing (Homeless Persons) Act. They claimed that "under existing legislation, what should be a safety net has become a fast track into ['social housing' tenancies] with consequences that are often seen as unfair" (DoE, 1994, para 1.1). Accordingly, the 1996 Act omitted specific reference to homeless households in the statutory list of people entitled to special consideration when allocating 'social housing', limited the duty of local authorities to provide temporary accommodation to two years and restricted the help obtainable from registered social landlords if private landlord accommodation was available.

New Labour claimed that "Homelessness has more than doubled under the Conservatives. Today more than 40,000 families in England are in expensive temporary accommodation" (Labour Party, 1997, p 26). A new duty would be imposed on local authorities "to protect those who are homeless through no fault of their own and are in priority need" (Labour Party, 1997). The Allocation of Housing (Reasonable and Additional Preference) Regulations (1997) added statutory homeless households to the list of 'need' categories to which local authorities were required to give 'reasonable preference' when allocating dwellings. However, significant proposals for reform were postponed until the publication of the Homes Bill in 2000. This contained provisions to impose a duty on local government to prepare a homelessness strategy. Moreover, local authorities would no longer be able to discharge their obligations to homeless people by offering short-term private landlord tenancies unless the homeless person gave written consent. Homeless people were to be given the same choice of accommodation as others on the housing register and local authorities would be obliged to provide suitable short-term accommodation until 'settled' accommodation became available. In addition, the government promised to make an order under existing legislation to extend the 'priority need' category to cover those leaving care, 16- and 17-year-olds, people 'vulnerable' as a result of violence and harassment and those from an 'institutionalised background' (ex-service personnel and ex-prisoners). The homelessness charities gave the Homelessness Bill a warm welcome but it did not restore homelessness policy to the position before the passing of the 1996 Housing Act. Then, when allocating 'social' housing, it was policy and practice to give precedence to homeless people in priority need *above* other categories of need. The Homes Bill fell on the dissolution of Parliament.

Homeowners

When in opposition, Blair's keynote housing speech championed the homeowner. He branded the Conservatives "the 'homewreckers party' – the party of negative equity, repossessions, broken dreams and falling house prices" (Blair, 1996, p 192). The Conservatives had "lost touch with the insecure majority", whereas Labour was "back in touch – the party of social housing, but the party of private housing too" (Blair, 1996, p 192). These 'warm words' on home ownership were sustained by token rather than robust policies. New Labour promised a more flexible, regulated mortgage market, better protection against gazumping and the introduction of a new 'commonhold', enabling people living in flats to own their homes individually and to own the whole property collectively. According to the Green Paper *Quality and choice: A decent home for all* (DETR/DSS, 2000b), the government had worked with the financial services industry to produce flexible mortgages and had strengthened the regulation of the financial services sector via the Financial Services Agency. The Homes Bill required sellers to put together a 'seller's pack', giving evidence of title, responses to standard preliminary enquires, a draft contract and a home condition report, thereby, so the government claimed, cutting delays in the selling process and helping fulfil the Manifesto pledge to reduce opportunities for 'gazumping'. Nonetheless, following the demise of the Homes Bill on the dissolution of parliament, no new Bill to implement the 'seller's pack' proposals was announced in the 2001 Queen's Speech, despite the inclusion of the idea in New Labour's 2001 Manifesto.

In August 2000, the DETR and the Lord Chancellor's Department jointly published the Commonhold and Leasehold Reform Bill, with a consultation paper setting out proposals to introduce a new form of tenure. 'Commonhold' would allow flat owners to share ownership and management of the common parts of the development they were living in and make it easier for leaseholders of flats to collectively purchase their freehold. The Commonhold and Leasehold Reform Bill failed to complete its passage through Parliament.

Despite its enthusiastic endorsement of owner-occupation, New Labour took a firm line on the subject of state assistance to homeowners to help with the cost of repairs and improvement. "We expect owner occupiers to maintain their homes from their own resources", it said (DETR/DSS, 2000b, para 2.15), and, in promoting maintenance, declared it would seek greater resources from individual equity withdrawal. Policy shifted to a rigorously selective, area-based programme. This was aimed at those cases "where the household is most at risk from poor housing, the owner cannot afford to repair the house" and "the poor condition of a house or group of houses is having a negative impact on the wider area" (DETR/DSS, 2000a). The consultative document *Private sector housing renewal* (DETR, 2001a) proposed the ending of statutory entitlements to improvement grants. The DETR claimed that such entitlements undermined local authority flexibility in dealing with the physical decay (DETR, 2001, para 1.2). However, in the absence of performance targets on housing renewal, the abolition of statutory based claims made it easier to cut state investment in private sector housing.

Renters

In its Manifesto, New Labour welcomed a revived private landlord sector, but promised to give greater protection to tenants living in multi-occupied dwellings and to licence private landlords operating in this sector. These promises were not kept. Indeed, in an attempt to convince landlords that there was no 'political risk' in investing in private renting, New Labour backed away from involvement in the operations of the assured shorthold tenancies introduced by the Conservatives, claiming that "excessive regulation ... can stifle growth to the detriment of tenants and responsible landlords" (DETR/DSS, 2000b, p 16).

New Labour extended the Conservative policy of transferring local authority housing to 'alternative' landlords. In 1996/97, 20,000 dwellings were transferred, but this figure increased to a projected 150,000 in 2000/01 as New Labour geared up to its target of 200,000 transfers each year (DETR/DSS, 2000b). In Scotland, the 2001 Housing Act was aimed at accelerating stock transfer and, via a new form of tenure and a common regulatory regime, at blurring the distinction between local authority housing and accommodation provided by other registered social landlords. New Labour justified its stock transfer policy as a mechanism of tenant empowerment. Tenants would become more involved in local authority housing management via 'tenant compacts', but they would also be able to choose between a more diverse range of landlords. It was also argued that, given the remote possibility of finding all the resources necessary from public sector borrowing, then stock transfer was a tried and tested method of using private finance to reduce the £19 billion backlog in council house repairs and improvements. The transfer programme contained the safeguard that dwellings could be transferred only after tenant endorsement in a ballot, and alternative routes to tapping new resources were made available to local government. Selected local authorities could use the Private Finance Initiative and, primed by an earmarked fund of £400 million, local authorities with a proven record of excellence were allowed to set up "arm's-length management arrangements" and enjoy "extra scope to borrow for investment". Whether this is a short-term inducement for local government to take a first step towards stock transfer or a long-term feature of housing policy remains to be seen (Murie and Nevin, 2001, p 40).

Capital spending

The Manifesto pledge to allow local authorities to use their housing capital receipts was qualified by statements on their use. In contrast to the commitment in Labour's 1992 Manifesto, 'right to buy' receipts were not specifically allocated to local councils to build 'homes for the homeless'. Instead, New Labour promised to support a three-way partnership between the public, private and

Table 6.1: Capital spending on housing (1993/94 to 2001/02)

	£ billion
1993/94	3.99
1994/95	3.33
1995/96	2.79
1996/97	2.70
1997/98	1.93
1998/99	1.73
1999/2000[a]	1.78
2000/01[b]	2.84
2000/02[b]	3.25

[a] Estimated.
[b] Projected.
Source: House of Commons, Hansard, Written Answers, 16 November 2000, col 723W

housing association sectors to promote 'good social housing'. An early start was made in releasing capital receipts, but the first three years of New Labour governance were lean years for housing investment. The government adhered to the cutbacks in local authority borrowing and in capital support to housing associations drawn up by the Conservatives, and the 1998 comprehensive spending review promised scant resources for 1999/2000. Only in 2000/01 did resources start to flow at a faster rate than under the last full year of the Conservative government (see Table 6.1).

Welfare-to-work

Social inclusion via work is the dominant theme of Blair's social policy and the housing Green Paper listed "reducing barriers to work, particularly in relation to benefit and rent policy" as a key principle of housing policy. This objective was reflected in the initial downward pressure applied to the rents charged by registered social landlords, in amendments made to the regulations governing housing Benefit and in changes to the rules on Income Support.

New Labour continued the Conservative policy of controlling the rents charged by registered social landlords. For three years, the government also tried to link local authority rent increases to inflation. Then, as part of an agenda to promote rent convergence across the registered social landlord sector, the government announced that local authority rents would increase by 20% above inflation, phased over 10 years. Moreover, New Labour proposed to impose a uniform rent structure on all 'social housing' tenants, on the formula of 30% capital value and 70% on average county earnings. According to some estimates, this will involve an additional real rent increase for 560,000 local authority tenants (Smith–Bowers and Taylor, 2001). Although increases will be limited to £2 per week above inflation each year (DETR/DSS, 2000b, p 11), it seems that the long-standing DETR objectives of creating a single 'social housing' category and supplying financial incentives for local authority tenants to vote for stock transfer had taken precedence over reducing barriers to work.

In the early 1990s, the cost of Housing Benefit soared as it took the strain of greater reliance on the private landlord sector to meet housing requirements and the push towards market-level rents. The escalating cost of Housing Benefit – £3.9 billion in 1987/88 to £11.1 billion in 1994/95 (Wilcox, 2000a, p 213) – prompted the Conservatives to introduce measures to cut expenditure. New maximum 'reference rent' limitations on entitlement produced a dramatic increase in the number of households subject to Housing Benefit reductions – from 269,000 in 1994/95 to 439,000 in 1996/97 – but no stabilisation of private sector rents. New Labour retained the Conservatives' 'reference rent' restrictions and did not remove the rule, applied in October 1996 to people aged under 25, restricting Housing Benefit to the rent of a single room. However, it did not implement a Conservative proposal – included as a reduction in public expenditure in New Labour's inherited financial targets – to extend the single-room limitation to those aged 25 to 60.

The Housing Benefit system is a major obstacle to reducing barriers to work; the higher the rent (up to set thresholds), the larger the benefit entitlement. The introduction of Working Families' Tax Credit – taken into account in assessing Housing Benefit entitlement – modified the 'poverty trap', but a couple with one child and a rent of £70 per week are still not free from the Housing Benefit taper until their gross weekly income reaches £266 (Wilcox, 2001). Housing Benefit was the subject of an internal government review but, although the housing Green Paper for England put forward a number of options for change, reform was shelved. The policy of stock transfer depended on the availability of Housing Benefit to service debt, and the cost crisis had abated due to lower unemployment, the operation of Working Families' Tax Credit (National Association of Citizen's Advice Bureaux, 2001) and the impact of the Conservatives' restrictions on Housing Benefit eligibility. The existing administrative chaos presented a further obstacle to change. In many areas local authorities struggled to deliver a scheme made increasingly complex by the introduction of new regulations aimed at reducing fraud. Ninety changes in Housing Benefit regulations were made in New Labour's first term of office. In the absence of Housing Benefit reform, the welfare-to-work dimension of housing policy was pursued on a piecemeal basis. Foyers, where homeless young people are housed and trained, were encouraged, and rough sleepers, having 'come out of the cold', were to be put on welfare-to-work schemes as promised in the 1997 Manifesto. Claimants recently returning to work became entitled to Housing Benefit at the full rate for four weeks and claims for 'in-work' Housing Benefit were fast-tracked.

Rights and responsibilities

Blair made his first keynote speech outside parliament as Prime Minister at the Aylesbury estate in London, an area with a reputation as a 'problem estate'. His theme was the 'underclass' and how the government was going to tackle it.

> There is a case not just in moral terms but in enlightened self-interest to act, to tackle what we know exists – an underclass of people cut off from society's mainstream, without any sense of shared purpose.... The basis of this modern civil society is an ethic of mutual responsibility or duty. It is something for something. A society where we play by the rules. You only take out if you put in. That's the bargain. (quoted in Anderson and Mann, 1997, p 205)

As part of its rights/responsibilities agenda, New Labour warned it would strengthen existing measures to deal with 'anti-social' tenants. Twelve-month probationary tenancies and the Anti-Social Behaviour orders of the 1998 Crime and Disorder Act were implemented. The housing Green Paper promoted the idea that authorities should be given the powers to reduce Housing Benefit for unruly tenants as an alternative to, or as part of, the process of pursuing an Anti-Social Behaviour order (DETR/DSS, 2000b, para 5.47).

New Labour's 'rights equals responsibility' agenda extended beyond 'anti-social' behaviour. One of the SEU's first tasks was to report on the policies necessary to tackle the problems of deprived neighbourhoods. The report concluded that past policies had often intensified the problems. There had been a tendency to parachute solutions in from outside rather than engaging local communities; too much emphasis on physical renewal instead of better opportunities for local people and too many initiatives. Above all, a joined-up problem had not been addressed in a joined-up way (SEU, 1998b). These conclusions were reflected in a new government programme, New Deal for Communities, with £800 million over three years to promote 'bottom-up', 'joined-up' solutions to neighbourhood deprivation. This was followed by the creation of the Neighbourhood Renewal Fund to nurture community commitment, joint working between 'mainstream' services and neighbourhood management. More resources would be offered to communities if they took greater responsibility for improving their neighbourhoods (SEU, 2001).

Balanced communities

> We would not expect schemes funded with Social Housing Grant to reinforce existing high concentrations of social rented housing. Where schemes are on, or close to, existing social housing estates, particular emphasis should be given to producing homes that cater for a mix of households and schemes that cater for a mix of households and income groups. (DETR/DSS, 2000a, para 8.30)

This exhortation to avoid concentrations of social housing in new developments was accompanied by attempts to change the social mix of existing estates by encouraging greater flexibility in the allocation schemes used by local authorities. 'Choice' took a place alongside 'need' in the official language on lettings, and local authorities were encouraged to supply a lettings service rather than a lettings system (Cole et al, 2001). The Starter Home initiative, which allocated £250 million to assist key workers to afford homes in high housing cost areas, was also linked to the idea of creating balanced communities. Central guidance on planning procedures supplied an additional dimension to building mixed communities. Planning Policy Guidance Note Three (PPG3: www.planning.detr.gov.uk/ppg3/index.htm) declared that "The Government believes that it is important to help create mixed and inclusive communities", adding "the community's need for a mix of housing types, including affordable housing, is a material planning consideration which should be taken into account in formulating development plan policies and in deciding planning applications involving housing" (DETR, 2001b, paras 3.11, 3.13). However, New Labour's lukewarm approach to the creation of 'balanced communities' was reflected in its failure to champion tenure specification as a legitimate element in establishing a requirement for 'affordable' housing. New Labour was also willing to allow developers to meet affordable housing requirements outside their main developments but failed to set out indicators of success in promoting 'mixed and inclusive' communities. Indeed, there appears to be very little monitoring of the impact of PPG3. A parliamentary question asking for information on affordable housing in London produced by PPG3 elicited the following response:

> A full breakdown of information on affordable housing provided as part of individual development schemes is not available. The Department, working with the Greater London Authority, is taking steps to ensure that consistent and accurate data are collected for the provision of affordable housing in London. (House of Commons, *Hansard*, 25 April 2001, col 275W)

Housing and regeneration

In 1995, the Conservative government published household projections indicating that, between 1991 and 2016, there would be an additional 4.4 million households in England (DoE, 1995b). These projections presented difficult issues for New Labour. Having pushed its electoral base well beyond its urban heartland, the government "faced resistance to building in the countryside from a new batch of Labour members representing shire constituencies and well versed in the rhetoric on environmental sustainability" (Bramley, 1998). New Labour removed part of the problem by commissioning new household formation calculations that reduced the anticipated growth in new households from 176,000 to 150,000 households per year. The government delegated the main responsibility for planning to meet housing needs to 'regional stakeholders', but established a target of 60% for the reuse of previously developed land in meeting housing demand and required local planning authorities to consider using existing property and previously developed land before releasing greenfield sites. As in the 1930s and 1960s, the needs of city and country were reconciled with the claim that restrictions on rural and suburban development would lead to an 'urban renaissance'.

The Final Report of the Urban Task Force (Urban Task Force, 1999), chaired by Lord Rodgers of Riverside, supplied a blueprint to promote this 'urban renaissance'. Having considered estimates of how many additional dwellings were likely to be accommodated on recycled land, the Urban Task Force predicted significant pressure to release more greenfield sites, especially in the South East and South West. But, "if we manage our land and building assets differently" (Urban Task Force, 1999, p 189), it said, then the pressure to release greenfield sites could be reduced:

> Through a combination of a strong regional economic development policy, the strategic application of the planning system, the use of economic instruments, changes in design policies, increased regeneration investment, improved assembly and reclamation of previously developed land, and a commitment to recycle under-used and empty buildings, we can do much better ... (Urban Task Force, 1999, p 189)

Greatly increased resources were deemed necessary to achieve these objectives and the task force noted the decline in government regeneration expenditure between 1993 and 1999, commenting that under the 1998 Comprehensive Spending Review:

> For the first time in many years, the Government promised to increase its regeneration expenditure over each of the next three years. In real terms, however, the increase in expenditure only means that by 2001/02 we will have just overtaken the amount that the previous Government was spending in 1993/4. (Urban Task Force, 1999, p 286)

New Labour's urban White Paper, *Our towns and cities: The future delivering an urban renaissance,* reflected the broad strategy recommended by the Urban Task Force and expressed a commitment to channelling more mainstream service resources into deprived areas. Moreover, the Comprehensive Spending Review 2000 and the 2001 March Budget delivered new resources to kick-start the urban renaissance. The capital resources available to local authorities were boosted mainly by the introduction of an earmarked Major Repairs Allowance for local authority housing, to be concentrated in the most deprived areas. Registered social landlords received extra capital provision; resources were made available for the Starter Home Initiative; provision was made to pump-prime local authority stock transfers and selected local authorities were granted more freedom from capital spending controls. There would be: exemption from

Table 6.2: Progress against Manifesto/Annual Report housing targets

Pledge	New Labour's assessment	Score/10
86: Encourage flexible mortgages	On course: (a) We will reject the boom and bust policies which caused the collapse of the housing market. (b) We will work with mortgage providers to encourage greater provision of more flexible mortgages to protect families in a world of increasing job insecurity.	5 6
87: Stronger protection for home buyers	Mortgage buyers also require stronger consumer protection, for example by extension of the Financial Services Act, against the sale of disadvantageous mortgage packages.	7
88: Consult on ways to tackle gazumping	On course. Those who break their bargains should be liable to pay the costs inflicted on others, in particular legal and survey costs.	0
89: Protection for tenants in housing in multiple occupation	On course: (a) Capital receipts from the sale of council houses, received but not spent by local councils, will be reinvested in building new houses and rehabilitating old ones. (b) We will provide protection where it is most needed: for tenants in houses in multiple-occupation: there will be a proper system of licensing by local authorities which will benefit tenants and responsible landlords alike.	3 0
90: Simplify leasehold enfranchisement	On course: We will simplify the current rules restricting the purchase of freeholds by leaseholders.	0
91: Introduce 'Commonhold'	Not yet timetabled. Draft legislation is in progress: We will introduce 'Commonhold', a new form of tenure enabling people living in flats to own their homes individually and own the whole property collectively.	0
92: Duty on local councils to protect homeless	On course: (a) We will place a new duty on local authorities to protect those who are homeless through no fault of their own and are in priority need. (b) We will attack the problem of homeless young people by the phased release of capital receipts from council house sales to increase the stock of housing for rent and by leading the young unemployed into work and financial independence.	4 8

Stamp Duty on all property transactions worth less than £150,000 in 'disadvantaged' communities; accelerated tax credits for cleaning up contaminated land; 100% capital allowances for creating 'flats over shops'; VAT reductions to encourage conversions of properties for residential use; zero VAT for the sale of renovated houses empty for 10 years or more and a Community Investment Tax Credit.

Table 6.3: Dwellings started (UK) (1994 to 2001, 000s)

	Private	'Social'	Total
1994/95	163.2	42.2	205.4
1995/96	140.5	34.5	175.0
1996/97	162.1	31.8	193.9
1997/98	171.6	26.5	198.1
1998/99	161.4	24.2	185.6
1999/2000	169.4	22.9	192.3
2000/01	165.7	20.3	186.0

Source: DTLR (2001) Housing Statistics (www.dtlr.gov.uk/research/hss/index.htm)

Table 6.4: Households in temporary accommodation

	England		Scotland		Wales
	Bed and breakfast	All	Bed and breakfast	All	All
1995	4,500	44,140	449	4,028	
1996	4,160	42,190	454	4,214	
1997	4,520	45,030	355	3,772	388
1998	6,930	51,520	360	3,764	446
1999	8,060	62,190	413	3,864	538
2000	9,860	72,440	462	4,089	459

Sources: Scottish Executive (2000); Welsh Assembly (2000); Wilson (2001)

Intrinsic evaluation

Judged in terms of meeting its specific Manifesto pledges on housing, New Labour merits a low overall mark (three out of 10) for an insipid attempt to achieve modest objectives (see Table 6.2).

On the credit side, the pledge on statutory homelessness and was met in part, rough sleeping was reduced, interest rates were reasonable and, despite the boom in the house prices in many areas, there was no bust. On the debit side, New Labour did not introduce legislation to regulate lettings in multi-occupied properties, and the Homes Bill and the Commonhold and Leasehold Reform Bill were the victims of the early General Election. The initial failure to inject capital into 'social housing' – the release of capital receipts was offset by reductions in mainstream allocations – produced a decline in new 'affordable' housing (Table 6.3). Thus, it is unsurprising that the number of households in temporary accommodation increased under New Labour (Table 6.4). Although no specific commitment to reducing statutory homelessness was made in the 1997 Manifesto, Blair promised to "do everything in our power to end the scandal of homelessness, to tackle the spectacle of people sleeping rough on the streets and to end the waste of families sleeping in bed and breakfast accommodation" (Blair, 1996 quoted in *Housing Today*, March 2001).

Extrinsic evaluation

A number of 'extrinsic' criteria are available on which New Labour's achievements can be assessed, but 'social justice' seems to be an appropriate overarching concept to apply because, although the idea of equality has been abandoned, New Labour uses the language of social justice (see Chapter Two of this volume). A variety of specifications of social justice are available but John Rawls' 'maximin' principle will be adopted here as it is closest to New Labour's formulation of the concept. In *A theory of justice* (1971), Rawls presented a reasoned case for evaluating social action according to the 'maximin' principle. Social and economic inequalities are to be arranged, says Rawls, so produce "the greatest benefit of the least advantaged" (Rawls, 1971, p 101). Has New Labour's housing policy benefited the 'least advantaged'?

Income

The series *Households Below Average Income* gives statistics on the distribution of income before and after housing costs. The latest published figures relate to 1999/2000 and do not include the full impact of Working Families' Tax Credit or the most recent changes in taxation and in universal and selective benefits. Nonetheless, New Labour's record is disappointing. In 1996/97, 19% of children were living in households with an income below 50% of the mean *before* housing costs. This increased to 25% *after* housing costs, an indication, perhaps, of the lack of assistance to people in work with low incomes in the owner-occupied sector (Wilcox, 2000b). In 1999/2000, after three years of New Labour governance, the figures were the same as for 1996/97 (DSS Analytical Services Division, 2001, p 151). Compare this to 1979, when 7.5% of children were living in households with an income below 50% of the mean *before* housing costs and 9% *after* housing costs (DSS Analytical Services Division, 2000, p 83).

Social justice: the tenure dimension

The academic analysis of housing policy in terms of tenure has declined in recent years. This has led to the neglect of the distributive impact of tenure-related housing policies. In an attempt to force all rents to market levels, the Conservatives added the cost of Housing Benefit to the debit side of every Local Authority Housing Revenue Account. This meant that 'better-off' tenants, not receiving Housing Benefit, contributed to the cost of providing help to poorer tenants, whereas homeowners, the tenants of private landlords and housing association tenants made no such direct contribution. New Labour retained this accounting devise with the result that the so-called 'tenants' tax' increased until it reached £1.5 billion in 2000/01 (Wilson, 2000, p 9).

Wealth

The value of dwellings is an important element in personal wealth. New Labour's 1997 Manifesto promised to avoid 'boom and bust' in the housing market, but, despite attempts to dampen demand by the withdrawal of mortgage income tax relief and a steep increase in Stamp Duty, house prices increased by 45% between May 1997 and April 2001 (Proviser Property Prices: www.proviser.com/property_prices/). House price inflation varied between and within regions. In some areas, house prices declined, whereas, in adjacent neighbourhoods, they increased rapidly. In Oldham, for example, the £2,000 drop since May 1997 in the average value of a terraced house in the most deprived postal district, combined with a rise in the value of detached houses in the most affluent postal district, increased the 'wealth gap' by £39,000 in three years (Upmystreet: www.upmystreet.co.uk).

Policy developments since the 2001 General Election

New Labour passed no primary housing legislation in its first term, leaving it in the embarrassing position of having to repeat most of its 1997 housing pledges in its 2001 Manifesto. The major policy recommendations of the 2000 Housing Policy Statement were added to these pledges. The Manifesto promised the annual transfer of 200,000 houses "to social landlords like housing associations" (Labour Party, 2001, p 14), to bring all social housing to a decent standard by 2010 and to help 10,000 key workers buy their homes in high-cost areas. In addition, a pledge was made "to examine ways in which tenants can be helped to gain an equity stake in the value of their home" (Labour Party, 2001, p 14). As in all the elections since 1979, housing was an insignificant issue in the election campaign (Paris and Muir, 2002).

One of first actions of New Labour in its second term was to return the homelessness provisions of the Homes Bill to Parliament as the Homelessness Bill. The steep increase in the number of statutory homeless families – up from 48,000 in 1997 to 80,000 in 2001 (Rahman et al, 2001) – led to the establishment of a Bed and Breakfast Unit to tackle one dimension of the problem. The Unit issued a consultation document declaring the government's determination to reduce reliance on bed and breakfast accommodation and seeking advice on performance criteria necessary to monitor the policy. The Green Paper, *Planning obligations: Delivering a fundamental change*, declared the government's concern "at the shortage of affordable housing in many areas" (DTLR, 2001b, para 2.6) and supported the extension of planning obligations to facilitate the supply of affordable housing to commercial developers. The Commonhold and Leasehold Reform Bill was reintroduced to Parliament and the government declared its intention to allow local authorities to licence landlords operating in low-demand areas.

Conclusion

New Labour's 1997 Manifesto was directed towards reassuring electors that a Labour government would not tax, spend and redistribute to the disadvantage of 'Middle England'. This produced fallow years of diminishing investment in housing and regeneration but the opportunity to formulate policies for the effective use of 'stored' resources and the fruits of economic growth. New Labour's 2001 Manifesto promisingly placed most of its housing proposals in the context of regional and urban renewal policies rather than social inclusion. It promised £1.8 billion additional housing investment plus £2.7 billion spending on New Deal for Communities and the Neighbourhood Renewal Fund over the following three years (Labour Party, 2001, p 14). These promises helped to compensate for the years of low investment but their sufficiency in relationship to New Labour's objective of offering "everyone the opportunity of a decent home and so promote social cohesion, well-being and self-dependence" (Labour Party, 1997) remains in question.

Given that, in the domains of housing and regeneration, policy changes and investment decisions take time to produce robust outcomes, Blair's claim that New Labour required a second term for 'delivery' rings true. There will be no such dispensation at the end of a second term, especially as the reports on the 2001 urban riots (Clarke, 2001; Home Office, 2001; Ritchie, 2001) have underlined the salience of housing to issues of race relations and law and order. The publication of the results of the English, Scottish and Welsh House Conditions Surveys will supply an indication of the improvements made to the condition of the housing stock since 1996. The homelessness statistics will continue to reveal the impact of general housing policies on the more vulnerable in the housing market. The Department of Work and Pensions' series, *Households Below Average Income* (www.dss.gov.uk/asd/online.html; DSS, 2000), which provides information on the distribution of incomes before and after housing costs, will indicate the extent to which the housing system has contributed to the alleviation of poverty. The Inland Revenue Statistics, plus the Office for National Statistics' series on the redistributive impact of taxation, service provision and benefits, will uncover the impact of New Labour governance on the distribution of wealth and income.

By 2005, despite the absence of 'robust' performance indicators on crucial policy outcomes such as 'affordability' and 'balanced communities', we will be in a better position to know if 'joined-up' social engineering – aimed at guaranteeing 'floors' of well-being – has reduced social exclusion.

References

Anderson, P. and Mann, N. (1997) *Safety first*, London: Granta Books.

Blair, T. (1996) *New Britain: My vision of a young country*, London: Fourth Estate.

Bramley, G. (1998) 'Signs of panic in middle England', *New Economy*, vol 5, no 3, pp 168-74.

Cameron, S. and Field, A. (2000) 'Community, ethnicity and neighbourhood', *Housing Studies*, vol 15, pp 827-43.

Clarke, Lord (Chair) (2001) *Burnley Task Force Report* (www.burnleytaskforce.org.uk/).

Cole, I., Iqbal, B., Slocombe, L. and Trott, T. (2001) *Social engineering or consumer choice*, London: Chartered Institute of Housing.

Cowan, D. and Marsh, A. (2001) 'Analysing New Labour housing policy', in D. Cowan and A. Marsh (eds) *Two steps forward: Housing policy into the new millennium*, Bristol: The Policy Press.

DSS Analytical Services Division (2000) *Households Below Average Income 1994/5 to 1998/9*, London: DSS.

DoE (Department of the Environment) (1994) *Access to local authority and housing association tenancies: A consultation paper*, London: DoE.

DoE and Welsh Office (1995a) *Our future homes: Opportunity, choice, responsibility*, Cm 2901, London: HMSO.

DoE (1995b) *Projections of households in England to 2016*, London: HMSO.

DETR (Department of the Environment, Transport and the Regions), Rough Sleepers Unit (1999) *Rough sleeping: The government's strategy*, London: DETR.

DETR/DSS (2000a) *Quality and choice: A decent home for all: The way forward for housing*, London: The Stationery Office, December.

DETR/DSS (2000b) *Quality and choice: A decent home for all: The Housing Green Paper*, London: The Stationery Office, April.

DETR (2001) *Private sector housing renewal: A consultative document*, London: DETR.

DTLR (Department of the Transport, Local Government and the Regions) (2001a) *Government meets target on reducing rough sleeping* (www.housing.dtlr.gov.uk/rsu/pn/rsu19.htm).

DTLR (2001b) *Planning obligations: Delivering a fundamental change* (www.planning.dtlr.gov.uk/consult/planoblg/index.htm).

Hall, S. (1998) 'Street Tsars to have big budget', *The Guardian*, 8 July.

Home Office (2001) *Building cohesive communities*, London: The Stationery Office.

HM Treasury (2001) *Choosing the right fabric*, London: The Stationery Office.

Labour Party (1997) *New Labour because Britain deserves better*, London: Labour Party.

Labour Party (2001) *Ambitions for Britain: Labour's manifesto 2001*, London: Labour Party.

Murie, A. and Nevin, B. (2001) 'New Labour transfers policy', in D. Cowan and A. Marsh (eds) *Two steps forward: Housing policy into the new millennium*, Bristol: The Policy Press.

National Association of Citizen's Advice Bureaux (2001) *Work in progress: Client experience of Working Families' Tax Credit*, London: National Association of Citizen's Advice Bureaux.

Paris, C. and Muir, J. (2002) 'After housing policy: housing and the UK General Election 2001', *Housing Studies*, vol 17, no 1, pp 151-64.

Rahman, M., Palmer, G. and Kenway, P. (2001) *Monitoring poverty and social exclusion 2001*, York: New Policy Institute/Joseph Rowntree Foundation.

Rawls, J. (1971) *A theory of justice*, Oxford: Oxford University Press.

Revell, K. and Leather, P. (2000) *The state of UK housing: A factfile on housing conditions and housing renewal policies in the UK*, (2nd edn), Bristol/York: The Policy Press/Joseph Rowntree Foundation.

Ridley, N. (1991) *'My style of government': The Thatcher years*, London: Hutchinson.

Ritchie, D. (Chair) (2001) *One Oldham, one future*, Oldham: Oldham Metropolitan District Council.

Scottish Executive (2000) *Operation of the Homeless Persons Legislation in Scotland*, Quarter Ending 30 June, Edinburgh: Scottish Executive.

Smith-Bowers, B. and Taylor, T. (2001) 'Tenants Extra', *Inside Housing*, 16 March, p 2.

SEU (Social Exclusion Unit) (1998a) *Rough sleeping – Report by the Social Exclusion Unit*, Cm 4008, London: The Stationery Office.

SEU (1998b) *Bringing Britain together: A national policy for neighbourhood renewal*, London: Cabinet Office.

SEU (2001) *A new commitment to neighbourhood renewal: National Strategy Action Plan*, London: Cabinet Office.

Urban Task Force (1999) *Towards an urban renaissance*, London: E. & F.N. Spon.

Welsh Assembly (2000) *Housing Statistics*, Cardiff: Welsh Assembly.

White, G. (2001) 'Charity questions rough sleepers' cut', *Housing Today*, 6 December, p 3.

Wilcox, S. (1999) *Housing Finance Review 1999/2000*, York: Joseph Rowntree Foundation.

Wilcox, S. (2000a) *Housing Finance Review 2000/2001*, York: Joseph Rowntree Foundation.

Wilcox, S. (2000b) 'Left in their own', *Roof*, November/December, p 31-2.

Wilcox, S. (2001) *Housing Finance Review: Online update* (www.york.ac.uk/inst/chp/hfonkine).

Wilson, W. (2000) *Rent rebates and local authority Housing Revenue Accounts*, House of Commons Research Paper 00/87, London: House of Commons.

Wilson, W. (2001) *The Homelessness Bill*, House of Commons Research Paper 01/58, London: House of Commons.

SEVEN

Cheques and checks: New Labour's record on the NHS

Calum Paton

Introduction

In some ways, New Labour has presented a tale of two health policies. In opposition, and in the early years of government, the general line was that improving the NHS required the abolition of the internal market rather than a major injection of extra resources. However, as the Conservatives found, claims of improved statistics of health policy failed to convince the public, who perceived that the service was getting worse. The most significant evolution of New Labour's health policy came not with the White Paper of December 1997, *The new NHS: Modern, dependable* (DoH, 1997), but two years later. The decision by the Chancellor of the Exchequer and the Treasury to "stick to the Tory spending limits" for the first two years of the New Labour government meant that structural tinkering (as promulgated by the December 1997 White Paper) did not materially change the public's perception of the NHS. It was arguably an 'evaluation' in January 2000 by the independent-minded Labour peer Lord (Robert) Winston in the *New Statesman* that the NHS was in a worse state than the health service in Poland, and that New Labour had failed to keep its promises (including the abolition of the internal market) that prompted the second phase (cf Timmins, 2001). Although some of this was later qualified, the message was clear: the jewel in New Labour's crown, the NHS, required significant polishing. This came in the form (first) of the Prime Minister's announcement of new money in February 2000 and (second) of the NHS Plan, announced in July 2000. This clearly shows that the context for New Labour's health policy, and consideration of the future of the NHS, is the background environment of political economy (Paton, 2000, 2001).

At one level, the key political objective for the NHS (Paton, 2001), in New Labour's eyes, is its preservation. However, at another level, the fact that New Labour claims that it had largely achieved its pledges on health before launching its NHS Plan (DoH, 2000) suggests that, in health policy, New Labour may have met its more limited objectives yet failed to achieve much. This chapter focuses largely on the two phases of New Labour's health policy in its first term, but it also examines the evolution of policy during the second term.

Health policy developments 1997-2001

The first major statement of health policy arrived fairly quickly towards the end of 1997 (DoH, 1997; see, for example, Paton, 1999; Powell, 1999, 2000). This set out the agenda of abolishing the 'internal market', but retaining the Conservatives' provider/purchaser split. The main change was that 'commissioning' would be in the hands of new Primary Care Groups (covering an average of 100,000 patients) rather than health authorities and general practitioner (GP) fundholders. Collaboration and partnership would replace competition. Commissioners and providers would draw up a plan rather than exist in a principal–agent relationship. This would be complemented by longer-term agreements, resulting in moves from 'spot' or 'adversarial' contracting, to 'relational' contracting. Over time, Primary Care Groups would evolve into Primary Care Trusts (PCTs). Two new national bodies were set up: the National Institute for Clinical Excellence (NICE) would set standards, and the Commission for Health Improvement (CHI) would enforce them. This would result in national standards rather than 'postcode prescribing'. National Service Frameworks (NSFs) were to be developed. The issue of a 'one-nation NHS' – or 'fair access' to healthcare – would be matched by an emphasis on fair outcomes, or narrowing the health gap between the rich and the poor (for example, Acheson, 1998). At the local level, clinical governance (an evolution of the Conservatives' medical audit) would enforce clinical standards.

The new NHS would have a new NHS Performance Assessment Framework (PAF), based on an approach known as the 'balanced scorecard', which aims to ensure that objectives are achieved in a balanced manner – and that some objectives do not crowd out others. For example, an emphasis on waiting lists and access could 'squeeze out' indicators from the realms of health improvement and/or 'patient/carer experience'. The PAF highlights six areas of performance, which, taken together, seek to give a balanced view of the performance of the NHS:

1. Health improvement
2. Fair access
3. Effective delivery of appropriate healthcare
4. Efficiency
5. The patient/carer experience
6. Health outcomes of NHS care (as opposed to health status overall reflecting factors other than the NHS, as in 1).

The overall aim was to move from the Conservatives' 'narrow' Efficiency Index to a framework that measured quality and outcomes for individuals, areas and classes. The question is, how SMART (specific, measurable, achievable, relevant and timed) were the targets? To consider this, the PAF's specific Performance Indicators (PIs) should be assessed, as this framework is supported by a set of national NHS PIs. *The NHS Plan* endorsed the PAF (DoH, 2000, 2001).

Indicators in the realms of primary care, the 'patient/carer experience' and health inequalities have gradually been included. The aim is to develop a long and ambitious list of indicators by both clinical area and what might be termed 'management priority' or functional discipline (for example, workforce issues, controls assurance, information governance, and so on). This list ranges from coronary heart disease and cancer through to diabetes, older people, smoking, child food, dentistry, 'patient/carer experience', access and so on.

The NHS Plan of July 2000 represented a perceived need by the government to 'relaunch' its NHS policy. The acceptance of previous Conservative administrations' spending plans for its first two years of office, only amended after the New Labour government's first Comprehensive Spending Review conducted in 1998/99, had resulted in rising waiting lists (and times) and the public perception, punctuated by the usual media attention, that the NHS was not coping. The significant investment announced by Tony Blair in February 2000 and detailed in the Budget later that year was deemed to acquire a quid pro quo: it was inconceivable that the government would sign a blank cheque for significant investment in the NHS. *The NHS Plan* was fundamentally about what had to be delivered in return for the money. The new elements were new Care Trusts that would provide unified health and social care provision; a 'concordat' with private medicine; and a 'traffic lights' scheme of 'earned autonomy'.

Prior to the political decision in February 2000 to increase NHS funding more than hitherto, a new Strategy Unit had been created in the Department of Health, geared to the task of 'modernising' the NHS. This Unit predated *The NHS Plan*. The Plan's contents represented the different, and often piecemeal, priorities and issues already being worked upon in the Department of Health, but the decision to pull it all together in the grand plan represented a perceived need to relaunch health policy (not least to achieve results with extra money).

The NHS Plan also reflected the denting of public confidence in the NHS following the crisis of winter 1999 (echoes of the Thatcher Review following the crisis of winter 1987), and there was a growing sense of a public impatient for change, requiring faster progress. As a result, the whole panoply of priorities (with targets to follow), prefigured in *The NHS Plan*, became the route to putting things right. Additionally, the No 10 Policy Unit, working closely with the Prime Minister as well as administrators in the Department of Health, saw a need to prioritise empowerment of the patient and ensure that professional domination did not thwart modernisation. To that extent, there was continuity from the previous Conservative administration. Finally, the Prime Minister personally was concerned by what he considered to be evidence of significantly variable performance in efficiency access and outcomes across the NHS. The Plan therefore was an initiative based upon benchmarking – that is, using 'evidence-based management' – to raise standards, and to ensure that these standards were monitored through a system of performance management, with sanctions at the end of the line if necessary.

The first New Labour term therefore closed with a relaunch of health policy, which actually begs the question whether the more modest 'first-term' targets were met or not. Even so, with the possible exception of waiting lists and waiting times (and, to a lesser extent, issues around costing and 'reference pricing' of NHS services), there is as yet no unequivocal 'empirically verifiable' record of achievement. To use the time-dishonoured phrase, 'it is too early to tell'. The earlier reforms, based on the 1997 White Paper, were more about the reshaping of institutions (although the government denied it was engaging in a structural reorganisation) such as the creation of PCTs and the movement towards Care Trusts combining both health and social care. The 'hard targets' are increasingly being met, but as yet they are based on access and 'process' rather than clinical outcomes. All this is set to change from 2002 onwards.

Intrinsic evaluation

The 1997 Manifesto was a curious mixture of grand, broad claims and modest, specific intentions. The broad claim was that New Labour would 'save' or 'rebuild' the NHS. However, the key pledge (one of the five on the famous election pledge card) to was to "cut NHS waiting lists by treating an extra 100,000 patients as a first step by releasing £100 million saved from NHS red tape…" (Labour Party, 1997).

The main aims of the pledges are concerned with reducing waiting lists and cancer waiting, abolishing mixed-sex wards and introducing a new Patients' Charter. There was a certain 'déjà vu' about the pledge to reduce waiting lists. This was a crude target that had potential tensions with clinical priorities. In opposition, Labour had criticised the Conservatives' waiting list initiatives. Such initiatives always peak before a general election, and the picture changes again thereafter – which it soon did.

Some progress has been made on reducing cancer waiting times. Since April 1999 all breast cancer patients are guaranteed to see a specialist within two weeks by 2001. The promise has broadly been kept from 2000, and the guarantee extended to all kinds of cancer. However, the record is patchy although improving, and there are areas where under-capacity and underinvestment is preventing swifter progress. The National Service Framework for cancer set out a framework that provides targets for achievement in terms of waiting time and access to appropriate levels of care for patients with different clinical needs.

There has been some progress in abolishing mixed-sex wards. However, this aim has not always been achieved (but is not necessarily the best priority given scarce resources and the possibility of single-sex 'bays' in wards). Moreover, this pledge has largely been eclipsed by the recent attention given to waiting times on trolleys in mixed-sex corridors. A new Patients' Charter concentrating on quality and successful treatment was announced (but not 'fleshed out'), in order to replace the Tories' Efficiency Index with an outcome index. Greg Dyke (later to become BBC Director General) eventually produced a revamped Charter, but it was never adopted.

The other pledges relate more to means rather than ends: abolishing the internal market; introducing GP commissioning; longer agreements; more representative boards; more spending in the NHS; a greater proportion of spending devoted to patient care; overcoming PFI problems; appointing a Minister of Public Health; and setting up a Food Standards Agency.

New Labour promised to raise spending on the NHS in real terms every year. This was quite a modest promise, in that nearly all governments had raised spending on the NHS in real terms since 1948 (with the exception of two years after 1976, and the possible exceptions in 1983 and early 1990s after the 1992 General Election). Money was initially drip-fed into the system, before the announcement of a major cash transfusion. It sounded too good to be true: 'beyond our wildest dreams', in the words of one manager. And it was: the announcement in 1998 of £20 billion extra for the NHS over three years was criticised as double or triple counting – with justification, in that the increases were all counted from the base year rather than as annual increments. Larger increases of 6% 'real' growth for five years (announced in the more usual accounting procedure) in the NHS Budget were to be announced in 2000 and later.

The pledge of spending of money on 'patients not bureaucracy' was linked with the other pledge to abolish the internal market and the administrative costs associated with it. Some of this may be achieved by reclassifying 'grey suits' as 'white coats'. There is a lot of work being done by relatively few managers – which means low administrative costs (in one sense of the term), yet arguably almost relentless pressure throughout the organisation to deliver an increasing array of targets. Unfortunately, however, the 'reorganisation–itis' that has been afflicting the NHS for some time worsened (in England more than in Scotland and Wales). PCTs are quite a disaggregated and bureaucratic way of organising commissioning in the NHS, for example. A further reorganisation was announced in April 2001, replacing health authorities with larger strategic 'regulatory' agencies. Later in January 2002, yet more reorganisation was announced, involving three grades of hospital ('autonomous'; directly-regulated; and 'franchised' to private or external management). These grades reflected a continuum from 'good' to 'bad' performers, as measured by the government's indicators. There was an overtone of 'back to the future' of 1991.

The replacement of fundholding by Primary Care Groups or PCTs allows 1 April 1999 to be chosen as the date that the 'abolition of the internal market' was achieved. However, the devolution of commissioning in England to PCTs, set out again in *Shifting the balance of power within the NHS* (DoH, 2001), means that sharp and adversarial relationships between relatively undeveloped PCTs and hard-pressed acute hospitals consortia of individual PCTs may lead to the 'market ethos' remaining. Against this can be set the fact that provision (especially acute provision) is being networked over wide catchment areas, and hospital/hospital competition in the style of the internal market is a thing of the past. GP commissioning has been done formally but de facto commissioning is still (inevitably) steered by health authorities. In any case, GP commissioning of acute services may not be the best way to proceed. It is, however, a mast to which New Labour has nailed its colours.

New Service Level Agreements (SLAs) covering 'local health economies' for three- to five-year periods replaced the annual contracts of the internal market from April 1999. Yet there are sometimes dissonances between SLAs (essentially cost/volume), regional targets for waiting lists and times and the wider targets of the Health Improvement Programme. Moreover, the 'stuff' of service agreements is still annual. Service and Financial Frameworks (SaFFs) are conducted annually – whether this changes or not remains to be seen. The Health Improvement Programme is a rolling programme but is less relevant to the 'nuts and bolts' of what is contracted (to use the old-fashioned term). Service-level agreements between commissioners and hospital trusts, for example, are a kind of amalgam between old-style contracting and new service agreements.

Waiting times targets and regional targets for health authorities (or PCTs) are based on residential population, while those for hospitals or other NHS Trusts are based on catchment populations. Thus the hospital's target probably – but not necessarily – has to be met in order for a health authority to meet its target, and vice versa. For example, even if a hospital failed to meet its target, the health authority might still meet its target (in terms of numbers waiting from its residential population) *if* hospitals outside the area without service agreements did better than expected. Equally, a hospital might still meet its target even if the host health authority did not, on the grounds that work for commissioners outside the hospital's area allowed the hospital to meet its workload targets in aggregate.

The PFI has been 'cleaned up' and speeded up, and has quickened the process, albeit in a politicised way that may store up budgetary problems for the future. In a purely quantitative sense, the number of NHS PFI projects has risen significantly (for example, to 31 by June 1999, and 29 new projects agreed in February 2001). The Conservative PFI was derided on the grounds that it had failed to deliver, not on the grounds that it was intrinsically wrong (see extrinsic evaluation below).

There are still claims about politicisation of trusts and health authority boards but there is less politicisation than in the time of the internal market. The representation of local communities may be a good thing if one is looking for representation; it may be less of a good thing if one is looking for 'business management'. To be fair, New Labour is seeking a creative amalgam of the two.

The government promised to create a new post of Minister of Public Health who would attack the root causes of ill health, in particular the social and environmental causes. Tessa Jowell was appointed at the level of Minister of State in 1997. Her replacement, Yvette Cooper, appointed at the level of Under-Secretary of State, suggested that this 'important' new post was being given a lower priority. The Food Standards Agency has been set up, but its effect is yet to be gauged.

One major problem is that sometimes these targets are insufficiently 'joined-up' (the key aim of the Blair government). For example, directives to cut

Table 7.1: Progress against Manifesto/Annual Report targets for health

Pledge	New Labour's assessment	Score/10
53: Reduce waiting lists by 100,000	On course	5
54: Introduce GP commissioning	Done	6
55: Introduce three- to five-year agreements between health care teams and hospitals	On course	4
56: Hospital boards to better represent communities	Done	6
57: Reduce spending on administration and increase patient care	Done	7
58: Raise spending in real terms every year	Done	7
59: End waiting for cancer surgery	On course	7
60: End the NHS internal market	Done	7
61: Introduce a new Patients Charter	On course	3
62: Work towards eliminating mixed-sex wards	On course	5
63: Overcome NHS PFI problems	Done	5
64: Create a new Minister for Public Health	Done	6
65: Independent Food Standards Agency	Established	6

waiting lists may clash at least in the short term with directives to cut trolley waits for acute medical emergency admissions. Hard-pressed hospital Trusts may find it difficult to obey all the directives – with trade-offs between different priorities not acknowledged in the itemised or piecemeal system of command control which exists in today's NHS. Should they put their energies into helping New Labour to meet its pledges, hitting their PAF targets, passing Commission for Health Improvement (CHI) inspections, or waiting to see whatever the latest telephone call from the Secretary of State suggests is the most recent priority?

Extrinsic evaluation

How sensible or relevant are the government's 'waiting'/access targets? Press headlines in the summer of 2001 suggested that a change in priorities, by moving away from 'waiting list' policy to a waiting time policy, represented one of the biggest changes in NHS policy for years. Such an interpretation would be exaggerated, however. Overall waiting list targets will remain, albeit 'lower down the list' of priorities. In any case, such lists are clearly correlated with waiting times.

Comment has focused on the possibility that less serious conditions can be prioritised over more serious conditions. For example, to ensure that nobody is waiting longer than 12 months in a region, varicose veins might, in theory, be prioritised over heart bypass surgery (with more serious heart conditions waiting, say, 11 months rather than seven months as a result). New Labour had criticised the Conservatives' waiting list initiatives of the 1990s on these grounds; the Conservatives have likewise criticised Labour. It is rather a sterile debate.

The debate has incidentally been fuelled by a National Audit Office report, based on interviews with 500 clinicians in the NHS, suggesting that there has been pressure by managers to change clinical priorities to meet political targets. There is in fact no systematic research into the extent of this. Many clinicians may refuse to change clinical priorities; but with elections pending, pressure mounts. For example, there was pressure to 'clear' the small numbers of very long 'waiters', who were in danger of exceeding the government's 18-month maximum wait policy, before the 2001 General Election.

Regarding public health more generally, one of the NHS's biggest challenges is to combine the 'downstream' challenge of being an illness service (which it has to be) with an appropriate 'upstream' strategy for public health that improves the health of the nation on an equitable basis. The previous Conservative government's *Health of the nation* strategy was amended to form the New Labour government's *Our healthier nation* strategy.

It is worth pointing out that, up to the medium term at least, the NHS as an 'illness service' will be required on a greater scale; and that an effective public health strategy therefore is no more likely to diminish the need for hospitals, doctors and nurses, than was Nye Bevan's original belief that a successful NHS would diminish the need for healthcare likely to come true.

The challenge is to devise public health targets, including targets on health inequalities – on which New Labour has made progress – that stress equity as well as qualitative (or 'utilitarian') achievement. That is, it may be easier to meet targets by focusing on groups that are healthier to begin with. Equally, it is important to avoid 'easy targets', which actually diminish managerial urgency.

Furthermore, national targets should not be translated mechanistically into local targets. This can mean local effort in areas that are less salient in 'adding years to life and life to years'. Instead, areas for priority, as well as targets within these, should be tailored to local circumstances. This may sound centralist, but it is actually the best way to combine national planning with local sensitivity – and to 'build in' the search for greater equity, not only in access to healthcare but also in health status across the social classes and strata. (For example, suicides may be a problem in one area but not in another; the same may apply to accidents, teenage pregnancies and coronary care.) The best approach is to address – in each locality – these areas of the highest preventable mortality and morbidity, against the backlog of national targets around such factors.

Equally, other agencies have an important effect upon health status. Therefore *implementing* public health policy must be collaborative – it must not rely on the NHS, nor must it assume that the NHS is not significant (vis-à-vis housing, poverty, and so on).

New Labour's record on public health is a good one in making policy objectives more salient and (in more cases) specific. Yet just how 'joined-up' both policy *and* implementation will eventually be is a key issue. Furthermore, whether 'micro' initiatives (for example, on health inequalities) can compensate for the macroeconomic background of widening social inequality – and widely varying working conditions, in the knowledge that one's degree of autonomy at work is a significant prediction of health status – remains to be seen.

New Labour has reaffirmed its belief in diminishing inequalities in health. Targets exist for reducing deaths from specific conditions (principally heart disease, cancer and mental health-related problems). In the first term, these latter targets are not class-related; that is, they are not linked intrinsically overall to the 'health inequalities' approach. (In the second term, however, 'targeting of targets' seems to be more on the agenda.)

In seeking appropriate access to effective care in a timely manner, New Labour is seeking to ensure that there is equity in access to 'repair', if not to the conditions of life that produce more equitably distributed good health. New Labour is, however, hamstrung by its adherence to the economic dictates of global capitalism, which do not allow national prioritisation of social objectives above the economic. New Labour is therefore dependent on a range of 'micro' initiatives to even out or seek to even out specific, localised manifestations of health inequalities.

Equally, New Labour can be judged on the basis of whether improved access to improved services produces improved results for poorer and disadvantaged sections of the community. To this end, the continuing consultation on NHS PIs requires prioritisation of 'health inequalities' in public health. Targets will need to be devised both at national and at strategic health authority level – and devised innovatively at the latter level so that it is not simply a case of applying standard norms across the country but tailor-making local targets to produce the desired national improvements in health inequalities.

New Labour's 'intrinsic' targets do not easily address class or geographically based ill health, although the funding formula is to be amended further to recognise health inequalities. Such amendment is overdue in the light of data at the end of 2001, emphasising how far some areas still are from their expected resource allocation target.

Regarding efficiency, everybody (it now seems) criticised the Conservatives for their one-dimensional, 'one-club golfer' approach to incentives in the NHS – market means to market ends. However, one frequently hears the criticism of New Labour's policy that it is too diffuse as regards incentives, and that there is no single, overriding, clear incentive. If the previous criticism were true, then presumably this is a virtue.

At the micro level, in its first term, New Labour instituted the policy of reference costing for the purposes of 'benchmarking' efficiency. At a broader level, efficiency and accountability overlap, in that New Labour's reforms of structure are substantial, ongoing and likely to effect the overall efficiency and effectiveness of the service. Given New Labour's strong agenda on performance in the health service, many of the mechanisms it is using to achieve results are arguably cumbersome. PCT policy at source derives from both the Total Purchasing Pilot initiatives from the last Conservative administration as well as from the earlier Primary Care Groups under the New Labour administration, and in turn the total purchasing pilots emerged from an attempt to reconcile some of the fundholding ethos in practice with a more integrated approach to commissioning services.

When it comes to the key agenda for New Labour – fair access to high-quality services – the mechanisms needed to achieve this are quite intricate. The 'local health economy' comprises Acute Trusts, evolving (diminishing) Community Trusts, PCTs, local authorities and others. On the positive side, if all these players signed up to an effective health plan, then such a plan is more likely to be implemented and to stick. On the negative side, achieving that commitment and regular monitoring is a major opportunity cost for scarce senior management time. Given the need to manage across boundaries and 'at the margins' in order to achieve performance targets, investment in senior management is actually a prerequisite for an effective NHS and, as with nearly all governments, New Labour faces both ways here. It is always easier for politicians to add initiatives and add agencies – 'initiative-itis' is an occupational hazard for politicians – and it would be nice to think that the NHS has reached a stage whereby rationalisation and consolidation initiatives are necessary.

On quality, the key initiative has been clinical governance, fuelled not least by poorly performing doctors in Bristol producing tragically poor outcomes. There are now moves to unify clinical governance with the broader agenda of corporate governance. (In the early days this stressed finance and probity, spreading to cover risk management and its modern variant 'controls assurance', and has now broadened further to ensure that 'clinical' and 'non-clinical' quality improvement are not artificially divorced.) The key questions for a hospital Trust Board are, 'Do you know whether or not a 'Bristol' is happening in your hospital?'; and, 'If you suspected so, what information would you seek; and then what would you do?'

At the local level, Trusts' clinical governance procedures are increasing in importance. Clinical governance embraces the weeding out of poor performance and the diminution of adverse incidence; it also involves broader continuous quality improvement, both of which are overseen by Trust Boards (both generic Trust Boards including non-executives and executive boards and top management teams within Trusts). In the medium term, indicators to suggest success in this realm will be based on diminution in adverse incidence by certain categories; and a similar approach to complaints and clinical incidents generally. Quarterly or half-yearly indicators might include the implementation or otherwise of NICE guidelines, national recommendations from the Committee of Enquiry in Perioperative Deaths and similar committees, progress reports on sickness and absence rates for staff, number of infection outbreaks for certain categories, compliance with specialty-specific access times, and so on. Annual information will concern death rates in hospital as a result of surgical intervention, death rates for emergency admissions for particular conditions, unscheduled readmissions or theatre returns, and so on and so forth.

The PFI has featured strongly in New Labour's lexicon, from almost as soon as it took office. It is New Labour's main source of new hospital facilities, and therefore part of its intrinsic policy to modernise the NHS. This is a continuation of a Conservative policy, but with some amendments. For example, PFI-financed buildings will now be owned by the NHS after the period of 'payback'; and it is intended that there will be a more rational prioritisation of schemes run through the Capital Priorities Advisory Group. But it might still be more sensible to let regions allocate capital in response to need, heralded as long ago as 1976.

Every major project under the PFI has a 'public sector comparator' (that is, it is compared to a similar project carried out with public funding). Research has shown that the key factor in determining which approach 'wins' – always the private route – is the quantification of the value of risk transfer (without which the public alternative would usually win). The revenue consequences of PFIs over the next 25-30 years will be substantial, and growth in total NHS budgets to cover this will have to be greater than currently assumed officially.

Is this irrespective of other debates about the PFIs? Does it cost more (involving significant profit for the private partners)? Does the private sector have expertise in planning new hospitals and services that the NHS does not? (It seems not, in that the 'Output Based Specification' that forms the basis of the project is always produced 'in house'.) As a result, is the PFI's 'efficiency' attributable to changed terms and conditions for staff? In this connection, it should be noted that – even where the PFI leaves (all) staff employed by the NHS (as some pilot projects announced in June 2001 will do) – 'reprofiling' (that is, redesigning) jobs and increasing 'flexible working' may be the key element. The intention presumably is that changed working practices spread to the whole NHS over time.

Overall, public–private partnerships and PFIs may vary in terms of financing, ownership, management and labour contracts. A multi-criteria evaluation is therefore necessary. The recent Institute for Public Policy Research (IPPR) report on public–private partnerships 'faced both ways' on the issue, reflected in the fact that diametrically opposed 'spin' was put on it by different media reports. Some saw it as asking for more privatisation, others as striking a cautionary note. It seemed to suggest more caution in health and education, yet, even there, placed what this commentator would consider a naïve faith in the capacity of the private sector to design health services. The reality is that complex NHS services involving intricate collaboration between primary and acute or specialised care are virgin territory for even the big private players, who rely on NHS expertise. The PFI is at heart a macroeconomically imposed constraint rather than an opportunity.

Developments in New Labour's second term

The agenda of New Labour's health policy is a huge one – and a complicated one. The 2001 Manifesto was devoted primarily to the 10-year NHS Plan and to the latest reorganisation, principally devolution to PCTs. It lists as an achievement (from a promise of 2000 rather than 1997) the fact that there are

17,000 more nurses, over 6,000 more doctors, and so on. Targets for improving and cutting inequalities in health include two new national targets to reduce health inequalities: infant mortality and life expectancy. Significant additional targets are being added almost daily to the PAF, to include human resources issues such as labour turnover, locum or agency expenditure, and so on.

The 2001 Manifesto promised 10,000 more doctors and 20,000 more nurses by 2005 (however, the base year was unclear, as was the full-time/part-time status of both cadres). There were specific promises regarding privacy in hospital wards, good food and cleanliness in hospitals, and so on. Specific promises were made about 'extra beds' – although the balance between core acute hospital beds and 'intermediate care' beds were unclear. Targets set for modernisation of general practice as well as the hospital service were significant. On improving health generally, the Manifesto promised that making the fight against cancer, heart disease and stroke top priority would help to tackle the long-standing causes of ill health and health inequality. Specific targets were made for recruitment of new cardiologists; the waiting times for cancer treatment were reinforced as a priority for attention; avoidable deaths and the closing of the health gap by cutting deaths in poor communities were prioritised; and prevention was again stressed in a whole range of areas.

It is possible to focus on two very broad themes for the second term. The first main theme continues the recognition of the second phase of the first term that spending must rise. Health spending is targeted to increase in real terms by 6% for at least three more years, from 2001 to 2004. To reach the European average, a promise made by the Prime Minister in early 2000, would mean sustaining increases of at least this nature for a significant number of years. (There are different interpretations of what the European average means, with differing degrees of generosity involved.) The political economy, or fiscal politics behind this objective, is an expanding one (Paton, 2000). Without this, higher taxes, more government borrowing, or both, would be necessary. In February 2002, Blair and Brown started to think the unthinkable: that taxes might have to rise in order to achieve more spending on the NHS. However, it was also stressed that improving the NHS would be a long-term project (see Powell 2001). It takes time to build new hospitals and train new staff. The recruitment of key staff is related to the whole national and international economy – as more doctors and nurses depend upon the attractiveness of medicine, nursing, and other clinical specialisation as a career choice at the outset for young people. Additionally, recruitment and retention to NHS posts requires competitive conditions. The government is taking a number of 'micro-initiatives' in the realm of staff pay and conditions – again, the jury is out as to whether or not this will be enough. In the short term, there is an increased reliance on importing staff (for example, nurses) from other countries and exporting patients to be treated in countries such as France and Germany.

The second theme stresses that there must be reform in return for the investment. The NHS must 'modernise', finding new and innovative (although not always thought-out or proven) ways of working. The second term may see a policy cocktail of new means and ends that resembles a 'blur-print' rather than a blueprint (Powell, 2001). It is likely that the waiting-time targets will be 'hard' – in both senses of the term – and therefore the ones that reoccur at election time in the future. There is no reason, again by international comparison, why they *should* not be met, although the challenge in British terms is a huge one. Patients' rights (such as booked appointments) are also key objectives, and changed working practices (reprofiling of the workforce and of jobs in the NHS) will be required on a large scale to achieve them. Regarding the private sector more generally, the government wishes to use it for solving waiting-list problems (nothing new here), but fails actively to recognise the trade-off between investment in a public NHS on a greater scale that would make this unnecessary or less necessary. Similarly, regarding the government's policy of private 'elective surgery centres', the reality is that these will be part of PFIs for new acute hospitals or modernised hospitals.

A big questionmark remains over the future of elderly care, where no pledges have been made in England, unlike in Scotland, and whether there is to be a 'social insurance' or private solution to improving the social and nursing care of the elderly. A BBC telephone poll in February 2002 found that long-term care was by a significant margin the top NHS priority for viewers. Clearly, this affects the prospects for efficient and effective use of acute hospitals. 'Bed blocking' and uncoordinated NHS and social service budgets are still a big problem, despite various initiatives from the 1980s onwards.

At the structural level, the NHS and social services are to be brought much closer together – from the Department of Health downwards – but it remains to be seen whether this structural approach produces rewards on the ground. Structural change (such as the mergers and new roles for SHA created by *Shifting the balance of power in the NHS* [DoH, 2001]) plus incentives (such as failing NHS hospitals to be taken over by the private sector or by successful hospitals, and successful ones to be 'floated off') require significant investment in effective NHS management and significant trust in the 'loyalty to the NHS' of self-governing hospitals – as well as their coordination with PCTs. More structural reorganisation in particular (not least, removing an identifiable 'strategic commissioner' for services above the level of the inexperienced PCT, with its additional capacity for 'conflict of interest') will be debilitating in the context of a mountainous agenda and plethora of targets. It would arguably have been more sensible to allow new SHAs to commission directly the new 'networks' of acute care (which they may eventually do, anyway) and to have PCTs as provider organisations, as in Scotland.

In terms of the future of the NHS, despite it being gradually rebuilt (in terms of investment in staff), doing so by 'cutting administration' takes us into a hall of mirrors. There is a need for more strategic capacity and operational management, not for the administration of perpetual reorganisation or changing strategy.

Equally, the structure based on PCTs is a cumbersome one, and not easily compatible with the 'new' wider-area strategic planning of acute services. Like the Conservatives before them, New Labour has found the bureaucratic consequences of its reforms to be substantial. This stems from 'reform-itis' and political amnesia, which itself leads both to reinventing of wheels and 'tacking on' new institutions to old ones. In 1997, New Labour initially sought to avoid 'more structural reform', yet ended up with far-reaching reforms, which furthermore tended not to replace the Conservatives' institutions but to add to them.

Despite a promise in *The NHS Plan* (DoH, 2000) to prioritise the ever-lengthening number of priorities, numerous targets remain and are overlapping. Key indicators linked to incentives were originally to be built into as NHS Performance Traffic Lights Systems: organisations were to be classed as red, amber or green, with different consequences for their autonomy and access to different kinds of funds. Later, as an alternative, organisations were classed by a star system (from zero to three stars) assigned to organisations on the basis of how well they met national targets.

In September 2001 there were six basic targets and nine additional targets, as well as a possible report following an inspection by the CHI. The six core targets included waiting lists and times, 'trolley waits' and cancelled operations. The nine additional targets comprised three on clinical quality, three on staffing and three on patient satisfaction. The CHI report could be crucial: a bad report on clinical governance (basically, quality) could negate good performance on the other targets (as it did in the case of, for example, the Walsgrave NHS Trust in Coventry).

High-performing organisations are rewarded with greater autonomy (and less ongoing inspection by the CHI) and national recognition for the automatic access to the new 'performance fund'. At the other extreme, 'poor' organisations may be 'taken over' by successful organisations or, at least, 'directly managed'. 'Middling' organisations are to be supported by the Department of Health's Regional Offices (presumably now SHAs as well as, or instead of, Regional Offices) and the Modernisation Agency in order to improve performance, and have limited access to the privileges of earned autonomy.

Not only are targets numerous and ambitious, but often inadequate attention is paid to implementation as opposed to simply 'command and control'. A whole range of new agencies has been developed in the second term to seek to address implementation issues.

There is a plethora of mechanisms for implementing central NHS policy and the NHS Plan in particular. The *NHS Plan Implementation Programme* (21 December 2000) is a document that sets out the planning cycle and service objectives to be achieved through *milestones* on the way to overall *targets* (for example, access to primary and secondary care, standards of accommodation, cleanliness and food), as part of the Patient Environment and Access Initiative (PEAI), as well as specific quantitative targets regarding production of mortality rates from cancer, coronary heart disease and mental health-related causes of death and injury. Tackling the 'health gap' in childhood as the major component of inequalities between social and economic groups is important.

At the local level, NHS trusts have service improvement plans (replacing the business plans of the internal market era). At the regional level, the Regional Offices as currently exist are to be abolished. Performance management is to be taken over by 30 SHAs (with direct commissioning to be undertaken in the main by PCTs – perhaps even for specialised services, to be purchased by consortia of PCTs). The Regional Offices and SHAs will therefore have to work closely with the Modernisation Agency, CHI, NICE and the Department of Health nationally, as well as with service users and local health communities. The key question therefore concerns potential overlap – for example, between the CHI and the Modernisation Agency in seeking improvement. Coordinating the different agencies and ensuring that valuable complementary, and not overlapping, work is done by all will be an important task.

On the other hand – although not incompatible with what I have just described – a whole raft of ambitious new targets and initiatives adopted through *The NHS Plan* often do *not* have earmarked money alongside them. In other words, it is still up to local management to make hard choices yet remain 'accountable' both to the public and to their political masters if key national initiatives have not produced results.

There is a problem, however, with this type of incentive. Poor organisations, for example, 'may be taken over'. However, improving a failing organisation will be far from easy. "It is not possible for example to roll out enthusiasm, personalities or local pride" (OD Partnerships, 2000). In other words, there is a real job for the Modernisation Agency to do in reconciling its creative and facilitative role on the one hand with its responsibilities for performance management (shared with other agencies) on the other. Implementing the performance improvement agenda through traffic lights and earned autonomy (or otherwise) may be in conflict, to say the least, with wider developmental objectives and alternative ways to stimulate improvement of performance. Furthermore, top-quality managers in the NHS are hard-pressed (the NHS is 'undermanaged', despite the rhetoric): real achievements, say, in one trust may depend upon exceptional commitment to the 'home patch'. This cannot easily be 'rolled out'. Perhaps this is the charitable interpretation of why the policy soon seemed to be superseded by the 'privatisation' or poorly performing trusts (approved on 15 January 2002 by Secretary Milburn).

Conclusion

My report card reads 'well-intentioned'. New Labour is trying hard against a difficult background of political economy but, despite huge majorities in 1997 and 2001, it is too defensive. Unproven 'right-wing' ideas are given far too much intellectual credence as the 'threat', although it is sensible to take them seriously as a political threat. A positive strategy to defend the NHS would have less truck with 'private involvement' (on economic and pragmatic, not ideological, grounds). It would also expose the irony inherent in right-wing attacks on the NHS model that advocate a French or German alternative. These are expensive systems that are much more publicly funded than, say, Iain Duncan Smith acknowledges. (It is hilarious yet tragic to find the terms of debate set by 'Euro-sceptics' eulogising the core European healthcare systems.) The challenge for the NHS to survive in an international environment of low taxes, among other things, is a great one. But if we believe in universalising quality services, it is (still) the best model. The problem is mobilising enough long-term expenditure upon the NHS in an era of less progressive geared taxation. The key challenge for New Labour is whether it can 'save' the NHS quickly enough. One understands their impatience, but it should be managed with a steady hand on the till. 'Agency-itis' as well as 'reform-itis' may in the end be debilitating.

References

Acheson, D. (1998) *Independent inquiry into inequalities in health*, London: The Stationery Office.

DoH (Department of Health) (1992) *The health of the nation*, London: HMSO.

DoH (1997) *The new NHS: Modern, dependable*, London: The Stationery Office.

DoH (1998a) *A first class service: Quality in the new NHS*, London: The Stationery Office.

DoH (1998b) *Our healthier nation*, London: The Stationery Office.

DoH (1999) *NHS performance assessment framework*, London: DoH.

DoH (2000) *The NHS Plan: A plan for investment, a plan for reform*, Cm 4818-I, London: The Stationery Office.

DoH (2001) *NHS performance indicators: A consultation*, London: DoH.

Milburn, A. (2001) Speech to launch the NHS Modernisation Agency, 26 April.

NHS Executive (1999) *Improving working lives*, London, DoH.

NHS Executive (2000) *NHS plan implementation programme*, London, DoH.

NHS Executive (2001) *The NHS Plan – Implementing the performance improvement agenda*, London, DoH.

OD Partnerships (2000) *Modernising the NHS: Six ideas that may repay further thought* (www.odpnetwork.co.uk).

Paton, C. (1999) 'New Labour's health policy', in M. Powell (ed) *New Labour, new welfare state? The 'third way' in British social policy*, Bristol: The Policy Press, pp 51-75.

Paton, C. (2000) *World class Britain: Political economy, political theory and British politics*, London: Macmillan.

Paton, C. (2001) 'The state in health', *Public Policy and Administration*, vol 16, no 4, pp 61-83.

Powell, M. (1999) 'New Labour and the Third Way in the British National Health Service', *International Journal of Health Services*, vol 29, no 2, pp 353-70.

Powell, M. (2000) 'Analysing the "new" British National Health Service', *International Journal of Health Planning and Management*, vol 15, pp 89-101.

Powell, M. (2001) 'Saving the NHS in 14 days or 14 years', *Critical Social Policy*, vol 21, no 4, pp 528-30.

EIGHT

A decent education for all?

Rajani Naidoo and Yolande Muschamp

Introduction

Education has occupied a pivotal position in relation to New Labour's overall political, economic and social strategy. By 1997 it headed the Election Manifesto and was declared to be the Party's first priority (Muschamp et al, 1999). An evaluation of policy developments in New Labour's 'priority' area at the end of its first term of office is an important component of a more general analysis of New Labour's welfare reforms. This chapter provides an assessment of New Labour's education reform by focusing on policy initiatives in relation to 'access' and 'quality', two areas that have taken centre stage in the government's public pronouncements and which are of considerable importance to an assessment of whether New Labour has fulfilled its election promise of providing a 'decent education for all' (Labour Party, 1997). Our analysis concentrates on two sectors in education: the school sector, in which reform has been highly interventionist, and the university sector, where the approach to reform has been relatively more cautious and respectful of institutional and professional autonomy.

We begin this chapter with a discussion of why education, particularly in relation to access and quality, has emerged as a priority area and how education is expected to contribute to the twin aims of 'equity' and 'economic development' espoused in the third-way political programme. In the second section of this chapter, we provide an outline of the aims and objectives presented by New Labour to the electorate. The third section provides an intrinsic analysis, measuring the government's achievements against its aims. The final section complements this 'intrinsic' evaluation by analysing the tensions and unintended consequences of various policy strands. We also analyse the potential of education reforms to contribute to New Labour's goal of a more socially equitable and economically competitive society.

Policy developments

While education has always been expected to play a part in the economic, social and political changes taking place in Britain, these expectations have gained increasing importance in the context of the third-way political strategy adopted by the New Labour government. Although there have been numerous interpretations of the third way, it is generally agreed that it reflects an overall desire on the part of New Labour to forge a political and intellectual enterprise that moves beyond the traditional fault lines of 'old left' and 'new right' (see Giddens, 1998, 2000). One aspect that makes this approach distinctive is that economic prosperity and social inclusion are positioned simultaneously as key goals of social policy. In this vision of a society built on social justice and competitiveness, education is perceived as playing a key role. The 1997 Election Manifesto states that "Education remains the bedrock of the Government's programme to modernise and reform the country and provide opportunity for all". New Labour has argued for increased access to education at all levels by drawing on the argument that economic prosperity in the new 'knowledge' economy (see Castells, 1996) depends on raising both the degree of productivity as well as the quality of human capital. The Election Manifesto states that a focus on education "is vital if Britain is to have the highly skilled and talented workforce needed to compete in the modern world". In relation to higher education, the Green Paper, *The Learning Age*, asserts that "*everyone* must have the opportunity to innovate and gain reward" as the "most productive investment will be linked to the best educated and best trained workforces" (DfEE, 1998a, p 10; emphasis in original). Access to education has also been linked to equity and social cohesion. Education is represented in the Manifesto as "the most effective route out of poverty" and higher education according to *The Learning Age* offers a way out of 'dependency and low expectation' and is 'capable of overcoming a vicious circle of underachievement, self depreciation and petty crime' (DfEE, 1998a). A great deal of attention has also been placed on the quality of higher education. According to the Manifesto, while education is an "economic necessity for the nation", the quality of education is essential since Britain will "compete on the basis of quality or not at all". As the pledges from the 1997 White Paper show, diversity, a competitive environment and the marketisation of institutions would be central to the drive to raise quality and standards. Further development of the rigorous regime of inspection, continued prescription and the publication of results would act as levers to enhance the performance of education institutions and to create relations of accountability between education institutions and external stakeholders.

New Labour's promises

In this section, we outline the promises and pledges made by New Labour in the run-up to the elections and in its first term of office. We focus in particular on the 1997 Election Manifesto, White and Green Papers and speeches by government spokespersons. We begin by analysing the school sector before turning to higher education.

The government's Annual Report (1999-2000) confirmed that education remained 'the bedrock' of the programme to modernise and reform the country, with the claim that "Education is the most effective route out of poverty". Excellence in schools, they argued, would provide equity by ensuring that the talents of all could be developed to the full. This access for all had begun with the pledges made in the White Paper of 1997 in relation to places in nurseries and infant classrooms:

- high quality of education for all four-year-olds whose parents want it;
- an Early Years forum in every area, planning childcare and education to meet local needs;
- effective assessment of all children starting primary schools;
- class sizes of 30 or under for five-, six- and seven-year-olds.

The provision of Early Years places would be complemented by increased access to a common curriculum by the introduction of standardised literacy and numeracy hours.

- At least an hour a day devoted to both literacy and numeracy in every primary school.

Greater equity would be achieved for secondary school pupils by 'modernising the comprehensive principle'. Again the White Paper pledged equity of access both to places and to an appropriate (although not a common) curriculum:

- Schools setting pupils according to ability and further development innovative approaches to pupil grouping.
- Education Action Zones (EAZs) providing targeted support and development where they are most needed.
- An extensive network of specialist schools benefiting neighbouring schools and the local community.

A raft of further initiatives would ensure that the training of teachers kept pace with the development of institutions. A new pact with parents and the community would widen the responsibility for children's achievement:

- more family learning schemes;
- a home–school contract in all schools;
- better school–business links;
- better programmes of work-related learning, citizenship and parenting;
- a new framework for foundation, community and aided schools;
- fairer ways of offering schools places to pupils;
- a more positive contribution from independent schools to our goal of raising standards for all children, with improved partnership and links with schools and local communities.

Raising standards in schools?

The government's Annual Report set out its continuing commitment to high standards in education in terms that had moral overtones and that also specified the approach to be taken. Education of a high standard was a 'decent' education, and "A decent education means concentrating on the basics". The basics, however, no longer involved the standardisation of schooling through a comprehensive system of education (see Muschamp et al, 1999). The link between the Labour Party and comprehensive education that had dogged the Party for so long was finally to be dropped regardless of David Blunkett's 'Read my lips' comment, promising no selection, at the 1995 Labour Conference. As the pledges from the 1997 White Paper show, diversity and a competitive environment would be central to the drive to raise standards. Further development of the rigorous regime of inspection, continued prescription and the publication of results would ensure the continued marketability of institutions.

The pledge to raise standards in schools was unequivocal. Standards of achievement would rise and, as Toynbee and Walker comment, "Blunkett had the guts to stake his job on it" (2001, p 46). The White Paper read like a creed:

- There will be a greater awareness across society of the importance of education and increased expectations of what can be achieved.
- Standards of performance will be higher.

Principles were set out to underpin the approach to be taken; and the pledges relating to every phase of schooling declared:
We will have:

- a network of early excellence centres to spread good practice;
- great improvement in achievements in maths and English at the end of primary education, to meet national targets.

In addition:

- Each school will have its own challenging targets to raise standards, and will be held responsible for achieving them.
- Most failing schools will have been improved, and the remaining few closed or given a Fresh Start.
- The Office for Standards in Education (OFSTED) will have improved its schools inspection process, and will also have inspected a large number of local education authorities (LEAs).
- Schools will be taking practical steps to raise ethnic minority pupils' achievements and promote racial harmony.

Again, the training and assessment of teachers would match that of the pupils. New core requirements for an initial teacher training course, training for newly qualified teachers, existing teachers and headteachers, and a streamlined procedure for dealing with incompetent teachers made it clear that the teaching profession was responsible for underachievement in schools.

Expansion and improvement in universities

The increasing recognition that high-level skills and knowledge are critical in determining the nation state's ability to compete in the global economy has resulted in a focus on access to higher education. As higher education institutions are major contributors to the knowledge economy, one of the main concerns reflected in government documents is how existing institutions can 'transform' themselves to increase and widen participation (DfEE, 1998a, p 13). The 1997 Manifesto drew attention to the fact that Britain has a smaller share of 17- and 18-year-olds in full-time education than any major industrial nation. In this context, New Labour set the following goals:

- 50% of those under 30 would have access to higher education by 2010;
- current low levels of participation in higher education by students from disadvantaged social and educational backgrounds would be raised;
- lifelong learning would be promoted.

Both the Manifesto and the Annual Report have argued that it was no longer possible for funding for the expansion and improvement of higher education to come out of general taxation. The Annual Report declared that a better system would include:

- a fairer system for repaying loans, together with fees for better-off parents;
- a fairer and more efficient system of student maintenance.

The highly controversial changes introduced by New Labour to the student financial support system has therefore been presented as a strategy to promote inclusion and raise the standards of higher education. New Labour has argued that the 1998 Teaching and Higher Education Act, which abolished student awards for support and maintenance and introduced contributions towards tuition fees, would bridge the deep divide between those who benefit most from higher education and those who benefit least. The government has argued that the previous system of full public support for tuition fees and maintenance to which the Labour Party had historically subscribed did not facilitate access and in fact failed to transform the socioeconomic mix of the student intake (Blunkett, 2000). New Labour has also indicated that savings from the new student funding arrangements would be used to provide financial support where it was most needed (DfEE, 1998b, 2000). In a similar vein, the introduction of student contributions to tuition fees has been linked to an enhancement of quality. New Labour has argued that when individual students contribute financially to their education, by 'investing' in student loans and tuition fees, they become 'critical consumers' with 'choice' and certain rights, and hence reinforce the accountability of higher education providers (Blackstone, 1999).

The shift from elite to highly diverse mass systems, and the increasing competition between national university systems to recruit international students and develop research 'products' for the knowledge society, has resulted in increasing government concern over quality in higher education. New Labour has sought more and more to implement new forms of measurement to assess and enhance the performance of educational institutions and to ensure external accountability. In higher education, quality assurance procedures have reflected the marketisation strand of the third-way political programme and have been highly interventionist in forcing institutions into competitive relations.

Intrinsic evaluation

We begin our evaluation of the government's success in achieving greater access and higher standards of education in the different phases of schooling and in higher education by comparing New Labour's achievements against its stated aims. We also refer in this section to the findings of the government's own monitoring and evaluation agencies. We conclude the section with an assessment table of New Labour's success in meeting its promises. However, there is insufficient space to discuss each of the 25 education pledges that appear in the Annual Report, which accounted for 14% of *all* pledges. Moreover, the government's own list is also selective, and pledges from the Manifesto that we discuss in this chapter do not necessarily appear in the table within the Annual Report.

Schools: laying the foundations

The frameworks for inspection have multiplied during the government's term of office and the much sought-after release from inspection by teachers and educators did not materialise. The assessment of pupils at entry to primary schools, at the end of key stages and at ages 16 and 18 through the national programmes of examination provide valuable data for this intrinsic evaluation of the performance of pupils. Inspections by OFSTED and the Quality Assurance Agency (QAA) of schools and higher education institutions and the assessment of research outputs provide data on the performance of teachers and tutors. Further independent evaluations were commissioned by the government, such as the evaluation of the National Literacy and Numeracy Strategies by the University of Toronto. These are drawn upon to complement the evaluation.

There were early moves by the new government to establish nursery education as the foundation for lifelong learning. As Toynbee and Walker comment, "They began at the beginning, hoping to create a generation of Labour babies whose early success would carry them through to higher attainment later on" (2001, p 49). The Tory voucher system for nursery places was abolished and the Early Years Development and Childcare Partnership introduced. Local plans brought together childcare and education and the nursery education provided within the plan became subject to the guidance and regulation of the Qualifications and Curriculum Authority (QCA) and OFSTED. QCA provided standardised Early Learning Goals designed to meet children's diverse needs and to provide them with a smooth transition to the national curriculum at the end of the school reception year. OFSTED will take on the regulation of daycare and Early Years education, including the registration of childminders, from the local authorities. Although the work of this new inspectorate has yet to begin, the Annual Report of Her Majesty's Chief Inspector of Schools (HMCI) was able to report that the provision for under-fives in nurseries and reception classes is good and that "the assessment of attainment is generally good, although the use of baseline assessment to monitor and evaluate pupils' progress is still relatively under-developed" (OFSTED, 2001d). For the under-fives in settings receiving a nursery education grant, provision was not as good but improving. Nearly nine in 10 settings for four-year-olds were promoting the desirable learning outcomes, set by the QCA, compared with only six in 10 two years ago.

When beginning compulsory education, young pupils are receiving the new slimmed-down version of national curriculum. This curriculum revision has gone further than reducing content. There are new priorities for the 'basics', literacy and numeracy, and an unprecedented attempt to determine teaching methodology through the prescriptive guidance within the National Literacy and Numeracy Strategies (NLNS).

The National Literacy Strategy provided guidance for teachers which specified the regulation of the hour-long daily literacy lessons. The National Numeracy Strategy, implemented a year later, followed a similar format, with emphasis on calculation, especially mental calculation, a template for daily lessons and detailed planning. The OFSTED evaluation of the Literacy Strategy has been very supportive, and the response from schools shows general acceptance. HMCI was able to report that "The Literacy and Numeracy Strategies have led to considerable improvements in the teaching of reading and mathematics", allowing us to award seven out of 10 in our assessment table for piloting literacy summer schools and for the pledge to increase reading ages for all pupils on leaving school. Some other subjects are showing clear benefits, but as yet there has been less impact on the teaching of writing. The evaluation of the NLNS, commissioned by the government and carried out by the University of Toronto, appeared more cautious: "As an instance of large-scale reform, NLNS compares favourably with other such efforts anywhere. But it also faces some serious challenges" (Earl et al, 2000, p 8).

To ensure equity in access to education in the secondary phasing of schooling, the Excellence in Cities project has been central to the attempt to reduce underachievement by pupils in inner-city schools. The project was initially launched by the Prime Minister and David Blunkett in March 1999 in six urban areas. Since then, there have been two successive expansions, and the initiative now covers 58 authority areas (DfEE, 2001). The programme continued to integrate childcare with education through the provision of on-site welfare officers to tackle truancy and special units to remove disruptive pupils from the classroom. OFSTED figures for 2001 show that city schools are improving with outstanding examples of successful secondary schools serving severely disadvantaged communities, but there is considerable variation in the attainment of schools in disadvantaged area (OFSTED, 2001b, p 8, 2001c). OFSTED's Chief Inspector of Schools concluded that one in eight secondary schools and one in 10 primary schools is ineffective. In these schools, weaknesses in leadership or teaching lead to substantial underachievement by pupils. For pupils, teaching is only unsatisfactory in one in 20 lessons. Recruitment and retention of suitably qualified teachers are increasing problems for schools, particularly in urban areas. For these reasons we have awarded 10 out of 10 for the Fresh Start programme, and agree that over 200 schools have benefited from this initiative; seven out of ten for the introduction of homework guidance; nine of 10 for the pilot of referral units; and seven out of 10 for the introduction of the mandatory qualification for headship as a response to the weaknesses found in school leadership.

The considerable variation in access to high-quality education is not a new condition of inner-city education, as Toynbee and Walker (2001) point out. The division of community schools along class lines has been fundamental to the disparity in provision in our cities. This division is in addition to that existing between the state and private sectors, which had been recognised by Labour in opposition: "the educational apartheid created by the public/private divide diminishes the whole education system" (Labour Party, 1997, p 7).

The EAZs have been an important element of the Excellence in Cities programme. The establishment of a further 23 new small EAZs in August 2001 brought the total number in operation to 81, allowing us to award seven out of 10 in the assessment table. The government's existing target is to increase the total number of EAZs to 100 by April 2002. OFSTED's Chief Inspector remains critical of the lack of strategic direction and coordination of education and training for 16- to 19-year-olds, which has led to the duplication, waste and patchy provision in many inner-city areas. In some cases, high numbers of students are obliged to travel considerable distances to study (OFSTED, 2001c). The right to appeal over the allocation of secondary school places is welcome, but the award of five points for this initiative reflects our concern over school choice generally.

Improving access to higher education?

 New Labour's approach to widening participation envisages a larger role for the state and for public funding than that envisaged by the Conservative government (see, for example, DES, Scottish and Welsh Office, 1987). New

Labour has developed a variety of mechanisms to increase and widen access to higher education. The cap on student numbers imposed by the previous government has been lifted, thus increasing the number of places in higher education. A variety of funding levers have been developed with regard to policy mechanisms aimed at encouraging institutions to develop strategies to widen participation. Extra funding, for example, has been set aside to promote partnerships and development work between universities, schools and further education colleges to promote access to groups of students that are traditionally excluded from higher education (DfEE, 1998c, p 13). The government has also proposed an increase in sub-degree provision to attract non-traditional groups of learners. The introduction of a new two-year programme of study, the 'foundation degree', was announced by David Blunkett in his speech at Greenwich University in which he also introduced New Labour's plans to introduce half a million foundation degree places over the next 10 years (Blunkett, 2000). Other funding levers have also been developed to support institutions that recruit and retain groups of students who have been traditionally excluded from higher education. In addition to receiving premiums for part-time and mature students, institutions also receive extra student-related funding for disabled and young full time undergraduate entrants from disadvantaged backgrounds (HEFCE, 1998). The government has also set up mechanisms to assess and monitor the effects of the various policies designed to encourage the development of a more inclusive system of higher education. Such mechanisms include performance indicators for widening participation developed by the funding councils (HEFCE, 1999a).

New Labour's success in increasing and widening access to higher education has been uneven. The total higher education population has risen by 3% between last year and this year and currently, 41% of those under 30 are in some form of higher education, 9% below Tony Blair's target of 50% by 2010. Government sources, however, believe the target may be reached as a result of factors such as the projected increases of students going on to take A-level and other third-level qualifications who are likely to enter higher education. Much also depends on the extent to which the government adapts its definition of 'participation' in higher education in order to meet its target.

Widening participation and the promotion of lifelong learning, however, has been generally unsuccessful and for this reason we award a score of four, although a higher score could have been awarded for the development of policy levers to encourage universities to widen participation. Unfortunately, students from unskilled and partly-skilled backgrounds still count for little more than one in 10. The number of students from unskilled backgrounds in 1995 was 5,000. In 2000, after widening participation measures were put into place, the figure rose to a mere 5,500. However, the numbers from partly-skilled families grew more steeply, from 19,800 in 1995 to 24,200 in 2000. Students from professional and intermediate backgrounds still count for more than half of all entrants. In addition, bodies such as the National Audit Commission have pointed out that much of the funding to universities for improving access went to middle-class graduates returning to higher education instead of to poor first-timers. The postcode premium intended to support poor students has also been attacked as a crude measure that often subsidises wealthy students who happen to live in less affluent neighbourhoods. There are also indications that the foundation degree is struggling to recruit students, since the two-year sub-degree qualification is valued neither by students nor employers.

Government changes in student financial arrangements as a way of financing the expansion and improvement in higher education has encountered a great deal of difficulty. We therefore award this initiative a score of four in the assessment table. When New Labour came into office, it rejected the main recommendations on student funding in the Dearing Report and announced its own student support arrangements. The major changes introduced were the abolition of maintenance grants and the introduction of means-tested fees. The government has put into place various financial support measures, including non-repayable bursaries for young students from disadvantaged backgrounds, a limited amount of support in the form of grants for lone parents with dependants, and 'access funds', which are distributed at the discretion of individual institutions. However, it is questionable whether changes in student funding arrangements have resulted in increased access to education for many categories of students including those from disadvantaged backgrounds. Rather than facilitating access, loans may actually act as a disincentive to students from lower socioeconomic groups seeking higher education. Recent research by Callender and Kemp (2000) has indicated that students most dependent on student loans come from the lowest socioeconomic classes. The study also found that this group was the most debt-averse. These students were least likely to take out loans because they were concerned about borrowing and getting into debt. They were also concerned that higher education study may not automatically lead to improved employment prospects. Research has therefore questioned whether the financial support mechanisms targeted at these groups will be adequate to compensate for the deterrent effect of student loans. The National Audit Office has also confirmed that the removal of the means-tested grant is likely to have widened the gap between social classes. The government has implemented a review of student support in light of the risk that the system of up-front tuition fees and loans might deter the poor and jeopardise the participation target for higher education.

Improving higher education quality?

Since coming to power, New Labour has strengthened crucial aspects of the Conservative government's quality framework. The current approach to quality continues to rely mainly on assessment carried out by external regulatory bodies using output indicators endorsed by the government. The model of achieving excellence in research remains a market-driven one, with the underlying assumption that a competitive model in which institutions bid against each other will enhance the quality of academic research in Britain. The Research Assessment Exercise (RAE) consists of a seven-point scale, through which research ratings are translated into a funding scale. The underlying assumption is that research excellence is enhanced and safeguarded by its concentration in a small number of universities. David Blunkett has argued that government support for research must be selective in order to "retain world class university research in an increasingly competitive environment" (Blunkett, 2000).

Accountability has been imposed on the higher education system through the development of a plethora of performance indicators designed to make the higher education market work better by enabling the consumers of education to make judgements about the effectiveness of institutions. The government has instructed the funding councils to develop indicators and benchmarks of performance for the higher education sector. The Performance Indicators Steering Group was established in 1998, with membership drawn from government departments, funding councils and other representative bodies. The task of this group was to formulate performance indicators that provide a 'snapshot' of an institution's performance in specific areas, such as student progression, learning outcomes including non-completion, and efficiency of learning and teaching (HEFCE, 1999b).

A quality assurance process for teaching, termed the Teaching Quality Assessment (TQA), has subjected universities to a high degree of external scrutiny. A single agency, the QAA for Higher Education, which is directly contracted by the funding councils, was set up in 1997. It was originally established to assess the quality of programmes in each subject, a process termed the Subject Review (SR), and to review each institution's internal processes for maintaining standards of awards and academic quality. The method combined self-assessment by the institution with visits by trained external assessors. Assessors award grades and publish an assessment report identifying good practice and areas for improvement. Where any aspect receives a poor grade, the institution is required to take action to remedy shortcomings as a condition of future funding (HEFCE, 1999c, p 6).

Higher education practitioners have objected to the government's mechanisms for ensuring quality at the same time as the National Union of Students has welcomed such measures. There has been a great deal of opposition from university staff to the SR. The estimated cost of the TQA has been £250 million in 2000/01 and the exercise has taken up 33% of lecturers' time. The elite group of Russel Universities has spearheaded the charge of grade inflation and gamesmanship, and has called for the withdrawal of the SR. The group has argued that the national model for quality assurance should be one of institutional review, not the current joint model of institutional and subject review. In response, HEFCE and the QAA have announced a rethink of the university quality assurance regime and have all but abolished the SR. A more recent development is the constitution of a working group headed by Professor Cooke, recently retired Vice-Chancellor of York University, which has developed

Table 8.1: Progress against Manifesto/Annual Report targets for education

Pledge	New Labour's assessment and our comments	Score/10
1: Increase proportion of GDP spent on education	Kept	
2: Cutting class sizes to under 30 for all five- to seven-year-olds	On course: Compares unfavourably with many European countries	5
3: Guaranteed nursery education for all four-year-olds	Met: Substantial progress	8
4: Piloting early learning centres	Done	
5: Link all schools to information super-highway	On course	
6: Introduce homework clubs with football clubs	Done	
7: Create a National Grid for Learning	Done	
8: Fresh Starts for failing schools	Done: We recognise the benefit to schools	10
9: Pilot literacy summer schools	Done: Pilot is logical response to NLS	7
10: Every child leaves school with reading age of 11+	On course: Reflects to success of the NLS	7
11: Introduce EAZs	Done: An attempt to meet inner-city needs with diversity of approach, a cautious welcome	7
12: More parent governors	Done	
13: Independent committee on technology in schools	Done	
14: Improve school buildings	Kept	
15: National Homework Guidelines	Done: Guidelines welcome, but is content satisfactory?	7
16: Pilot new referral unit	Kept: Better provision for excluded pupils must be welcome	9
17: Right of appeal to independent panel on admission	Done: Concerns remain over choosing schools	5
18: Improve teacher training	On course	
19: New advanced skills teachers	Done	
20: Speedy but fair removal procedures for teachers	On course	
21: Mandatory qualifications for head teachers	On course: Logical response for recognition of leadership	7
22: Efficient and fair student maintenance grant scheme	Done: Confusing array of student support schemes	4
23: Create 'University for Industry'	On course: Need for further development and coordination	5
24: Broaden A-levels/upgrade vocational courses	On course: Design acceptable. Implementation poor	6
25: Use £150 million to set up Individual Learning Accounts	On course: Suspended amidst allegations of fraud	3

proposals on information such as summaries of external examiners' reports and student feedback surveys that universities will need to make public under a new regime of quality assurance.

The substantial improvement in research quality in the sector has led to the HEFCE experiencing a funding shortfall. The consequence of this is that the HEFCE has failed to fund the outcome of the RAE. The HEFCE has maintained funding for the top-rated 5* departments only. Funding has been reduced for 5-rated departments by 15%, for 4-rated departments by 20% and for 3a departments by 70%. Departments rated 3b and lower will not get any funds. Universities UK (UUK) and other bodies have attacked this decision and have pointed to the damage caused to the research potential of universities rated 3 and 4 that have struggled to improve. The measures for assuring research quality appear to have preserved the international standard of the top research universities while destroying the research potential of many of the post-1992 universities.

Extrinsic evaluation

The difficulty of relying solely on the targets set by New Labour, which are often either vague or narrowly defined, makes extrinsic evaluation a useful complement to intrinsic evaluation. In this section, we analyse New Labour reforms in education against criteria and aims that have not been explicitly set by government. In particular, we examine the reforms against more traditional welfare state criteria such as equality. We also examine the tensions and contradictions of various policy streams, whereby policies satisfying one demand displace or undermine policies developed to satisfy other demands.

Mixed and diverse initiatives in schools

In the mixed and diverse initiatives that the government has implemented, with their aim of providing the diversity needed to enhance choice for parents, pupils and students, there appears to have been a shift towards pragmatism and away from ideology. Although it is too early to judge the impact of the reforms in Early Years education, there have been warnings from Early Years educators that the introduction of formal curricula into large classes may be counter-productive. Diane Hofkins (1995), for example, concludes from her research that many children in the early years of schooling are over-directed. The target size for Early Years classrooms is 30, which, although in the right direction, is simply too large and will not address this problem. Her concerns reflect critics' views of the formality of the National Literacy Strategy in an Early Years context. Many countries in Europe do not start the formal teaching of reading until much later than in England. Although large-scale research is now underway in England to monitor the Early Years, the effect of different types of provision is still not known.

The guidance developed for the involvement of parents in their children's education reflected the attempt by the government to spell out in detail the responsibility of parents and carers. Macnamara et al identify this as a development of the traditional partnership between home and school: "Recent shifts in government thinking about home–school relationships have begun to spread the mantle of accountability wider: all stake holders (governors, parents, teachers, children, local education authorities [LEAs] etc) are now obliged to accept the responsibility for the success or failure of the national educational venture. In this the support of parents in promoting effective education is seen as particularly crucial" (2000, pp 473–3). Such a dramatic reorganisation of childcare provision and nursery education has brought Britain more in line with Europe and ensured that Labour met its promise of a free nursery place for every four-year-old whose parents wanted it. We therefore award eight out of 10 for early years education in our assessment table. Local plans ensure that the number of places available for three-year-olds is now increasing.

Early evaluations of the Numeracy Strategy from OFSTED and the Department for Education and Skills (DfES) are less positive than we have reported above. Brown et al warn that the strategy moves away from an emphasis on work set in 'real-life' contexts, that the strategy itself is open to many interpretations by teachers and that some of the curriculum changes, such as the mental calculation, "may well be shown to have gone too far and necessitate eventually a counter-movement towards the synthesis and meaning needed for creative application, problem-solving and investigation" (2000, p 469). They argue that the Numeracy Strategy was in fact inherited from the Conservatives' National Numeracy Project and "what has changed since then, apart from the media attention and the financing of professional development is mainly the tone of the texts and the degree of prescription" (Brown et al, 2000, p 461). However, as they point out, it is not safe to assume that this approach is built on secure strategies: "The juxtaposition of the pragmatic and policy statements would seem to imply that there is clear evidence that the methods suggested improved effectiveness. However, in reality any evidence which can be quoted is far from robust" (2000, p 463). They also comment that the degree of central control over teachers is particularly ironic in view of Tony Blair's belief that "The democratic impulse needs to be strengthened by finding new ways to enable citizens to share in decision-making that effects them" (Blair in Brown et al, 2000, p 462).

In relation to the revised curriculum for primary schools, there is also no clear evidence that the new guidelines are based on 'what works'. Alexander remains critical: "England has twice taken the wooden spoon: first, when in the 1988 and 1996 Education Acts it propounded a meagre brace of goals which were even more meaningless as touchstones for practice than they read; then, in 1999, when in the context of national curriculum review it over-compensated and threw down a statement so comprehensive – a veritable rag-bag of values – as to have not even a rhetorical purpose" (2000, p 155).

In relation to secondary education, the EAZs have received a cautious welcome. Jones and Bird describe them as a new form of education institution that promises to accomplish an "historic shift in the governance of education" (2000, p 491) and to increase the influence of the private sector. As Toynbee and Walker point out, however, the EAZs add to the confusion over the form that secondary schooling should take. The government did not know "how to balance the right of parents to choose a school and the right of a school to choose a parent" (p 53). The attempt to remove the 'apartheid' in education by a direct threat to remove the charitable status of private schools was dropped and the message over selection, if not subjected to a U-turn, meandered through pragmatic and localised approaches to selection and choice. "The new line up was 'community' (council), 'aided' (church) and 'foundation' (ex-GM) the latter two selective on the basis of subject specialism and religious affiliation. Specialize sounds better than select" (Toynbee and Walker, 2001, p 53). We therefore award only five for achievement in these pledges. It is difficult to know how the problem facing parents in choosing a secondary school for their children can be reduced without a radical increase in the number of good neighbourhood schools. Unless all parents have confidence in their neighbourhood schools, local authorities will always be faced with the dilemma of restricting parental choice in order to create balanced catchment areas or giving parents choice and risking the creation of unpopular sink schools alongside oversubscribed popular schools. Reform of secondary schools may remain the government's greatest challenge.

Tensions and contradictions in higher education reform

New Labour's concern with equity and social justice has been reflected in the policy changes that have occurred in relation to widening participation. The allocation of special funds for widening participation projects is likely to provide support for widening participation strategies initiated by institutions such as the University of Bradford (Goddard, 2000) and will hopefully encourage universities to bid for funds to implement high quality projects to recruit students that have been traditionally excluded from higher education. The extra funding allocated to institutions in recognition of the additional resources needed to successfully teach students from educationally disadvantaged backgrounds is particularly welcome. While the performance indicators and targets for widening participation do not directly steer institutions towards widening participation through formulae funding, or link widening participation to other measures such as quality, they are nevertheless to be welcomed because they place the development of a more inclusive system of higher education in the public domain, alongside such measures as research excellence. It is likely that such publicity will apply pressure on elite universities to be more attentive to the social backgrounds of their student constituency.

However, as Sir David Watson, chair of the UUK longer-term strategy group warns, great tensions in the structure and function of higher education have been created by New Labour's agenda, which demands that universities be globally competitive while making themselves accessible and equitable to promote social inclusion (Watson, 2000). We agree with this concern and our analysis is that the unintended effects of the marketisation of higher education and the introduction of an extensive audit culture may actually inhibit the potential of the widening participation strategies developed by New Labour. We believe that the logic of the competitive policies developed to maintain and enhance quality, which require institutions to demonstrate student success and progression in the shortest time possible and to maximise research output, mitigate against the development of a more inclusive higher education system in at least two ways. First, institutions that have not traditionally included widening participation in their missions are unlikely to develop admission strategies to recruit students from underrepresented groups as they would fear that admitting students from non-traditional educational backgrounds would be time- and resource-intensive. As one of us has shown in a different national context (Naidoo, 1998, 2000), such students would be perceived as a threat to institutional arrangements around core activities such as research, through which universities accrue academic status and financial resources. In addition, such students would be unlikely to enhance the institutions' 'output' indicators. Marginson (1997) has also indicated, in the context of Australia, that the marketisation of higher education has not resulted in universities becoming more accountable to the consumers of education or more responsive to student choice. Since the demand for places at elite universities far outstrips the number of places available, it is the elite higher education providers that 'choose' the student, rather than the other way around. In addition, in cases where there is great demand and no possibility of charging differential fees, higher education providers simply increase the 'price' of access in the form of raised entry requirements. Analysis of student enrolment figures indicate that the Russel Group of universities, comprising elite universities such as Oxford, Cambridge, Warwick, Bristol and Imperial College London, failed to meet basic targets for widening participation set by the funding council for 1998/99.

Second, the extensive machinery of quality assurance makes the case for an explicit stratification of universities by implementing an institutional framework that is likely to continue selectively to empower and disempower individuals and institutions largely on the basis of historical and social disadvantage. The quality machinery as a whole, operating within a quasi-market framework, combines to apply pressures on universities to achieve a type of productivity that can be measured by quantifiable outputs, such as the progression rate of students, the number of postgraduate students and the numbers of research-active staff producing publications of 'good standing'. Such output-based numerical measures of quality are not set up to differentiate between different categories of students, different systems or the different means required to produce a successful 'outcome'. As such, the model is inevitably blind to social and educational factors generally associated with widening participation strategies. Institutions that absorb students from groups traditionally excluded from higher education, as well as students on sub-degree provision such as the new two-year foundation courses, are therefore likely to be financially penalised. This is particularly the case since the quality framework does not differentiate between categories of students with regard to social disadvantage and differences in prior educational attainment.

The highly selective research assessment framework, through which institutions receive a sizeable proportion of their block grants, functions to disempower non-elite universities. The Dearing Committee noted that the 1996 RAE resulted in five universities (out of 176 higher education institutions in the UK, 115 of which are titled universities) in England receiving almost one third of the available research funding. The concentration of research in a few institutions is also compounded by the funding methodology of the research councils, which award funds on a competitive tendering basis. Fifty per cent of research council grants were awarded to individuals in a mere 12 universities in 1996 (NCIHE, 1997, p 41). More recently, a report by Sir Brian Ramsden (2001), retiring chief executive of the Higher Education Statistics Agency, revealed that the 10 most research-intensive universities, all pre-1992 universities, receive 43% of the total research funding available from HEFCE. Geoffrey Copland, chair of the Modern Coalition of Universities, has indicated that until 1992 no dual funding for research was available for the post-1992 universities, which put them at a serious disadvantage in terms of the RAE. He has also indicated that the government's strategy to research appears to exclude new universities. For example, the Science Research Initiative Fund, worth £675 million, is to be allocated to universities with top RAE scores. There is no such funding for the post-1992 universities that are attempting to build their science and research capacity and which are starved of basic equipment. The concentration of research in a small number of universities has grave implications for the development of a more highly and widely skilled society, which New Labour proposes as Britain's route to gaining a competitive edge in the global economy. The success of this enterprise depends not only on having world-class research, but also on having well-educated and trained graduates, the majority of whom are located in post-1992 universities.

Policy developments since the 2001 election

Policy developments since the 2001 Election maintain the focus on 'economic development' and the resulting need to continue to raise standards. The twin aim of equity also remains. The reelection of the Labour government in 2001 was followed by a reorganisation of government departments. The work of the new DfES has been seen as central to achieving both these aims (see DfES, 2001b). The new department reflects these priorities in school education by continuing with the development of key skills; by promoting the enhancement of vocational education; and by continuing to address the problems experienced by disadvantaged communities. Targets in both the school and university sectors continue to build on the initiatives of the previous term of office. The most radical change in schooling is the refocusing of priorities on secondary education. Through the Key Stage 3 National Strategy, the aim is to 'transform' secondary education for pupils from the age of 11 to 14. There is an emphasis on 'the basics' in order to boost standards within literacy and numeracy, and there are government attempts to raise the status of vocational education by introducing new subject options for students to take as GCSEs or A-levels, such as tourism and leisure, business and engineering. The most radical change in relation to higher education is likely to revolve around proposed government plans to differentiate the sector into an elite tier of research universities and a tier of teaching universities with little research infrastructure. Senior university sources have already revealed that they have been in discussions with the government on the possibility of channelling extra funds to elite universities outside of the existing funding formulae. These developments, together with developments in schools, thus appear to be leading to the greater stratification of education systems. These policy developments are likely to result in pockets of excellence rather than the 2001 Election Manifesto's promise of "excellence for the many, not just for the few" (Labour Party, 2001).

Conclusion

Our evaluation of New Labour's achievement in education has focused on the access to, and quality of, educational provision from nurseries to universities. Using both intrinsic and extrinsic measures, we have shown how New Labour has kept its pledge to make education its number one priority through its efforts to ensure a decent education for all. Widening participation has remained central to education policy as demonstrated by steps taken to expand nursery education, improve both primary and secondary schools and increase access to higher education.

On the whole, participation strategies developed by New Labour may play an important role in increasing the access of certain groups of disadvantaged learners to all phases of education. However, there are dangers within its third-way approach to policy reform. New Labour continues to present market measures (albeit with policy mechanisms aimed to temper some of the consequences of the marketisation) as one of the main devices for creating diversity of choice for the consumer and therefore the appropriate means to tackle differences in quality across institutional programmes and institutions. In the reform of the secondary school system, there is every indication that there will be continued diversification. For universities this market measures attempt to draw diverse institutions into a unified system. For schools it is difficult to anticipate when sufficient high-quality institutions will be available to satisfy parental demand, whereas for universities it is feared that the impact, in reality, will encourage the development of a system within which status and resources will be inversely proportional to institutional and student disadvantage. Therefore, the education system will be characterised not only by less equality of opportunity, but also by greater highs and lows of quality. This will lead to a less inclusive higher education system and lower overall standards, which is inconsistent with the high-skills economic theory espoused by the New Labour government.

References

Alexander, R. (2000) *Culture and pedagogy: International comparisons in primary education*, Oxford: Blackwells.

Blackstone, T. (1999) 'Students are now "critical consumers"', DfEE Press Release, 16 September.

Blunkett, D. (2000) 'Modernising higher education – facing the global challenge', Speech on higher education at Greenwich Maritime University, 15 February.

Brown, M., Millett, A., Bibby, T. and Johnson, D.C. (2000) 'Turning our attention from the What to the How: the National Numeracy Strategy', *British Educational Research Journal*, vol 26, no 4, pp 457-71.

Callender, C. and Kemp, M. (2000) *Changing student finances: Income, expenditure and the take-up of student loans*, London: Policy Department for Education and Employment.

Castells, M. (1996) *The information age: Economy, society and culture. Volume 1: The rise of the network society*, Oxford: Blackwell.

DfEE (Department for Education and Employment) (1998a) *The Learning Age: A renaissance for a new Britain. Higher education: Meeting the challenge*, Green Paper, London: HMSO.

DfEE (1998b) 'Blunkett welcomes Teaching and Higher Education Act', Press Release, 17 July.

DfEE (1998c) *Higher education for the 21st century: Response to the Dearing Report*, London: HMSO.

DfEE (2000) 'Blunkett announces major student support package to widen access and tackle hardship in higher education', Press Release, 25 January.

DfEE (2001) *Excellence in cities: Schools, extending excellence*, London: DfEE

DES (Department of Education and Science) with Welsh Office, Scottish Office and Northern Ireland Office (1987) *Higher education: Meeting the challenge*, White Paper, Cm 114, London: HMSO.

DfES (Department for Education and Skills) (2001a) 'Timms congratulates GCSE and GNVQ students on their results', Press Release, 22 August.

DfES (2001b) *Education and skills: Delivering results: A strategy to 2006*, London: DfES.

Earl, L., Fullan, M., Leithwood, K., Watson, N. with Jantzi, D., Levin, B. and Torrance, N. (2000) 'Watching Learning OISE/UT', *Evaluation of the Implementation of the National Literacy and Numeracy Strategies*, Toronto, Canada: Ontario Institute for Studies in Education, University of Toronto.

Giddens, A. (1998) *The third way: The renewal of social democracy*, Cambridge: Polity Press.

Giddens, A. (2000) *The third way and its critics*, Cambridge: Polity Press.

Goddard, A. (2000) 'Unequal opportunities: a university challenge', *Times Higher Educational Supplement*, 10 March.

HEFCE (Higher Education Funding Council for England) (1999a) *Performance indicators in higher education*, Report 99/11, First Report of the Performance Indicators Steering Group (www.niss.ac.uk/education/hefce/pub99/99_11.html).

HEFCE (1998) *Widening participation in higher education: Funding proposals*, Consultation Paper 98/39 (www.niss.ac.uk/education/hefce/pub98/98_39.html)

HEFCE (1999b) *Reaching out*, 1998/99 Annual Report, Bristol: HEFCE.

HEFCE (1999c) *About the HEFCE: An introduction to the work of the Higher Education Funding Council for England*, April 99/23 Guide, Bristol: HEFCE.

Hofkins, D. (1995) 'Early Literacy "too imposed"', *The Times Educational Supplement*, No 4108, p 11.

Jones, K. and Bird, K. (2000) '"Partnership" as strategy: public–private relations in Education Action Zones', *British Educational Research Journal*, vol 26, no 4, pp 492-506.

Labour Party (1997) *New Labour because Britain deserves better* (Election Manifesto), London: Labour Party.

Macnamara, O., Hustler, D., Stronach, I., Rodrigo, M., Beresford, E. and Botcherby, S. (2000) 'Room to manoeuvre: mobilising the "active partner" in home-school relations', *British Educational Research Journal*, vol 26, no 4, pp 473-89.

Marginson, S. (1997) 'Competition and contestability in Australian higher education, 1987-1997', *Australian Universities Review*, vol 40, no 1, pp 5-14.

Muschamp, Y., Jamieson, I. and Lauder, H. (1999) 'Education, education, education' in Powell, M. (ed) *New Labour, new welfare state: The 'third way' in British social policy*, Bristol: The Policy Press, pp 101-21.

Naidoo, R. (1998) 'Levelling or playing the field? The politics of access to university education in South Africa', *Cambridge Journal of Education*, vol 28, no 3, pp 369-83.

Naidoo, R. (2000) 'Admission policies and the politics of access: a case study of two universities in South Africa (1985-1990)', Unpublished PhD dissertation, University of Cambridge.

NCIHE (National Committee into Higher Education) (1997) *Higher education in the Learning Society*, Main Report, London: HMSO.

OFSTED (Office for Standards in Education) (2001a) News Release, 11 January, London: OFSTED.

OFSTED (2001b) *Primary schools at a glance*, London: OFSTED.

OFSTED (2001c) *Secondary schools at a glance*, London: OFSTED.

OFSTED (2001d) *The Annual Report of Her Majesty's Chief Inspector of Schools 1999-2000*, London: OFSTED.

Ramsden, B. (2001) *Patterns of higher education institutions in the UK: A report the longer term strategy group of Universities UK*, London: Universities UK.

Riley, J. (2001) 'The National Literacy Strategy: success with literacy for all?', *The Curriculum Journal*, vol 12, no 1, pp 29-58.

Toynbee, P. and Walker, D. (2001) *Did things get better? An audit of Labour's successes and failures*, London: Penguin.

NINE

New Labour and social care: continuity or change?

Mark Baldwin

Introduction

In recent years, 'social care' has been used as a term encompassing not only its traditional meaning of the practical functions provided by personal social services, but also the professional function, primarily that of social work (Macdonald, 2000). It is this broad meaning of the term that will be utilised in this chapter scrutinising the expressed intentions of New Labour policy for social care. I will make both an intrinsic analysis of these intentions and an extrinsic critique of their social care policy. There is much detail to be evaluated in New Labour's social care policy targets and this chapter will focus on some of the key areas. A broad critique suggests that, where targets are explicit, they have proved of limited value in judging action against intention, and where they are less explicit, or more qualitative, it is hard to match outcome to original intention. In addition, many policy intentions are comparatively new and not embedded into practice sufficiently to provide evidence for evaluation.

The areas of social care policy that were mentioned in New Labour's Manifesto commitments (Labour Party, 1997) provide little to evaluate. The relevant 177 Manifesto commitments relate to:

- long-term care (100 and 101);
- reduction in time from arrest to court disposal for persistent young offenders (68);
- the introduction of child protection orders (73);
- the duty on local councils to protect the homeless (92);
- comprehensive civil rights for disabled people (147).

These add up to six pledges upon which to cast judgement (see Table 9.1). Many of New Labour's social care changes have come through other developments, such as the move from Compulsory Competitive Tendering (CCT) to Best Value (see Chapter Three of this volume). The changes resulting from Best Value in the social care policy arena are located in the Personal Social

Services Performance Assessment Framework (PSSPAF), and will be evaluated later in this chapter.

Despite this thin evidence of commitment, New Labour in government has produced an explosion of activity in relation to social care (Clarke et al, 2000; Toynbee and Walker, 2001). The government's first term produced a substantial policy agenda for social care, manifest within the White Paper *Modernising the social services* (DoH, 1998), and related policy initiatives such as the Quality Strategy for Social Services, the PSSPAF and the NHS Plan. I will look at some of these developments, although this late entry into the commitment stakes for social care means that many pledges are at too early a stage for comprehensive evaluation.

Although the White Paper and related policy initiatives have provided ample evidence to evaluate government progress, it is also important to explore other angles on social care policy development. After looking at the early and later pledges, I will offer some extrinsic evaluation by considering the following questions:

- Can the New Labour approach to social care be characterised as continuity with Conservative policy approaches to social care, or a change to something 'modern' as claimed?
- Are there targets among the Manifesto pledges that have implications for social care policy? Do pledges on poverty impinge on social care, for instance, and have these commitments to 'Old Labour' interests been successful?
- How has social care been conceptualised, and where does New Labour social care policy fit?
- What is meant by 'Best Value'?

Intrinsic evaluation

Stated Manifesto aims

Table 9.1 lists the commitments made at the time of the General Election in 1997, the claims to meet those pledges from subsequent Annual Reports, and the score awarded for success in achieving the aim. The Annual Reports are not as helpful in tracking developments as might have been hoped. The chart provided on the Number 10 website for the 1998/99 Annual Report helpfully listed the 177 commitments and the claims to progress so far. The most recent Annual Report (1999/2000) does not systematically tackle each commitment, and omits some. Table 9.1 cites Annual Report claims to success but it is necessary to look elsewhere for deeper or more recent claims for government progress. I will go through government claims of success in relation to these Manifesto pledges, providing some critical commentary.

The marks awarded reflect the limited scope and relevance of the government's pledges. They are soft targets, easily achieved. The implied targets, for reducing youth crime, making things better for looked-after children, improving long-

Table 9.1: Progress against Manifesto/Annual Report targets, relating directly or indirectly to social care

Pledge	New Labour's assessment	Score/10
68: Halve the time from arrest to sentencing for young offenders	"It was 142 days in 1996. It dropped to 108 days last year and is on course to meet the target of 71 days next year" (Annual Report 1999/2000)	10
73: Introduce child protection orders	"Done. In force since 30 September 1998" (Annual Report 1998/99)	10
92: Duty on local councils to protect homeless	"On course. Since September 1997, the Government has made sure that homeless people have been given reasonable preference for housing by local authorities" (Annual Report 1998/99)	5
100: Royal Commission on Long Term Care	"Done. The Royal Commission reported in March 1999 and the Government is considering its proposals" (Annual Report 1998/99)	10
101: Introduce a Long-Term Care Charter	"On course. A draft charter was issued for consultation in May 1999" (Annual Report 1998/99)	10
147: Comprehensive civil rights for disabled people	"We are also tackling the discrimination that excludes disabled people in the workplace and elsewhere through the powerful new Disability Rights Commission which started work this year" (Annual Report 1999/2000)	6

Source: Annual Report 1999/2000, Number 10 website

term care, and ending the social exclusion of disabled people, need much smarter indicators and better evidence of success. There are also all the other commitments that have been made since New Labour came to power. For many of those targets listed in the Performance Assessment Framework (PAF), which reflect those White Paper commitments, it is still too early to draw firm conclusions.

Taking all this into account, I would give the government a mark of five out of 10 for its social care reforms. It has not reached many of its stated targets, and the implied ones are still a long way from fruition.

Manifesto Commitment 68: Halve the time from arrest to sentencing for young offenders

Official information about this commitment prior to the June 2001 election was published in the 1999/2000 Annual Report. This commitment was not, then, achieved in Labour's first term, although Manifestos state clearly that the timescale for these commitments was a five-year parliamentary term. The Youth Justice Board, set up under the 1998 Crime and Disorder Act, issued a press release on 21 September 2001, indicating that the average time has now been cut to 69 days, thus surpassing the original target.

I argue that this policy area lies correctly within a chapter on social care rather than criminal justice. Successive governments have in fact shifted away from the 1969 Children and Young Persons Act and its welfare approach to youth crime. New Labour is much closer to previous Conservative government policy reflecting a punitive approach to young offenders, despite evidence that connects youth crime with poverty, family breakdown and other social problems (Carlen, 1996; Stone, 1998; Hayden et al, 1999).

There has been substantial investment in the bodies entrusted with delivering this commitment, and the Youth Offending Teams (YOTs), which were also a Manifesto pledge (69), seem to have successfully reduced numbers to this target. Given that the criminal justice system in general has been subject to 'an unprecedented expenditure review' since 1997 (McLaughlin and Muncie, 2000, p 182), it seems unlikely that this level of investment will be sustained. So, although the Manifesto aim has been met and the government can claim success, failure to maintain this level of disposal time will undermine claims that New Labour is dealing effectively with the problem of youth crime.

It is also questionable whether this is an effective target to set if reducing youth crime is the aim. With around a quarter of all offenders committing indictable offences being under 17 years of age (Ayres, 2000), it is hard to argue against this as a priority area. More efficiency will enable young offenders to connect their offending behaviour with the disposal of the courts, and this is argued as more effective in diverting young people from future criminal behaviour. The target has been met by increasing resources that manage the volume of juvenile offenders through the system more quickly. It is debatable what it achieves in reducing offending.

The government would, no doubt, argue that this target should be put together with other approaches such as the orders dealt with in the next section. Adopting a policy that focuses on court disposal rather than prevention and diversion has not generally proved successful in the past. Deterrence and retributive approaches to youth crime only deal with one half of the New Labour soundbite. They are 'tough on crime' but less geared to being 'tough on the causes of crime'.

Manifesto Commitment 73: Introduce child protection orders

This is part of a broader commitment to youth justice, in a range of 'community sentences' introduced by the government early in its term of office through the 1998 Crime and Disorder Act, to demonstrate its pledge to be tough on young offenders (McLaughlin and Muncie, 2000). On the bare pledge, the government has exceeded its target by introducing a range of disposals to reduce youth crime.

These options, which include final warnings, reparation orders and curfew orders, were promoted by Jack Straw, the Home Secretary in the first New

Labour government, but they did not initially prove attractive as disposals for magistrates. The Youth Justice Board Annual Review (2001) indicates increased use of these disposals. As there is no current analysis of their success in reducing youth crime, this can be seen as another Manifesto pledge in which the bare commitment has been met, but with little connection to the broader commitment.

Manifesto Commitment 92: Duty on local councils to protect homeless

The government recognises in the White Paper *Modernising social services* (DoH, 1998) that there is a high proportion of homeless young people who have been in the care of social services departments. Initiatives to pressure local authorities to improve after-care services (Statutory Instrument 2001 No 2874 The Children [Leaving Care] [England] Regulations August 2001) have demonstrated a commitment to tackling this Manifesto pledge, at least for children formerly looked after by local authorities.

Like many others in the social care arena, these commitments depend on effective local, rather than central, government action. This is a two-edged sword for New Labour, in that it can deflect responsibility for failure to meet targets, but could also lose control of the implementation process.

Manifesto Commitment 100: Royal Commission on Long Term Care

A Royal Commission on Long Term Care has been set up and has reported to government, thus fulfilling that limited pledge. Implementation of government policy in this area, as with many other aspects of health and social care, has become blocked by the 'Berlin Wall' described so graphically by then Secretary of State for Health, Frank Dobson, in New Labour's first term. Failure of effective collaboration by the NHS and social services departments appears to have been the spur to the White Paper, *Modernising social services*.

The government's initial reaction to the Royal Commission's report in January 2000 was to welcome its findings, list the areas already dealt with, and then to postpone its response. The government has quoted the White Paper, *The NHS Plan*, and the guidance entitled *Partnership in action* as evidence of its determination to tackle the 'Berlin Wall' (DoH, 1998). On 1 October 2001 it introduced a scheme for payment of nursing care costs in long-term residential care, but has not taken England down the Scottish route where residential care charges are to be abolished.

If setting up the Commission was the government's aim, then it has achieved its aim. If the aim was to tackle the problems identified by the commission, then it is too early to analyse this. Cynical analysis suggests that a Royal Commission is an effective way to kick costly policy areas into the long grass. The Commission has allowed government to declare it was 'considering the proposals' for most of its first term in office.

When it came, the response was mixed (DoH, 2000). The government accepted some of the less costly recommendations, such as the disregard of the value of long-term care users' homes, bringing 'preserved rights' payments into post-1993 funding, and the introduction of free nursing care into residential provision. It has accepted suggestions for organisational change, such as increased efficiency and quality, and a more client-centred approach. These recommendations were already listed as best practice in the PSSPAF, which I will look at later in this chapter.

The government rejected the recommendation that personal care should be paid for from general taxation to reduce the 'postcode lottery' of care provision. It claims that it is making 'unprecedented' investment in older people's services, but universal provision of free personal care would not be the best use of resources. This leaves the Royal Commission commitment as a limited gesture towards the problems of long-term care.

Long-term care has been argued as an illustrative example of how care has been commodified since 1979 (Player and Pollock, 2001). By the time New Labour came to power, 300,000 NHS long-term care beds had been closed and replaced in the private care sector. The privatisation "task had been accomplished" (Player and Pollock, 2001, p 239). New Labour's policy change shut the door, but the horse had bolted. Contracting out is now established practice in local authority commissioning. Best Value has done nothing to reverse the trend, and the major problem is that local authorities do not have the cash to purchase long-term care places at market value in many parts of the country. Tightening of eligibility criteria has resulted in service varying geographically and homes are closing at an alarming rate (Player and Pollock, 2001). Frequent movement of frail people is considered to be poor practice, but there is little sign of change in government policy. Indeed, Labour Minister Paul Boateng is reported as saying local authorities would answer for their actions if they undermined the private sector (Player and Pollock, 2001). Having rejected the Royal Commission recommendation for free, comprehensive long-term care, the government has been pronounced culpable of "severing the 1948 social contract" (Player and Pollock, 2001, p 252).

Manifesto Commitment 101: Introduce a Long-Term Care Charter

The government has produced a draft charter for local authorities to construct local charters. One hundred and thirty-four local charters had been completed by March 2001 when the Department of Health published a circular outlining investigation into the introduction of charters (DoH, 2001b). The main concern was variation through the country, although the deluge of charters indicates that the government has met its basic target.

Charters were introduced by John Major to provide clarity of expectations, and a set of benchmarks for service consumers and others to evaluate expectations. Citizen's Charters were criticised for being top-down policy imposition (Cochrane, 2000). Best Value, with its requirement to consult with service users and carers in the construction of targets, is claimed as a significant development (Clarke et al, 2000). I will look at Best Value later, but want to note two points here. The first is that charters provide little more than 'soft' and easily manipulated targets (Clarke et al, 2000) and that they have reduced local democratic accountability in favour of customer satisfaction. Second, given government failure to fund the Royal Commission's recommendations designed to improve services, local authorities are left with NHS colleagues to implement charters, but without the necessary resources.

Manifesto Commitment 147: Comprehensive civil rights for disabled people

The Disability Rights Commission has now started work. Therefore, on that basis, it could be argued that the legislative framework and the statutory body are in place to effect this policy commitment. It is early days to make judgements about effectiveness.

Despite the lack of adequate time to evaluate this commitment, the setting up of the Disability Rights Commission is a notable achievement for two reasons. First, this development has been long requested by disability groups, and adds to the Equal Rights and Racial Equality Commissions established in the 1970s. Second, the inclusion of a number of disabled people in the Commission demonstrates government commitment to participation.

Aims developed during the first term

New Labour has been active in the development of new policy for social care not mentioned in manifesto pledges. In order to manage the task of evaluating these new policy developments, I will focus on two key indicators of social care policy, the White Paper, *Modernising social services* (DoH, 1998), and the PSSPAF. This will provide an illustration of New Labour's policies and targets for reforms, which the government claimed in the White Paper were needed in working practices, local management and training in order to improve the quality of social services in England (DoH, 1998). The aim of these new policies, therefore, is to improve the quality of social care services, emphasising enabling those who can to live independently, and those who cannot to receive the quality services they require (DoH, 1998). There is also an aim to provide the framework for evaluating the success of health and social care agencies in meeting targets. Central government sets the targets but it is performance on the ground that will be scrutinised.

Modernising social services (DoH, 1998)

Modernising social services argues the need for social care services on the grounds that "any decent society must make provision for those who need support and are unable to look after themselves" (DoH, 1998, p 4). The White Paper demonstrates that the government is dissatisfied with social services, laying out values upon which change should be built, in particular making the system "more centred on service users" (DoH, 1998, p 12). Services will be characterised by high standards, responsiveness, meeting expressed need and respecting culture and lifestyle, and built upon service users' abilities to participate in society. The paper also reflects New Labour's third way, which moves "the focus away from who provides the care, and places it firmly on the quality of services" (DoH, 1998, p 8).

The details of the White Paper's commitments can be sought elsewhere (for example, Johnson, 1999), but, as with the Manifesto commitments discussed earlier, I will work through these, describing the commitment and then providing a critical commentary on progress in the implementation of each.

Improving evidence of what works in social care

The White Paper pledges to introduce a Social Care Institute for Excellence (SCIE). The remit is for the SCIE to evaluate evidence for what works in social care and then work with social care organisations to implement practice. Over time, the SCIE will build up a knowledge base founded on the experience of all involved in social care – managers, practitioners, service users and carers, to improve service quality.

The SCIE has now been established by the government, several months into its second term. The appointment of Ray Jones as Chief Executive, and Jane Campbell as Chair signals a government commitment to place service user involvement at the heart of this enterprise. Ray Jones in his former role as Director of Social Services in Wiltshire was supportive of service user organisations and Jane Campbell comes from the National Centre for Independent Living with strong user empowerment credentials.

There is concern (Jordan, 2000; Parton and O'Byrne, 2000) that these developments reflect a commitment by New Labour to particular forms of knowledge as effective for evaluating what works in social care. There are also voices in support of such an approach to policy and practice development (Davies et al, 2000). Much of this evidence base for social care comes from a scientific rationalist version of evidence. I will return to this point, but failure to acknowledge diversity, uncertainty and complexity within social care is at odds with the Department of Health exhortation to a holistic perspective on service user needs. In general this is a new development and evaluation will have to wait for the SCIE to bed down as an organisation.

Establishing a New Quality Framework

This development is intended to improve quality and consistency of social services across the country, avoiding 'postcode' accessibility. Apart from ensuring that there is service user involvement in social care developments, the White Paper has much else to say about standards. There are detailed suggestions for where improvements could be made in the Quality Framework, with a promise of rigorous assessment of "performance in achieving agreed goals" (DoH, 1998, p 109). This initiative fits with Best Value goals, and with virtually all White Paper commitments covered by the PSSPAF.

The targets listed in the paper are replicated in the PSSPAF and an illustrative selection of them is evaluated below. A White Paper is almost by definition a wish list. It is easy enough to make commitments about, for instance, improving preventative care for older people, or protecting vulnerable children. Many of the commitments are of a qualitative nature for which measurable targets have proved difficult to establish. Evaluation will depend on the degree to which targets are met, and it is early days for many of them, particularly those of a more qualitative character. In addition, these targets will need to be met through the efforts of local authorities working in partnership with health Trusts and other provider organisations in the independent sector as well as service users and carers. This is another example of targets set at the top by government, but which require action by others to facilitate their achievement.

Improved training and regulation of the social care workforce

The White Paper paves the way for a national curriculum for social care staff, to ensure consistency across the country. Training will be stimulated in the voluntary/private sector to deal with a shortfall of training in non-statutory organisations. The paper reiterates a long-standing government intention, started by the Conservatives, to introduce a General Social Care Council (GSCC) to regulate social care practitioners and the delivery of qualifying training.

Some of these developments are yet to start, let alone bear fruit. The GSCC was set up on 1 October 2001, but is not expected to start registering social workers until 2004. New occupational standards and qualifications are being developed in social care by the Training Organisation for Personal Social Services (TOPSS). A new degree in social work that will come on stream in 2003 should boost a profession attracting diminishing numbers of applicants. Occupational standards will give the government the opportunity to compare, judge and regulate the behaviour of social care staff, regardless of the level of resources with which they are provided to deliver quality services. This pledge to increase training and standards in social care practice is another example of New Labour's quest for quality in social care.

Better prevention and rehabilitation services

The government promotes independence as a general theme in the White Paper and prevention and rehabilitation are key aspects. It gives details of the amount of money that is to go into the 'partnership grant' and the 'prevention grant' (DoH, 1998, p 17), intended to stimulate preventative strategies in local authorities. The National Service Frameworks (NSFs) have been set up partly to guide such developments and the NSF for Older People (www.doh.gov.uk) lists some of the pilot projects set up using these resources, to provide services in what has become known as 'intermediate care', which is intended to manage patients/service users at the interface between hospital/home/residential care, in order to maximise the individual's opportunities to return home.

On the face of it, this would seem to be a commendable new direction for social care that has been dogged in the past by the consequences of targeting those in most need, originating from the White Paper *Community care in the next decade and beyond* (DoH, 1989). This policy resulted in ever tighter eligibility criteria being developed, culminating in a situation where informal care networks have to fall apart before help is offered (Baldwin, 2000). It is now argued that preventive services could help people live independently for longer. Some initiatives have been introduced using the money mentioned earlier, but these are new and too early to evaluate. Despite these initiatives, the principal evidence is of ever stricter eligibility criteria as resources get tighter and demand greater (Player and Pollock, 2001). Although policy stresses prevention, the published targets are not geared towards evaluation of effective prevention. There is a gap between the rhetoric of prevention and an actuality of 'targeting those in most need'.

Better coordination of services

This is a major theme, concerning the 'Berlin Wall' between health and social care. The White Paper proposes a "new statutory duty of partnership" (DoH, 1998, p 100) and the establishment of Primary Care Groups (PCGs) that will work closely with social services. Practice development is rapidly overtaking these proposals. Most PCGs have now developed into Primary Care Trusts (PCTs), and social workers will move from social services into these trusts by April 2003. The imperative for children and family services to work together better dates back as far as the Maria Colwell Inquiry (DHSS, 1974). The response again has been an organisational one, with the likely outcome that child protection services will be integrated within other local authority departments such as education.

There is little argument about the frustration involved in the continuing failures of health and social care staff (and others, particularly in child protection and youth justice) to work together. There is a long history of child death inquiry reports recording how blocks to cooperation between agencies contributed to failure to protect children (for example, Blom-Cooper, 1985, 1987). A number of factors seem to contribute to these problems. First, good practice in social care is greatly compromised where there are stretched resources. Second, the different value bases of collaborating professionals make it hard to cooperate. This is notable in health and social care where the medical model of disability and illness dominates health workers' views of patient needs and is contrasted with social care adherence to the social model. I think this is often a caricature of difference rather than actuality; many health workers – GPs and nursing staff – are influenced by a more holistic assessment of patient needs, and not all social workers are exempt from traditional professional approaches to determining need (Baldwin, 2000). Service user organisations are concerned that the switch to PCTs may result in a dilution of the preferred holistic approach that social workers are trained to embrace (CCETSW, 1995). Finally, the failure of health and social care staff to cooperate has habitually resulted in organisational responses. That reorganisation has failed to persuade professional groups to collaborate effectively would suggest that policy implementation should follow a participative approach rather than the imposition of policy imperatives (Baldwin, 2000).

General commentary on the White Paper

While the aims of the White Paper are clearly laid out, there are also some New Labour themes reflected more implicitly in its approach. The main one is decentralisation of responsibility, and centralisation of rules, regulations and regulatory authority (Langan, 2000). With this system, the government can say that it has met its aims in the White Paper. It has stated the problem, laid down the standards, specified the training necessary to improve practice, noted the organisational changes that will occur, and established the principle of service user involvement in social care services. The government has developed a system for identifying performance in comparison to targets, which is explored in the next section. In September 2001, the government published its first list of failing NHS Trusts. This will be the future for social services departments, assuming they have a future.

Personal Social Services Performance Assessment Framework (PSSPAF)

The PSSPAF (www.doh.gov.uk/paf/) is part of Best Value developments intended to bring improvements across all local authority services. This PSSPAF has to be implemented by social services departments, on pain of naming and shaming through single and joint reviews by the Audit Commission and the Social Services Inspectorate (SSI). The PSSPAF for social care is linked to the *Modernising social services* agenda, so that the intentions for change, development and improvement listed in the White Paper can be tracked through the success of social services departments in meeting their obligations under the PSSPAF. This is how it will happen:

- performance indicators will be centrally determined by the Department of Health;
- data will be collected locally;
- performance will be evaluated through SSI or joint review with the Audit Commission;
- monitoring of performance will take place through SSI Social Care Regions.

There is a plethora of Performance Indicators (PIs) in nine separate modules of the PSSPAF. Module 6, which is a list of 'National Targets' (www.doh.gov.uk/

paf/) is the list I will use to provide an illustration of the targets upon which government wishes its social care policy to be evaluated.

The following are an illustration of the targets social services departments are required to meet:

- Stability of placements of looked-after children (no more than 16% should have three or more placements by April 2001).
- Educational qualifications of looked-after children (at least 50% of care leavers over 16 should have one or more GCSE by 2003).
- Reregistrations on the child protection register (reduce proportion of reregistrations by 10% by 2002).
- Reviews of child protection cases (100% to be carried out).
- Emergency admissions of older people (promote independence by reducing emergency admissions over five years).
- Emergency psychiatric readmissions (similar target).
- Percentage of people receiving a statement of their needs and how they will be met (councils to set annual targets for improvement). (www.doh.gov.uk/paf/)

To evaluate whether these performance criteria have been met, we must look at the data collected so far by the SSI. A number of difficulties emerge. First, the latest statistics on the PAF from the Department of Health website (2000) (www.doh.gov.uk/paf/) reveal substantial gaps, making it difficult to evaluate overall performance. Second, most statistics collected so far are those most easily quantifiable (number of assessments done and so on). Where indicators concern the quality of service and user satisfaction or relate to equality issues (for example, racial equality), the SSI chart indicates 'no data collected' (www.doh.gov.uk/paf/). The rationale for PIs seems helpful, but, because of the lack of data, these remain to be tested.

The Department of Health website is, then, an unreliable source for evaluation. The Monitoring Report of the Social Care Regions Autumn 2000 (SSI, 2001) provides a little more analysis of progress in some target areas. The report puts the onus to deliver on social services departments, and states that only "between a third and a half of councils are making significant progress towards meeting DH targets" (SSI, 2001). 'Steady progress' on priority objectives is reported in children's services, although issues such as staff and carer recruitment, 'managing change simultaneously on many fronts' and dependence on the actions of other organisations, are cited as problems that are holding up the pace of change (SSI, 2001, p 3). As far as services for adults are concerned, "the agenda for promoting independence is moving forward steadily" (SSI, 2001, p 3), although there are problems, such as regional variation, poor take-up of Direct Payments by older people, and "continuing difficulty in resourcing improvements, especially at the interface with health services" (SSI, 2001, p 3).

Looking specifically at the national targets quoted above, this document only provides some information, including:

- *Reducing number of looked-after children with three or more placements.* Nineteen councils forecast that they will not meet the target by the end of March 2001.
- *Reducing reregistrations to the child protection registers.* The report indicates that "councils have succeeded in reversing the rising trend" (SSI, 2001, p 6). Ninety-five per cent of councils expect to meet the target by the due date.
- Three quarters of councils will *review at least 95% of child protection cases* (from a very low base) in 2000/01.
- Only 61% of councils expect to meet the target for *educational qualifications for looked-after children* by the due date.
- *Emergency admissions to residential care* are not looked at, although the picture more generally in this area is stated as patchy, geographically.
- There are no details of *emergency psychiatric admissions*.
- There are no details relating to the target on *people receiving statements of assessed need.* (SSI, 2001)

The PAF is a monumental statistical exercise. As yet, outcome statistics are thin, and do not allow valid evaluation, although presumably the process will gather pace and relevance. Evaluation is also not simple because figures relate to the performance of social services departments. The inspection system is designed to locate the source of failure to meet targets, thus deflecting responsibility away from government. In addition, lack of consistency in the provision of data from the various sources within the Department of Health makes it hard to compare like with like. New Labour claims to pursue 'joined-up' government, but the overwhelming detail of information for implementation makes it almost impossible to match targets with outcomes.

These concerns have not stopped the government using outcome measures to make political points. In October 2000, just months before the election, Health Secretary Alan Milburn and the Health Minister John Hutton provided press releases using this information. John Hutton used evidence of improved social care performance to demonstrate government meeting targets. Alan Milburn used evidence of poor performance to help emphasise a £284 million package to improve children's services. We are left pondering whether the indicators are positive or negative.

It remains to be seen whether the PAF will have any worth in providing evidence of service quality. For example, it will start to have real worth as an evaluative tool when it show links between resources and outcomes. Lack of resources is quoted by social services department returns (SSI, 2001) as a principle factor in the failure to reach targets. This raises a question about how reasonable the government's targets are. The PAF will also need to address other needs from the White Paper – for example, a properly trained workforce, empowerment of people, choice, protection – not indicated in the current PAF. These are longer-term objectives requiring time to bed in before full analysis. As the SSI report suggests, social services departments are going to have to learn quickly skills in "managing change simultaneously on many fronts" (SSI, 2001, p 3).

Where social services departments are proving effective is in meeting targets for the reduction of Public Service Agreements (the spending plans for local authorities). The report notes that, for the second year running, it is expected that the PSA efficiency target of 2% will be met or exceeded (SSI, 2001, p 3). These 'efficiency targets' are about the only ones being achieved by social services departments.

The government has claimed that its targets for policy implementation are SMART (specific, measurable, achievable, relevant and timed). On the basis of the above analysis of available data, the targets are not 'SMART'. Specificity is marred by failure to follow targets through from policy to practice outcome. Targets follow from the White Paper to the PAF with a degree of specificity but get lost in translation to SSI reports, which respond more to the concerns of implementation at organisational level and are not always congruent with the original target. Some targets are measurable and achievable, but dubious in relevance. For example, social services departments can count the numbers of assessments completed, or can reduce the numbers of reregistrations to child protection registers, so these targets are measurable. The link between them and the quality standards proposed by the White Paper is a much more sophisticated task than counting assessments and reviews allows. Other quantifiable targets, such as the rate of review of child protection cases, or packages of care for older people, are more helpful. They are more relevant to the unfolding of service development over time, and are related to quality of practice. For the social justice targets (for example, racial equality), the data is not yet available, so judgement is reserved.

Extrinsic evaluation

To make a comprehensive evaluation of the New Labour policy on social care, it is important to look not only at the targets set for itself, but also at other perspectives on social care developments. I will consider a number of wider issues.

Can New Labour's approach to social care be characterised as continuity or change? Is the government proposing a 'modern' social service?

The key change for social care under the Conservative government was establishment of the internal market following implementation of the 1990 NHS and Community Care Act. Social services departments have become residual authorities for social care, commissioning and regulating services from the private and voluntary sectors. This has continued under New Labour, with the task of privatisation largely complete by 1997 (Player and Pollock, 2001). New Labour's use of the word 'modernising' in the White Paper is a central part of New Labour discourse (Newman, 2000), but does it indicate a break with the past?

Compulsory Competitive Tendering (CCT) has been replaced by Best Value (see Chapter Three of this volume), indicating a change from CCT's reliance on the economic test to determine services (Mitchell, 2000). Best Value requires the involvement of service users in service planning and the consideration of equality issues. Other changes include the notion of partnership reflecting a diminishing belief that only business-led organisations can provide efficiency (Geddes and Martin, 2000). Another intention of Conservative reforms was to facilitate the matching of need to the service of choice for the individual consumer within a welfare market. The service user movement has successfully transposed this into a social justice approach to social care service provision. New Labour in government has to a degree gone along with this view. The White Paper emphasises user control (DoH, 1998) and the 1999 Disability Rights Commission Act provides a statutory body to oversee disability rights. These values for social care policy ends are reflected in the policy means of performance indicators, but setting overarching values indicates a governance stream for policy which is a shift from the Conservative welfare market approach. New Labour has specified its policy ends, but it is too early to tell whether it has moved beyond 'symbolic politics' and provided the policy means to meet objectives.

Benchmarks that imply a connection with social care

Depending on the way in which social care is conceptualised, commitments from other parts of the Manifesto will have an impact on meeting 'social care' pledges. These include:

- *Anti-poverty pledges.* Many of the problems for users of social care services are directly related to their poverty (for example, poor health), so we should look at the New Labour pledges to reduce child poverty and increase pensioners' incomes. The government has introduced the National Minimum Wage as pledged (Manifesto Commitment 46), and claims that it has made a difference to incomes at the bottom end are supported (Toynbee and Walker, 2001). Commitments to 'protect the basic state pension' (94) and provide 'help for the poorest pensioners' (95) proved rocky in the first term and most pensioner organisations would still argue that the government has not done enough, by failing to reestablish the link between pensions and earnings (Age Concern, 2001). Others have argued that these policy initiatives are so closely linked with the work ethic that they exclude old, young and disabled people who cannot engage within the employment market (Levitas, 1998; Drake, 2000). Whether it is carrot or stick, the New Labour approach to poverty is at odds with Old Labour values of protecting those on low incomes.
- *Social justice pledges (disability, anti-racism).* Most social care service users experience discrimination. Although the legal definition of a disabled person

medicalises the term, the word disabled is commonly employed in social care circles to conceptualise the marginalisation of individuals who have physical or learning difficulties from mainstream social processes (Morris, 1991; Oliver, 1996). This definition is implicit in the government commitment to introduce 'comprehensive civil rights for disabled people' (147), a pledge that has been partially met by the introduction of the Disability Rights Commission.

There is still a weight of evidence (Wall, 1999) that black service users are more likely to experience compulsory detention in psychiatric hospitals and less likely to receive therapeutic services. New Labour has produced race equality criteria within Best Value indicators, and this has been backed by the enactment of the Race Relations (Amendment) Act (2000). There is, however, some ambivalence. In race relations, the government has introduced the race equality imperative, but still speaks racist rhetoric in the asylum seeker debate (Jordan, 2000).

Contested knowledge and social care practice

Evaluation of government policy depends partly on our view of social care. We need to look at New Labour's intentions for social care and evaluate these against the different ways social care has been conceptualised. I will choose social work as an illustrative example, as it has been theorised extensively.

Commentators on the nature of social work have characterised it as a contested arena (Payne, 1997). Payne conceptualises social work in a three-part model. In the reflective-therapeutic tradition, social work provides services to alleviate social problems but without challenging the status quo. The individual-reformist tradition is about meeting individual needs through improving services, but again without an interest in structural disadvantage (Pinker, 1984). The socialist-collectivist tradition responds to poverty and marginalisation created by capitalism, by challenging power structures that recreate oppression (Brake and Bailey, 1980).

How does the New Labour approach to social care compare to this model? New Labour policy on social care reveals a rhetoric of social justice, but a social control ethos as well. *Modernising social services* (DoH, 1998) speaks the discourse of service user empowerment, for instance through its Better Government for Older People initiative, which aims to give older people a say in service delivery (DoH, 1998). It is less clear about who deserves this. New Labour says little about greater choice and control for social care service users who are mentally ill, young offenders or child abusers. This ambivalence is reflected in social work traditions, which are similarly unclear about the limits of empowerment and choice.

New Labour is keen to pursue policies that 'work'. The debate about what works is influential within social care (Hudson, 2000; Jordan, 2000), but there are two contrasting versions of what counts as evidence. The Centre for Evidence

Based Social Services (CEBSS) at Exeter University (Sheldon and Chilvers, 2000) has conceptualised evidence as meaning knowledge produced through natural scientific methods, most notably the 'gold standard' of randomised control trials (Macdonald, 2000). This approach has favoured rationalist methods for individual change such as cognitive behaviourist practice. On the other side of the argument, we have a reflective, pragmatic and contingent approach to social care suggesting development of practice through cooperative, inclusive methods, involving critical evaluation, and developed through reflection on experience, rather than through the laboratory techniques of the CEBSS approach. Using this contrast to make some extrinsic evaluation of the kind of approach that best describes social care under New Labour, we can conclude that it is the scientific method rather than critical reflection. Government rhetoric is strong on user participation and there are outcome indicators that relate to this value. In general, however, the technicality of the PSSPAF outcome regime reflects a managerialist ethos (Langan, 2000) that is rationalist in its design and expectation, in much the same way as the CEBSS evidence-based approach. The result is policy targets that are less SMART (specific, measurable, achievable, relevant, timed) than contradictory, reactive, unclear, disconnected and excessive.

Best Value and technical solutions

The government claims that Best Value will deliver better services through scrutiny of outcome measures, allowing targeting of identified problem areas. Resources will then be focused on meeting needs that are prioritised through the system as a whole. There is a seductive logic to this rationalist approach (Clarke et al, 2000). There are also political gains, given that certainty is always easier to sell than the lack of clarity that characterises the 'swampy lowlands' of social care (Schon, 1984). It is too soon to judge Best Value, but the concern is that efficiency and economy imperatives will supersede those of equity and effectiveness, simply because they are easier to measure.

Best Value's claim that it can deliver more service user-centred services is to be welcomed, given the long experience of social care as something done to people, sometimes with grave consequences for children (Waterhouse, 2000) or people with learning difficulties (Means and Smith, 1998) in public care. The problem for New Labour is that it will take time to change organisations built on the power base of 'technicist' professional expertise and managerial resource control (Clarke et al, 2000). PCTs, for example, will combine staff groups wielding considerable professional power, and to turn them into service user-centred organisations will require 'building greater capacity for learning', and a 'commitment to innovation and learning' (Martin, 2000). The incremental approach of the learning organisation to policy implementation can be seen in stark opposition to New Labour's punitive, top-down, outcome-orientated approach. We may admire the policy ends, but there is a big question about whether they have developed the policy means to achieve them (Jordan, 2000).

Social care developments in the second term

It is possible now to be a little clearer about New Labour's policy intentions for social care. What was implicit is now explicit, although it is still the case that organisational change often outstrips policy intentions. The quality framework still needs time before it can be evaluated as an effective tool for service development. The principle of central standards and regulation and local responsibility for delivery is now well established.

Organisational change from separate health and social care agencies to new organisations built on an ethos of interprofessional care is also well established. Initiatives such as the Single Assessment Process give clear guidance on the practices required to ensure better working across professional divides. Putting professional staff into the same organisations should not, in my mind, necessarily determine better collaborative practice. Again, however, the framework is established and it is up to the new organisations to demonstrate that they are delivering.

The regulatory framework for social care staff is emerging as I write, with new practice guidelines being published and regional workshops to consult on the implications springing up around the country. What is expected, therefore, of both organisations and the staff they employ, has never been clearer. New Labour is very upbeat about the new resources it has put into services covering all policy areas. Social care, however, continues to play Cinderella to more politically sensitive policy areas such as health. If the new organisations encompassing health and social care indicate the symbiotic nature of the two policy areas, then it should also be clear that the effectiveness of the one will depend on the adequate funding of the other.

Conclusions

The development of social care under the New Labour government is a good example of top-down policy implementation (Hill, 1997). So why has the government instituted these changes, and what does it tell us about them? One argument is that government policy on social care has been largely reactive. Moral panics associated with isolated murders by people diagnosed with schizophrenia or personality disorders hitting the front page of the tabloids has been a powerful incentive to government action. Reaction to the bed-blocking that is fouling up NHS systems as a result of the slowness (or is it lack of resources?) of social services departments in assessing the needs of people in hospital resulted in Frank Dobson referring to the 'Berlin Wall' between health and social services departments.

It is also of note that New Labour has a philosophical ambivalence about individualism and community. Identifying the need for social justice within geographical communities or communities of need is part of New Labour rhetoric and commitment (Manifesto Commitment 137). This is the bridging that the third way is supposed to achieve. Targets for delivery of social care, however, are couched in individual terms. Interestingly, social work has exactly the same ambivalence about individuals and community within its traditions. This ambivalence will need to be worked through. With mental health services now slipping out of social services departments into PCTs where the individual medical model associated with psychiatry will be ascendant, the community-orientated, holistic aspects of social care may become subsumed. In a similar way, New Labour's ambivalence between social justice and social control mirrors the social work legacy of tension between care and control. This is another social care tension needing to be managed.

Finally there is the New Labour obsession with 'modernising', reflected in the White Paper. I think this can be conceptualised as an obsession with 'modernism', a belief that rationality is the key to success in many areas of policy. It is illustrated in relation to business acumen through the threats of further privatisation of health and social care services. It is reflected within policy implementation, with Best Value demonstrating top-down rationalist expectations. It can also be found with the certainties expected by scientific managerialism, and the search for methods of intervention that 'work' in social care research and practice (for example, evidence-based social servics and SCIE).

There is plenty to hearten us within New Labour rhetoric on social justice, but it is going to have to learn that its method for implementation is unlikely to achieve the success it expects, and certainly not within the time scales it demands (Jordan, 2000). When the government realises this, I suspect it will have to return to some of the best of social work and social care in terms of values, knowledge, practice and organisation for direction. Service-user orientation requires structural disadvantage to be addressed. This is a central value for contemporary social work. Responding to service users' myriad needs requires services built on a contingent rather than fixed and established knowledge base, critically reflective and creative practices and a learning style of organisation (Baldwin, 2000). Such an approach is being demonstrated already in some pockets of social care organisation and practice. It will be necessary to demonstrate over time how successful these can be before we can pass any lasting judgement on New Labour's social care policy.

References

Age Concern (2001) *Dignity, security, opportunity: The Age Concern Manifesto for the new parliament*, London: Age Concern.

Ayres, M. (2000) *Cautions, court proceedings and sentencing: England and Wales 1999*, London: Home Office.

Baldwin, M. (2000) *Care management and community care: Social work discretion and the construction of policy*, Aldershot: Ashgate.

Blom-Cooper, L. (1985) *A child in trust: The report of the Panel of Inquiry into the circumstances surrounding the death of Jasmine Beckford*, London: Borough of Brent.

Blom–Cooper, L. (1987) *A child in mind: Protection of children in a responsible society. The report of the Commission of Inquiry into the circumstances surrounding the death of Kimberley Carlile*, London: Borough of Greenwich.

Brake, M. and Bailey, R. (eds) (1980) *Radical social work and practice*, London: Edward Arnold.

Brandon, M., Schofield, G. and Truder, L. (1998) *Social work with children*, Basingstoke: Palgrave.

Carlen, P. (1996) *Jigsaw: A political criminology of youth homelessness*, Buckingham: Open University Press.

CCETSW (Central Council for Education and Training in Social Work) (1995) *DipSW: Rules and requirements for the Diploma in Social Work*, Paper 30, (revised edition), London: CCETSW.

Clarke, J., Gewirtz, S. and McLaughlin, E. (eds) (2000) *New managerialism new welfare?*, London: Sage Publications.

Cochrane, A. (2000) 'Local government: managerialism and modernization', in J. Clarke, S. Gewirtz and E. McLaughlin (eds) *New managerialism new welfare?*, London: Sage Publications, pp 122-36.

Davies, H. (2000) *The Blackwell encyclopaedia of social work*, Oxford: Blackwell.

Davies, H., Nutley, S. and Smith, P. (eds) (2000) *What works? Evidence-based policy and practice in public services*, Bristol: The Policy Press.

DHSS (Department of Health and Social Security) (1974) *Report of the Committee of Inquiry into the care and supervision provided in relation to Maria Colwell*, London: HMSO.

DoH (Department of Health) (1989) *Community care in the next decade and beyond*, London: HMSO.

DoH (1998) *Modernising social services: Promoting independence, improving protection, raising standards*, London: The Stationery Office.

DoH (2000) *The NHS Plan: The government's response to the Royal Commission on Long-Term Care*, London: The Stationery Office.

DoH (2001a) *Statutory Instrument 2001 No 2874. The Children (Leaving Care) (England) Regulations August 2001*, London: The Stationery Office.

DoH (2001b) *Circular LAC (2001) 6 Annex: Better Care Higher Standards*, London: The Stationery Office.

Drake, R. (2000) 'Disabled people, New Labour, benefits and work', *Critical Social Policy*, vol 20, no 4, pp 421-39.

Fletcher, K. (1998) *Best Value social services*, Caerphilly: SSP Publications.

Geddes, M. and Martin, S. (2000) 'The policy and politics of BestValue: currents, crosscurrents and undercurrents in the new regime', *Policy & Politics*, vol 28, no 3, pp 379-95.

Hayden, C., Goddard, J., Gorin, S. and Van Der Spek, N. (1999) *State child care: Looking after children?*, London: Jessica Kingsley.

Hill, M. (ed) (1997) *The policy process: A reader* (2nd edn), Hemel Hempstead: Prentice-Hall.

Hill, M. (ed) (2000) *Local authority social services: An introduction*, Oxford: Blackwell.

Hudson, B. (ed) (2000) *The changing role of social care*, London: Jessica Kingsley.

Johnson, N. (1999) 'The personal social services and community care', in M. Powell (ed) *New Labour, new welfare state?: The 'third way' in British social policy*, Bristol: The Policy Press, pp 77-100.

Jordan, B. (2000) *Social work and the third way: Tough love as social policy*, London: Sage Publications.

Labour Party (1997) *New Labour because Britain deserves better (1997 General Election Manifesto)*, London: Labour Party.

Langan, M. (2000) 'Social services: managing the third way', in J. Clarke, S. Gewirtz and E. McLaughlin (eds) *New managerialism new welfare?*, London: Sage Publications, pp 152-68.

Levitas, R. (1998) *The inclusive society? Social inclusion and New Labour*, Basingstoke: Macmillan.

Macdonald, G. (2000) 'Social care: rhetoric and reality', in H. Davies, S. Nutley and P. Smith (eds) *What works?: Evidence-based policy and practice in public services*, Bristol: The Policy Press, pp 117-40.

Martin, S. (2000) 'Implementing "BestValue": local public services in transition', *Public Administration*, vol 78, no 1, pp 209-27.

McLaughlin, E. and Muncie, J. (2000) 'The criminal justice system: New Labour's new partnerships', in J. Clarke, S. Gewirtz and E. McLaughlin (eds) *New managerialism new welfare?*, London: Sage Publications, pp 169-85.

Means, R. and Smith, R. (1998) *Community care: Policy and practice* (2nd edn), Basingstoke: Macmillan.

Mitchell, S. (2000) 'Modernising social services: The management challenge of the 1998 *Social services* White Paper', in M. Hill (ed) *Local authority social services: An introduction*, Oxford: Blackwell, pp 179-201.

Morris, J. (1991) *Pride against prejudice: Transforming attitudes to disability*, London: The Women's Press.

Newman, J. (2000) 'Beyond the New Public Management? Modernizing public services', in J. Clarke, S. Gewirtz and E. McLaughlin (eds) *New managerialism, new welfare?*, London: Sage Publications, pp 45-61.

Oliver, M. (1996) *Understanding disability: From theory to practice*, Basingstoke: Macmillan.

Parton, N. and O'Byrne, P. (2000) *Constructive social work: Towards a new practice*, Basingstoke: Palgrave.

Payne, M. (1997) *Modern social work theory* (2nd edn), Basingstoke: Macmillan.

Pinker, R. (1984) 'The threats to professional standards in social work education', *Issues in Social Work Education*, vol 4, no 1, pp 5-15.

Player, S. and Pollock, A. (2001) 'Long term care: from public responsibility to private good', *Critical Social Policy*, vol 21, no 2, pp 231-55.

Powell, M. (ed) (1999) *New Labour, new welfare state? The 'third way' and British social policy*, Bristol: The Policy Press.

Schon (1984) *The reflective practitioner: How professionals think in action*, New York, NY: Basic Books.

Sheldon, B. and Chilvers, T. (2000) *Evidence-based social care: A study of prospects and problems*, Lyme Regis: Russell House.

SSI (Social Services Inspectorate) (2001) *Social care regions: Monitoring Report Autumn 2000*, London: The Stationery Office.

Stone, N. (1998) 'Children and youth justice', in M. Brandon, G. Schofield and Truder, *Social work with children*, Basingstoke: Palgrave, pp 166-98.

Toynbee, P. and Walker, D. (2001) *Did things get better? An Audit of Labour's successes and failures*, Harmondsworth: Penguin.

Wall, S. (1999) *A systematic review of the Mental Health Act (1983)*, London: The Stationery Office.

Waterhouse, R. (2000) *Lost in care: Report of the Tribunal of Inquiry into the abuse of children in care in the former county council areas of Gwynedd and Clwyd since 1974*, London: The Stationery Office.

Youth Justice Board (2001) *Annual Review: Delivering change in the youth justice system*, London: Youth Justice Board.

TEN

New Labour and the redefinition of social security

Martin Hewitt

Introduction

This chapter examines social security since 1997, focusing on developments in the latter half of the first term of the New Labour government and the start of its second term[1]. Although the story begins in 1997-98 when new policies were being proposed, an important stage was reached in the last two years of government when the first raft of policies were being implemented. The story, or rather this particular chapter in the story, concludes with the first year of the 2001 government when further policies were implemented and, of greater interest, earlier policies redefined. In terms of policy implementation, the chapter addresses the government's attempt to pursue a radical agenda for welfare that requires constant short-term tinkering and reassessment in order to achieve longer-term goals.

More specifically, this chapter focuses on three areas of the government's reform agenda that, it will be argued, have contributed most to New Labour's recasting of social security, namely welfare-to-work, pensions provision and, most recently, asset-based welfare. Other programmes associated with social security, such as family policy, are not discussed for reasons of space (see Chapter Five; Dean, 2002). These represent the essential elements of a welfare philosophy based on the new trinity of work, welfare and assets, by which New Labour is redefining welfare and citizenship. The good citizen is someone who works for a living (thereby making few or no claims on social security), saves a portion of their earnings, and uses their savings to contribute substantially to their own and their family's future welfare. This trinity develops the message of New Labour's first term: from 'work for those who can, security for those who cannot' (DSS, 1998a, p iii) to *savings for those who can, security for those who cannot.* This key message was prefigured in the pension Green Paper (DSS, 1998b, p 23) and the pensions credit White Paper (DSS, 2000b, p 15) and adumbrated in its proposals for asset-based welfare (HM Treasury, 2001a, p 1). The practice of saving is being elevated from a private aspiration of the prudent individual to a core duty of the good citizen supported by government, such that "those who can save have a responsibility to do so" and the "focus of the government's saving policy should be to encourage individuals to develop a regular saving habit" (DSS, 1998b, p 29; HM Treasury, 2001a, p 9). It represents part of New Labour's new definition of the welfare rights and responsibilities of citizen and state.

Following the introduction, the chapter comprises three parts. First, it examines policies between 1997 and 2001 for unemployed people, lone parents, disabled people and retired people. In examining provisions for these groups, the approach is to describe the aims, mechanisms and incentives of each provision. Secondly, it seeks, where possible, to assess what was achieved during the first term, drawing on the distinction described in Chapter One of this volume between intrinsic and extrinsic evaluation. In addition, this section follows the development of first-term policies into the second term. In giving more attention in this section to pension provision for retired people, it seeks to gauge some of the longer-term trends in social security policy, in particular the role of personal financial planning in promoting greater personal independence through the acquisition of private assets. Between 1997 and 2001, the government adopted a policy mind-set that divided individuals into two broad groups according to whether they work or receive welfare. A key question, therefore, must be whether groups in poverty and social exclusion are supported by this either/or classification, or whether some fall through the net of work activation policies only to end up in continuing exclusion. Developing this last thought, the third part of the chapter enters into a more speculative discussion of asset-based welfare, arguing that it is integral to the broad sweep of New Labour's social security reforms. However, this development is also the most problematic as to whether it can deliver outcomes during the second term and whether it will be accepted beyond this term as a serious social policy – rather than an aspect of financial regulation and consumerism.

Social security is something of a paradox for the New Labour government. It has been the prime focus of New Labour's welfare reform agenda; yet, unlike the reform programmes for health and education whose budgets have grown, the large social security budget has been subject to strict control. Social security spending in 1998/99 stood at £95.6 billion, which was 11.2 % of gross domestic product (GDP) and 28.9% of public spending, which the government forecast to rise to £98 billion in 2001/02 (DSS, 2000a, pp 5, 15). This moderate increase is due to economic stability as much as budgetary control. Nonetheless, social security reform has been shaped by the government's determination to limit expenditure as well as by the intrinsic benefits of reform. Within these budget constraints, the government has set itself several goals with material consequences for certain groups. Most significantly, it pledged in 2000 to halve the number of children in poverty by 2010 and abolish child poverty outright by 2020 (see Chapter Five). To this Gordon Brown has added pensioner poverty. Further, the 1997 New Labour Manifesto pledged to get 250,000 young unemployed off benefit and into work. The precise significance of these goals lies in the means for achieving them. Traditionally, social security was an area of public policy in which cash in the form of tax and NI contributions was transferred from one sector of the population to another as benefit. Now the stress on the individual's duty to work and save means that social security is extending its base and moving onto the new territory of markets for waged labour and personal finance. Nonetheless, the government still wishes to preserve the traditional role of social security of guaranteeing minimum security for those who cannot work. However, the definition of who cannot work has narrowed significantly, and the elements of provision have shifted from universal benefits based on NI contributions and taxation to means-tested and more targeted provision. While social security remains a matter of state benefits in cash, these shifts are also being sought by non-financial means. These involve redefining the subject of welfare and the scope of welfare in moral terms, especially by a structure of incentives and compliance that exhorts individuals to work and save for retirement rather than rely solely on government for support – all under the rubric of 'welfare-to-work', 'active welfare' and 'social inclusion'. Indeed, it is debatable whether some of the measures discussed in this chapter under social security – especially work activation and asset-based welfare – are social security in the traditional sense.

Several observers have noted that New Labour appears to be deflecting attention from the goal of achieving greater material redistribution and equality to the less tangible outcomes of greater 'social inclusion' (Levitas, 1998; Lister, 1998). However, its own penchant for performance measurement requires that the goals of inclusion are translated into operational and tangible measurements. In addition to the goal of ending child and pensioner poverty, the government has introduced 32 targets published in its first annual poverty report (DSS, 1999). However 'moral' the content of the government's anti-poverty agenda for 'social inclusion', the very concept itself must inevitably be turned back into operational and empirical terms by which the success of government reforms is measured. In view of its pledges on poverty and its standards for measuring achievement, Lister argues that "Whether the Government likes it or not, all this redirects the focus more sharply back onto income levels" (2001, p 66). In the conceptual cycle that passes from material problems to moral exhortations and finally to performance standards, a complex process of redefinition takes place in the process of transforming welfare provisions. Harker (2000), for example, suggests that the 32 targets may have little to do with traditional concepts of poverty and anti-poverty measures, and more to do with the details of programme design. In the minutiae of the implementation process, big picture goals are transformed into details on what is achievable given the resources available and the problems presented. The paradox opened up by investing welfare with new tasks and a new identity, but few additional resources, is to some extent managed, if not resolved, by redefining the routine tasks of formulating, measuring and implementing targets. The result can be more fundamental than merely adding new performance indicators to the existing inventory. The question is whether, in the *spiral of redefinition* that unfolds as means are redefined in terms of ends, and ends are imperceptibly transformed under a welter of practicalities, a transformed programme of social security provisions with a new identity and moral purpose can be forged. Alternatively, does evolution by piecemeal tinkering, as new measures are bolted on to old, lead to a loss of purpose and failure to achieve?

Social security and welfare-to-work 1997-2001

Whatever new targets for combating poverty and exclusion are devised, traditional estimates of poverty have remained substantially unchanged since the mid-1990s. The latest *Households Below Average Income* report (DWP, 2001) shows very small changes in the number of low-income groups between 1996/ 97 and 1999/2000. The number of children below the poverty line fell by only 200,000 to 4.3 million and the number of poor pensioners remained at 2.6 million. Overall, households on less than half-average equivalised income fell only slightly from 14.1 to 14 million. Of course, the new provisions for poverty take several years to be implemented, to affect family income, and then to be recorded in official data (Hills, 2000). The Institute for Fiscal Studies (IFS) has sought to short-circuit this problem by projecting to 2000 the impact on household income of fiscal policies announced since 1997, such as Working Families' Tax Credit (WFTC) and pensioners' Minimum Income Guarantee (MIG). These show that the post-tax income of average households in the bottom decile is 8.8% higher and that the other deciles gain proportionately less on average with the richest 30% of households experiencing falls (Myke, 2000, p 2). However, these calculations assume a full 100% take-up of means-tested benefits and WFTC and other assumptions leading to optimistic conclusions (Clark et al, 2001). On these extrinsic criteria, the debate continues. However, intrinsic criteria, according to how they are defined, suggest that some targets have been achieved.

The chapter now summarises the new policies of the government's first term for the four target groups. In addition, it considers how they are being developed in the first part of the second term.

Unemployed people

The new work-activation measures for different groups of unemployed people entail New Deals, tax credits and means-tested support. In addition, other measures provide support for particular groups, including childcare support through the National Childcare Strategy, the National Minimum Wage (NMW) and area-based measures such as Employment Zones and Sure Start. The first national tranche of six New Deals (NDs) was introduced between 1998 and 1999 to steer different non-employed groups through various gateways into the labour market. Each gateway provides a variety of 'carrot and stick' measures. All, bar the New Deal for Partners of the Unemployed (NDPU), provide a personal adviser and, with few exceptions, no one is allowed to claim benefits without receiving employment advice. Attached to the right to welfare is the minimum condition of considering employment. Further, the New Deals for Young People (NDYP) and for Long-Term Unemployed (NDLTU) (renamed New Deal 25+ in April 2001) contain measures including reduced benefits compelling individuals not only to receive advice, but also to participate in job search and training. The other four NDs – for Lone Parents (NDLP), Partners of the Unemployed, Disabled People (NDDP) and People Aged 50+ – require attendance at an interview with a personal adviser. McLaughlin et al echo a shared view that the New Deals are a "systematic experiment of significant proportions" (2000, p 163).

In 1999 the government introduced a range of tax credits for working families (WFTC), childcare (CTC) and disabled persons (DPTC) administered by the Inland Revenue. These provide work-based benefits paid by the employer as a supplement to wages. They are also paid at a higher rate than means-tested, out-of-work benefits, such as Income Support and the income-based Jobseeker's Allowance, as incentives to 'make work pay'. In replacing the Family Credit for working families, the WFTC offers higher income entitlement and a less steep taper for withdrawing WFTC as earnings increase, so slightly lessening the disincentives of high marginal rates of taxation associated with means testing. However, tax credits must be claimed, as are most means-tested benefits, and the level of benefit is determined by the size of the recipient's income up to a threshold.

By 2003, the government will have introduced some important modifications to tax credits that affect the separate payment of benefits to children and adults. First, the Children's Tax Credit, and the child rates for WFTC, Income Support, Jobseeker's Allowance, Incapacity Benefit, will be combined into an integrated Child Credit. The benefit rates for children in non-working households, presently paid through Income Support and income-related Jobseeker's Allowance, will be paid at the same high rate for all children whatever age – an 80% increase from 1997 to 2001 (Lister, 2001). Second, a new Employment Tax Credit will replace the adult elements of WFTC and DPTC and extend tax credits to single persons and childless couples in low-paid work. This rationalisation could provide further protection for child benefits in the government's commitment to end child poverty, while paving the way for further work compliance measures for adult recipients (Howard, 2000).

When the NDs were introduced, it was possible to distinguish between measures supporting the non-employed in reaching better informed choices about seeking and maintaining work and measures penalising them for rejecting work – that is, 'carrot and stick' measures. With more recent developments, this distinction is no longer so clear cut. In 2001, for example, the government replaced the different ND gateways with the single 'ONE' gateway through which all claimants must now pass (now succeeded by Job Centre Plus). This extends the machinery for 'advising' the non-employed, so placing additional requirements on other groups to attend interviews with personal advisers. It also paves the way for subjecting different groups to a regime that is increasingly the same for all. If this trend were to continue, its common features would tend to blur the distinction between carrot and stick measures. As suggested above, the rationalisation of tax credits in 2003 to provide a single tax credit for working adults fits with the unification of the ND.

In sum, the overall strategy of the ND, tax credits and the childcare strategy share in common a supply-sided approach to the labour market, targeted at the abilities of the non-employed rather than at job creation measures that increase the employer's demand for labour. Labour demand is left largely to market forces.

Lone parents

New Labour's approach to the problem of low income among lone parents is essentially one of work activation, as applied to the unemployed generally, using the financial incentives provided by the WFTC, the encouragement of ND personal advisers and childcare support. Although participation in the NDLP remains voluntary, the government has resolved to step up the compliance procedures applying to lone parents. The new, single, work-focused gateway uses mandatory annual 'work-focused' interviews for lone parents, and local officers can exercise discretion when deciding whether parents with children under school age can defer interviews (Gray, 2001). In the longer term, the 1999 Welfare Reform and Pension (WRP) Act makes provision for 'availability for work' requirements to be extended to all claimants at some future time, including lone parents and disabled people.

The shifting carrot and stick regime of the ND must be seen against the cash incentives (carrots) of tax credits. The Treasury anticipated that the WFTC would reach 50% more families than were covered by Family Credit in 1997 (McLaughlin et al, 2001, p 164). This target was achieved by November 2000, with numbers of lone parents receiving WFTC up 71% (*Working Brief*, 2001). The government expected the WFTC to provide an incentive for lone parents to enter the labour market (see Gray, 2001; Rake, 2001). However, McLaughlin et al suggest that there has been a fall in the number of lone parents claiming relative to the growing numbers of lone parents (2001, p 165). The decline in lone parent claimants is seen as caused by the greater impact of means-test disincentives on women, in particular the steep housing benefit taper and the loss of other means-tested benefits because WFTC is treated as income (McLaughlin et al, 2001, pp 166-7).

In encountering the limitations of the supply-sided approach of the ND, lone parents are likely to face further costs and benefits. Lone parents encouraged to enter the labour market will typically have lower skills than those already working and so will compete for jobs with other ND groups (Rake, 2001, p 216). On the other hand, higher-skilled lone parents may be helped by childcare provisions. The key issue is whether new dealers are reskilled sufficiently so that they can continually upgrade their basic skills.

Disabled people

For disabled people, as for unemployed people and lone parents, the government is fashioning a disability programme based on the same key provisions: the ND, tax credits and means-tested benefits when work fails, with each provision contributing to a new structure of incentives. Again, the focal issue is whether these reforms are truly inclusive in providing new opportunities for work and more secure provisions for the disabled who cannot work; or whether there are groups whose circumstances have worsened and who now suffer greater social exclusion. We will examine three types of provision.

First, like the NDLP, the NDDP provides a range of supply-sided measures based on a deficit model of disability, addressing the shortcomings disabled workers must overcome rather than their need for appropriate jobs. These measures include an ND personal adviser, £50 per week 'jobmatch' payments for individuals moving into part-time work and £200 'jobfinders' grants for those starting work. As with the other two groups, the 1999 WRP Act now requires disabled people of working age, other than the house-bound, to attend job-search interviews at job centres.

Second, the Disabled Persons Tax Credit was introduced in 1999. Third, social security benefits for disabled people have undergone fundamental reform since the 1970s when governments began developing different benefits for specific purposes (Berthoud, 1998; Burchardt, 2000). For example, compensatory benefits recompense individuals who have suffered injury or sickness resulting from work or military service, such as industrial injuries benefits and war pensions. Earnings replacement benefits, such as incapacity benefit, replace some of the earnings individuals have lost in being unable to work. Extra-cost benefits, such as the Disability Living Allowance (DLA), meet some of the costs resulting from disability. Means-tested benefits, normally available for the poor in general, provide additional income up to a threshold, such as IS with specific premiums for certain groups such as the disabled. The government's reforms are substantially modifying the balance between these different disability benefits towards reliance on means-tested benefits.

Drake (2000) describes some of the measures aiming to strengthen links between work and benefits. This includes anti-fraud initiatives such as: the 1997 Fraud Act; benefit review programmes, such as the benefits integrity programme in 1998 for the DLA and attendance allowance; and investigations in 2000 into error and fraud in Incapacity Benefit (ICB). Finally, there have been measures to end or restrict access to benefits, such as the substantial changes affecting ICB. Assessment for ICB has changed from focusing on incapacity to assessing an individual's capacity for work, as part of an 'All Work Test', now called a 'Personal Capability Assessment' (Drake, 2000, p 430). ICB is now means tested for claimants with personal or occupational pensions. In addition, entitlement to ICB is restricted to those paying contributions for at least one year during the two years prior to their claim. It is estimated that the cost of ICB will fall from £8.1 billion in 1996/97 to £6.6 billion in 2001/02 (DSS, 2000a, p 78).

Retired people

New Labour's reform theme of helping individuals to take on more responsibility for their own welfare by earning enough for present contingencies and saving for future ones, including retirement, is seen in its approach to pension provision for the retired. The pensions Green Paper echoes New Labour's welfare–work distinction in its three principal aims:

- to ensure that everyone has an opportunity to achieve a decent income in retirement;
- to enable people to see the benefit of saving for retirement. In short 'the pension system should reward work. It should also reward savings';
- to provide security for those who cannot save. (DSS, 1998b, p 29; also 2000, p 15)

In addition, it expects that in future: ·

- fewer people will rely on means-tested benefits as more people are able to develop good second pensions from the state and private sectors (DSS, 1998b, p 31);
- people will save more for their retirement. A higher proportion of national income devoted to pensions will come from private, funded pensions. The ratio of state to private support will reverse from 60:40 to 40:60 (DSS, 1998b, p 31).

The increasing emphasis on saving for retirement is a further reflection of the welfare-to-work ethic of making work pay and encouraging individuals to take greater responsibility for their welfare; in short *working to save, saving for retirement*. These ideas are central to pensions policy. The incentive structure underlying the ND for jobseekers and the National Minimum Wage, with traditional welfare confined to people with disability and very elderly people, is being extended to the government's pensions reforms.

The government's plans for realising these aims comprise seven types of provision, which will not be fully implemented until 2003. First, the basic state pension (BSP) is provided for everyone who has normally paid compulsory national insurance contributions. Its value in 2002/03 was £75.50 a week for a single person and £120.70 for couples with a *full* contributions record. This is all that remains of Beveridge's legacy. Like the 1948 state pension, it continues to provide 'the foundation of pension provision for all pensioners' (DSS, 2000b, p 12), although its long-term decline against earnings substantially weakens this role. However, for the first time in 20 years, when the pension was uprated with prices, it rose in April 2001 by more than earnings (DSS, 2000b, p 6), although the government does not intend to repeat this on a regular basis. Prior to this increase, the BSP for a single pensioner stood at 18% of median full-time earnings in 2000/01. If price indexation is retained, the BSP will fall to about 9% of median earnings by 2050 (FIA, 2001a, p 6).

Second, the MIG was introduced in 1999 for all pensioners claiming means tested IS. In 2001 the government replaced the different age-related rates with a single MIG set at the higher rate. Consequently, the MIG rose by more than the increase in national average earnings between 1999/2000 and 2001/2002 and will be linked to earnings in future. However, it is subject to capital limits whereby from April 2001 there is no entitlement at £12,000. Nonetheless, the new Pension Credit introduced in 2003 will involve removing all capital limits (to be discussed below). The problems posed by means testing were recognised in the 1998 Green Paper, which saw that the MIG, in common with all means-tested benefits, acts as a disincentive to savings (DSS, 1998b, p 37). Hence, the pension credit seeks to reward savings up to a means-tested income ceiling (DSS, 2000b, p 13).

Third, since April 2001, stakeholder pensions are available to employers who do not offer occupational pensions and to individuals who can purchase portable and low-cost pensions limited to 1% of the value of the pension – a not unattractive prospect for pension companies who see the value accumulate over time. There are currently 46 approved schemes available from insurance companies, banks and trade union groups (HM Treasury, 2001a). However, by August 2001, only 90,000 employers had designated a stakeholder scheme for staff, with half a million in danger of breaching the rules for all employers to have designated schemes by October 2001 (Jenkins, 2001). A further problem is the case by which well-off earners can use stakeholders as tax-efficient vehicles by purchasing them for their non-working partners, children or grandchildren.

Fourth, in 2002, the state second pension (S2P) is being introduced for low-paid employees and some categories of carers and the disabled and will initially be earnings-related. This will enable low-paid employees earning between £3,500 and £9,500 to be treated as though they had earned £9,500 (in 1999/00 terms), and so build up a more adequate second pension than under the State Earnings Related Pension Scheme (SERPS), which the S2P will replace. The government intends that when stakeholder pensions are established, people on S2Ps will transfer gradually to stakeholder or other funded schemes, and the S2P revert to a flat-rate scheme for lower earners (DSS 1998b, p 40).

Fifth, the Pension Credit will be introduced in 2003. This has two elements: a 'guaranteed income top-up' to the level of the MIG and an additional element in the form of a 'savings credit', that is a "cash reward for pensioners on low and modest incomes for every pound of income from their savings, second pensions or earnings" (DSS, 2000b, p 18). In practice, it will bring everyone up to the MIG level, whether or not they have savings, and reward savers with 60p for each pound of income from savings or current earnings. Significantly, capital limits will be ended and dividends from capital treated as income up to the income threshold (DSS, 2000b, p 24). By contrast, pensioners without savings will benefit only from the 'guaranteed top-up'. As of 2001, the precise terms of the Pension Credit, and its effect on means-tested Housing Benefit

Table 10.1: Progress against Manifesto/Annual Report targets for social security

Pledge	New Labour's assessment	Score/10
27: 10p starting rate for income tax	Done	10
28: Cut VAT on fuel to 5%	Done	10
46: Introduce NMW	Done	5
47: Get 250,000 long-term unemployed young people back to work	On course	8
48: Tackle long-term unemployment	On course	7
50: Help single parents back to work	Kept	5
52: Crack down on benefit fraud	On course	2
83: National Childcare Strategy	On course	8
85: Retain universal child benefit	Done	7
94: Protect the BSP	Done	7
95: Help poorest pensioners	Done	7
96: Retain SERPS	Kept	6
97: Produce framework for stakeholder pension	On course	5
98: Create citizenship pensions for carers	On course	4

and Council Tax Benefit, remain to be clarified by government (DSS 2000b, p 25).

Sixth, annual payments such as Winter Fuel Payments were introduced in 1997 for all pensioners and free TV licenses for pensioners aged 75 and over. Seventh, in addition, there are means-tested benefits for various groups including pensioners facing particular needs, such as IS, Housing Benefit, Council Tax Benefit, whose annual upratings remain tied to prices rather than earnings.

The total impact of these reforms means that pension provision will have risen by more than earnings between 2000 and 2002, so enabling pensioners to recoup a small share of economic prosperity lost during the preceding 20 years when all benefits including pensions were linked to prices rather than earnings. But this gain has been delivered by the means-tested elements of pension provision, especially the MIG, that have grown in value more than the basic pension. Consequently, the value of means-tested benefits has come to dominate pension provision over the past 20 years by increasing at a faster rate than the basic pension (FIA, 2001b). This method of targeting pension provision on the poorest by means testing has long-term consequences, which are discussed below.

Evaluating performance in social security policy

We can first summarise the government's performance in intrinsic terms by listing the key pledges for social security and related policies taken from the Annual Report, and assessing – somewhat subjectively – how well each has been honoured by awarding marks out of 10.

However, while we can note these achievements in intrinsic terms – and that success is partly a matter of the modest terms targets are defined by – not surprisingly, a more critical assessment depends on extrinsic evaluation.

Welfare-to-work and unemployed people

From an 'intrinsic' viewpoint, it is possible to credit government reforms with a degree of success. Bivand's (2001) analysis of government figures shows that by March 2001, 206,000 young people had left the NDYP and 57,000 unemployed people had left the NDLTU for sustained and unsubsidised jobs – the government's test for sustainable employment is jobs lasting 13 weeks or more. Eighty-four thousand lone parents on the NDLP started work, for whom the criterion of job sustainability does not apply. These achievements represent a small percentage of all the participants on NDLTU (16%), but larger percentages on NDYP (33%) and NDLP (45%). For young people, however, unemployment began to fall in 1993 long before the ND was introduced (House of Commons, 2001, p 1). Nonetheless, the same report notes (p 2) that since the introduction of the NDYP, unemployment among eligible groups has fallen more sharply than among ineligible groups. The success rate for NDYP suggests that the government is on course to reach its quarter million target by 2002 – a key five-year target set in 1997.

However, the assessment to date of the ND has drawn conflicting conclusions. On the upside, Millar (2000) points to the important role played by personal advisers who, if effective, were seen as friendly, helpful and approachable, and able to deliver a holistic approach to the needs and barriers participants face. This could instil a positive response in the participants, especially lone parents. However, with the implementation of the ONE programme, the different NDs could become more streamlined and personal advisers more generic in dealing with different client groups. This could lead, Millar suggests, to a potential tension between the welfare and control roles of the advisers.

Providing a more critical and extrinsic evaluation, Peck (2001) casts doubt at the 'deficit' reasoning behind the ND, seen particularly in the Treasury's belief that jobseekers should seek work further afield where jobs are available (HM Treasury, 2000). Peck argues that the success of the ND results from recent prosperity rather than the effectiveness of the policies themselves, and could bolster false expectations among New Dealers in high-unemployment areas. Peck points to the growing evidence of different experiences between ND areas (see also Millar, 2000). Given these foreseeable problems, Peck suggests that the Treasury is 'talking up' success in the way it constructs its indicators. In using the narrow benefit claimant count as the preferred measure of unemployment, it is understating unemployment in high unemployment areas. Peck argues that stepping up compulsion and tightening benefit conditions may displace the problem of social exclusion in deprived areas into the expanding market for casual, short-term jobs. He contends that such trends in deprived areas could be reflecting the 'growing fragmentation of jobs' as people bounce from one temporary job to another with increasingly frequent short breaks from the labour market. The result could be that the low paid and unemployed are merging into a new class of persistently underemployed workers.

Lone parents

Several commentators have referred to the contradictory motives underlying the government's approach to lone parents (Gray, 2001; Rake, 2001): balancing the desire to reduce welfare spending by maximising the rate of employment with relatively expensive tax credits; and improving the quality and quantity of childcare while diminishing the choice to parents opting to stay at home. Although on this last point, the government has responded by announcing increased maternity benefits and improved maternity leave. The new programme of ND and tax credits offers a mix of incentives and disincentives that can cause uncertainty in understanding the government's overall objectives. The structure of incentives may not always point in the same direction.

From a broader extrinsic perspective, several commentators have concluded that the WFTC has shifted resources unequally from women to men (Gray, 2001; McLaughlin et al, 2001, p 179; Rake, 2001). Gray (2001) has argued the case for an unconditional benefit for lone parents that provides a balanced choice between full-time parenting and working. She points out that the government's integrated Child Credit proposed in the 2000 Budget is a move towards bringing together Child Benefit, children's IS allowances and WFTC for children. However, for Barnes (2000) the new children's benefit is double-edged: extending universal provision for children and carers while preserving the possibility of the new credit disguising moves to freeze, tax and/or means test child benefit prior to its removal (see also Rake, 2001). For carers, whose work is now rewarded by a range of state benefits, the division between work for those who can and security for those who can't has proven a shifting distinction pointing increasingly in the direction of the labour market.

Disabled people

Burchardt has summed up the effect of these changes on the pattern of benefits for the disabled: "Compensatory benefits have to date maintained a steady role. Earnings replacement expanded in the 1970s but has since receded again in favour of greater means testing. The extra costs disabled people face have been recognised, although slowly and partially, and these benefits now form an important part of some disabled people's income" (2000, p 16). It remains an open question whether the circumstances of some groups have worsened, because "altered incentives ... function to eliminate the groups of people in-between – those who ... fall between the stools of 'work' and 'security'" (2000, p 16). However, for Drake the conclusion is clearer: the government "focuses more narrowly on people with severe impairments, older disabled people and disabled children" (2000, p 430).

Extrinsic evaluations of these kinds suggest that the government must design targets that are more appropriate for the disabled. The challenge for a government wedded to the view that labour market participation is the cure for social exclusion is to ensure that the changing nature of the labour market does not produce new forms of exploitative and low-paid exclusionary jobs from which the disabled – and the unemployed and lone parents – have limited escape.

Pension provision for retired people

This chapter has argued that the government is implementing a new trinity of work, welfare and asset-based reforms. For pensioners, the accumulation of assets based on savings accrued during the working life has become increasingly important, together with the enhanced role that means testing now plays in pensioner welfare. A full assessment of the combined effect of the basic pension, MIG, pension credit and second-tier pensions (S2P, stakeholder, occupational and private pensions) is of central importance. This effect is itself determined by the impact of wider trends in prices, earnings, shares and gilts on public and private provisions. Pensions policy is essentially a long-term project, and as such not deliverable in the lifetime of a single government. Given that short-term government targets cannot address – and often damage – the long-term aims of pension policy, policy assessment must be extrinsic in scope. In particular, the section considers how pension reform is likely to fall increasingly short of the two objectives of reducing reliance on means testing and increasing savings for retirement.

First, most people could end up with total state pensions at or below the improved but means-tested MIG. The majority of pensioners could be means tested. First, if in the long run the basic pension and SERPS benefits remain linked to prices, their value will fall relative to earnings. Further, for many people the value of the two benefits will be less than their full value because of incomplete contribution records, with the average basic pension worth 80% of its full value in 2000 (FIA, 2001b, p 5). Indeed, women and the low paid are more likely to have incomplete records because they experience more employment breaks. Second, lower-paid pensioners receiving S2P will, at some future time determined by government, move from earnings-related benefits whose value will range from high to low amounts according to the level of contributions paid, to flat-rate, price-linked, second pensions whose benefits will be the same for all (FIA, 2001a, p 7). Third, the MIG is linked to earnings – unlike the basic pension and the (eventually) flat-rate S2P – and increased sharply in 2001/02 (DSS, 2000b, p 11). If the MIG acts as the means-tested safety net for pensioners and increases in line with earnings while the basic pension and S2P fall in relation to earnings (because they are tied to prices), the MIG will become the basic level of income protection for pensioners. This in turn undermines the contributory principle of national insurance.

Second, with a higher means-tested level – the MIG – in place, an increasing number of people face a long-term dilemma as to whether it is worth saving for retirement or spending their earnings before retirement and relying on government means-tested protection in retirement (FIA, 2001b, p 5). This dilemma is heightened by the fact that there are parts of the government's plans where decisions have still to be made. Further, future governments could reverse current policies. Personal pension planning could be placed in jeopardy if governments over time constantly tinker with pensions policy. Such a prospect bodes ill for New Labour's plans for developing consumer financial support as the new 'pillar' of social policy (HM Treasury, 2001a). Further, for those of working age who do save, they must save larger sums than in previous years in order to provide the same level of pension. One illustration suggests that someone aged 45 now needs to save two and half times more every year than did their father at the same age in order to secure a similar retirement pension in real terms (Banham, 2001). This depicts the uphill struggle many people face in becoming more self-sufficient in retirement, and the widening 'savings gap' between what a growing majority are currently saving and what they need in retirement (Oliver, Wyman & Company, 2001), which the government must address realistically. In addition, there has been a worrying trend of companies moving employees from defined-benefit schemes, where the pension is tied to final salary, to defined-contribution schemes whose performance depends on the market and is unrelated to final salary. There is a distinct move to shift responsibility for pension provision from state and employer to the individual.

Third, some individuals in employment or preparing for employment will be excluded from the S2P (FIA, 2001a, p 7) by the government's entitlement rules, namely people in full-time education and the self-employed, and people earning below £3,500 a year (mainly women in part-time and casual employment). The rules defining carers are, moreover, narrower than for the Home Responsibilities Protection in the basic state pension (Ward, 2000, p 167). The government's pension rules seek to reward work, including those who work as carers. However, there are some groups who should be rewarded for work but are excluded from new pension provisions.

Fourth, a growing number of retired people with private incomes will also be means tested. The long-term actuarial implications of pension provision provide interesting pointers to the social world pensioners might inhabit in the decades ahead. This can be described by two scenarios. In one, growing numbers of pensioners on means-tested benefits also receive a proportion of their income from private sources. For the first time in British welfare history, there could be a growth in the number of pensioners who depend on both means-tested benefits *and* private income. This is not a new phenomenon. But it is one that could increase with the introduction of the proposed Pension Credit. This trend runs counter to the long-term trend of the past 50 years whereby savings as well as income were means-tested, so that savings had to be spent as income before an individual could claim means-tested benefits. With the pension credit in place, larger portions of savings will no longer be means tested as poorer pensioners live off income from private pensions and savings in addition to income from state and occupational pensions.

Traditionally, means testing tended to reinforce the social division between those who had and those who did not have private savings. By contrast today, the higher value of the means-tested threshold (the MIG) and the proposal to disregard savings in total will increase the number of pensioners who are dependent on means-tested benefits, pensions and income from private capital. The traditional social divisions between means-tested and non-means-tested pensioners could become more blurred. Were this to happen, it would accord with the government's aim of achieving greater social inclusion in old age. Further, it could be seen to presage particular social consequences of the move towards new public–private mixes in welfare.

However, a second scenario can be suggested, in which greater social inclusion for different groups of pensioners is thwarted by the impact of means testing on people's desire to save. In this scenario, means testing could undermine savings to such an extent that growing numbers of pensioners become dependent on state means-tested benefits and especially the MIG, with little in the way of savings. *Hansard* (9 November 2000, col 45; reported in Pension Reform Group, 2001, p 23) reports that in 2003, with the introduction of the Pension Credit, 50% of pensioners will be on means-tested benefits. This scenario does not accord with the government's aim of fostering greater independence and security through more people saving for retirement. In addition, Ginn and Arber (2000) have highlighted the ways in which occupational and private pensions are ill equipped to meet the needs of women and carers on a par with better off workers.

The trend towards extending means testing to cover increasing numbers of pensioners receiving private savings reflects the trend among the low-income sectors of the working population whereby increasing numbers of people in work are also receiving tax credits and other non-work means-tested benefits. By making work pay – through tax credits and the National Minimum Wage – the government is hoping to provide opportunities for the poor in work to save. The second scenario described earlier would suggest that in time the new divisions between those on in-work and those on out-of-work benefits may be reproduced in the divisions between pensioners who benefit from their savings and those who have none. Tax credits and pension credits are devices that may begin to change the social composition of the working-aged and retired poor, but more research is needed to examine the impact of the present raft of welfare reforms on incentives to work and save.

The response to the government's pension plans has ranged from the positive and encouraging to the overtly critical. For the Pension Reform Group, "It is clear that the changes the Government will make ... and the proposed introduction of Pension Credit in 2003 are a serious attempt to raise the income of the poorest pensioner and by a significant margin" (Pension Reform Group, 2001). For the Institute for Public Policy Research (IPPR), somewhat more questioningly, "there is a palpable sense in which government policy is seen to have unravelled to a significant degree" (Pension Reform Group, 2001, p 4). Throughout there is concern about the consequences of the government's slippage into relying on means testing.

Asset-based welfare: the third step to self-sufficiency

In the trinity of New Labour's welfare reforms, the first step is to pronounce that all who can should work (the work ethic). The second step that all who can work, and so earn, should save. The third step is to encourage individuals to take greater responsibility for saving for the future and asset building for retirement (a prudential ethic). Rowlingson has suggested that this is part of the 'new model citizen' at the heart of New Labour's vision of Britain (2000, p 1). These citizens are presumed to make rational decisions to behave responsibly and plan prudently. According to the government, this is the 'something for something' approach that underpins the different elements of the government's welfare reforms. In relation to savings, it means "If you save the government will reward you for your efforts" (HM Treasury 2001a, p 2).

The foundations of asset-based welfare (ABW) were laid by the new savings vehicles that governments introduced in the 1990s, such as Personal Equity Plans, Tax Exempt Special Savings Accounts and New Labour's Individual Savings Accounts and stakeholder pensions, with incentives to save based on tax exemptions. However, the Labour government's proposals for ABW, contained in the Treasury consultations *Savings and assets for all* (HM Treasury, 2001a), published just before the 2001 Election, and *Delivering savings and assets* (HM Treasury, 2001b), introduce a new approach to social policy in the form of state bequests for children and donations for adults that match the amount saved. This represents a new role for government in supporting people who save and instilling savings habits.

The IPPR heralded the idea in a series of seminars and publications such as *Assets and progressive welfare* (Regan, 2001). They were presented as government policies in the 2001 New Labour Manifesto before the ink was dry and consultation begun. As 'first thoughts', the Treasury proposal (HM Treasury, 2001a) is big on the motivational issues but small on detail. It dwells on the moral and psychological benefits of savings, the need to facilitate preparation for 'rainy day' contingencies and retirement, the pedagogic implications of encouraging 'financial literacy', and the linkages between asset-based policies and new government savings vehicles. The specific proposals, which are far from final, are two-fold. First, the government pays a child trust fund to all children at birth, with larger lump sums for children from lower-income families, adding further endowments at key stages in the child's life and permitting the child access to the fund at age 18 or 21. Parents could also add their contributions and the fund placed in tax-exempt vehicles such as an ISA or stakeholder. The Treasury illustrations suggest child trust funds of £300 or £500 (for children in low-income families) at birth, topped up by sums of £50 to £100 respectively three times during childhood. Second, the government is proposing a savings gateway for lower-income households which would match their savings by, say, a pound for every pound saved up to a maximum of £1,800 saved. Access would be limited over a fixed period, at the end of which the savings could be transferred into an existing vehicle. Both the Fund and Savings Gateway would require informational support, including perhaps a personalised financial 'health check'.

Running through several government documents is the importance of motivating people, especially lower-income families, to save not only because of the financial independence it brings, but "because the very act of saving encourages greater self-reliance, forward-planning and an increased willingness to make personal investments" (HM Treasury, 2001a, p 1). The government sees these asset-based policies as part of its broad approach to combating financial exclusion and poverty. It has agreed with banks, building societies and the Post Office to provide a universal banking service. It is has placed on the Financial Services Authority an obligation to promote greater public understanding of the financial system and wider financial literacy, especially among "the vulnerable and inexperienced" (HM Treasury, 2001a, p 2). The Number 10 Policy Unit has proposed developing financial education schemes as part of the neighbourhood regeneration programmes, possibly attached to credit unions (HM Treasury, 1999), and the Savings Gateway could be piloted in such programmes.

The IPPR has strongly championed ABW as the 'third pillar of the welfare state', beyond the traditional pillars of income-based benefits and services in kind (Paxton, 2001). Similarly, Regan asserts that "a growing body of evidence reveals that the ownership of assets can have a strong impact on life opportunities and indicates asset-based policies could have a significant role to play in modern welfare states" (2001). However, Rowlingson has addressed some of the wider issues that may confound the government's desire to encourage more personal financial planning. Noticeably, she identifies the tension behind such a move in the context of growing risk and uncertainty: "Individual planning is therefore increasingly difficult as we witness growing diversity and flexibility in people's economic and social lives" (2000, p 2). Evidently, asset-based welfare policies must contend with the widespread asset poverty running through the UK. The Treasury reports that in 1998-99, 46% of households earning less than £200 per week had no savings at all. A total of 57% of families with children where there were two or more adults had less than £1,500 in savings (HM Treasury, 2001a, p 7). Limited ownership of assets means that government faces an uphill struggle in using ABW as a contribution to overcoming financial exclusion. In conclusion, in common with the welfare-to-work programme, the government's proposals for widening asset ownership contains a strong streak of deficit thinking that seeks to overcome structural problems of poverty, unemployment and exclusion with a cocktail of incentives, penalties and personal mentoring.

Conclusion

Government policy has developed in a cyclical fashion as initial measures are readjusted in pursuit of its aims. But the cyclical nature of this exercise poses the question of whether piecemeal tinkering with means is contributing towards a longer-term redefinition of ends that are far removed from the original social democratic aims of social security policy. The separation of ends and means implied by the third way may turn out to be far more complicated as means and ends are constantly redefined in reaching for a radical transformation of social policy. The piecemeal tinkering of means produces not only a gradual redefinition of ends but a major recasting of social security itself. The resources of social security have been substantially widened to include private resources for future pension provision and market wages, enhanced by in-work benefits. Similarly, governance policy has involved replacing the Department of Social Security by a Department for Work and Pensions, vested with continuing welfare reforms for those who can and for those who cannot work. Moreover, much of the day-to-day operation of social security, including the administration of Child Benefit and the Child Support Agency, is to be undertaken by the Inland Revenue. The Treasury is playing an increasingly central role in policy innovation and overall guidance, a role it developed to some effect during New Labour's first term. It is now expressly committed to integrating taxes and benefits. However, it is also clear that the Treasury continues to exercise its traditional role of controlling departmental spending, a role supported by the economic prosperity than benefited New Labour's first term. Finally, the Financial Services Authority has now been given the task of developing financial education and extending financial information and advice throughout the population.

However, despite the government's fortune – and its fortitude – some of the objectives are unravelling in awkward ways. Pension reforms, for example, show signs of taking on the guise of a Heath-Robinson cartoon as the problems of means testing are addressed by bolting on further means-testing mechanisms such as the MIG and Pension Credit to produce what could be an unwieldy and unworkable structure. A similar commitment to means testing is evident in its ABW proposals. Yet the government clearly sees elements of these proposals as part of thought-through planning for pension and other provision, and not as reactive tinkering to problems encountered en route. The problem is that its grand scheme is in danger of being undermined by its dependency on traditional government solutions for budget management, namely means testing. Its moves to implement work activation and savings policies are heavily reliant on means-testing mechanisms of targeting and delivery. Further, the government must address the disincentive effect of housing benefit – as its Manifesto pledged (Labour Party, 2001, p 27).

Over the past five years, the government has sought to modernise social security provisions in order to achieve traditional objectives such as a noticeable reduction in child and pensioner poverty. For the IFS, "The four years of the New Labour government have seen a rise in living standards across the income distribution. This has been a period of consistent economic growth, during which time average earnings have risen, employment has grown and the generosity of many benefits, for those in and out of work, has risen" (Clarke and Goodman, 2001). While acknowledging these progressive but far from trumpeted achievements, Lister more cautiously suggests that "Doing good by stealth, while possibly astute politics in the short run, is unlikely to be sustainable and can go only so far in reversing the tide of poverty and inequality that has corroded society" (2001, p 69). There is a growing consensus in the policy community that the government's achievements in combating poverty and reforming social security are significant. However, the role of sustained economic stability since 1997 cannot be ignored. The test for the government in its second term, when economic good fortune has shown sign of waning, will be its ability to continue to advance its social goals.

Note

¹ The author would like to record his thanks to Agnes Michel for her assistance in researching the chapter.

References

Banham, Sir John (2001) 'In place of Micawber: empowering financial consumers', a Lecture by the Chair of the Inquiry into the Provision of Financial Information and Advice, set up by the Actuarial Profession, London: Institute of Actuaries.

Barnes, M. (2000) 'Ending child poverty – can New Labour succeed?', *Benefits*, issue 29, pp 1-5.

Berthoud, R. (1998) *Disability benefits: A review of the issues and options for reform*, York: Joseph Rowntree Foundation.

Bivand, P. (2001) 'New Deal jobs approach half million mark', *Working Brief*, Issue 125, pp 8-9.

Burchardt, T. (2000) 'Disability benefit reform: falling between the stools of "work" and "security"?', *Benefits*, issue 27, pp 12-19.

Clark, T. and Goodman, A. (2001) *Living standards under Labour* (Election Briefing Notes), London: Institute of Fiscal Studies.

Clark, T., Myck, M. and Smith, Z. (2001) *Fiscal reforms affecting households, 1997-2001*, London: Institute of Fiscal Studies.

Dean, H. (2002) 'Business versus families: whose side is New Labour on?', *Social Policy and Society*, vol 1, no 1, pp 3-10.

Drake, R.F. (2000) 'Disabled people, New Labour, benefits and work', *Critical Social Policy*, vol 20, no 4, pp 421-39.

DSS (Department for Social Security) (1998a) *New ambitions for our country: A new contract for welfare*, Cm 3805, London: The Stationery Office.

DSS (1998b) *A new contract for pensions: Partnership in pensions*, Cm 4179, London: The Stationery Office.

DSS (1999) *Opportunity for All: Tackling poverty and social exclusion*, London: DSS.

DSS (2000a) *The changing welfare state: Social security spending*, London: DSS.

DSS (2000b) *The pension credit: A consultation paper*, Cm 4900, London: The Stationery Office.

DWP (Department of Work and Pensions) (2001) *Households below average income 1999-2000*, London: DWP.

FIA (Faculty and Institute of Actuaries) (2001a) *The size of the state pension*, London: Institute of Actuaries.

FIA (2001b) *Means testing*, London: Institute of Actuaries.

Ginn, J. and Arber, S. (2000) 'The pensions cost of caring', *Benefits*, issue 28, pp 13-17.

Gray, A. (2001) '"Making work pay" – devising the best strategy for lone parents in Britain', *Journal of Social Policy*, vol 30, no 2, pp 189-207.

Harker, L. (2000) 'Tracking poverty: monitoring the government's progress towards reducing poverty', *New Economy*, vol 7, no 1, pp 14-17.

Hills, J. (2000) 'A long wait for the end of poverty', *Financial Times*, 22 March.

HM Treasury (1999) *Access to financial services*, Report of Policy Action Team 14, London: HM Treasury.

HM Treasury (2000) *The goal of full employment: Opportunity for all throughout Britain*, London: HM Treasury.

HM Treasury (2001a) *Saving and assets for all*, London: HM Treasury.

HM Treasury (2001b) *Delivering savings and assets*, London: HM Treasury.

House of Commons (2001) *Education and Employment Select Committee – Fifth Report*, London: The Stationery Office.

Howard, M. (2000) 'Designing the employment tax credit', *Poverty*, issue 107, pp 14-17.

IPPR (Institute for Public Policy Research) (2001) *A new contract for retirement*, London: IPPR.

Jenkins, P. (2001) 'Low take-up of new pension scheme', *Financial Times*, 13 August, p 2.

Levitas, R. (1998) *The inclusive society? Social exclusion and New Labour*, Basingstoke: Macmillan.

Lister, R. (1998) 'From equality to social inclusion', *Critical Social Policy*, vol 18, no 2, pp 215-26.

Lister, R. (2001) 'Doing good by stealth', *New Economy*, vol 8, issue 2, pp 65-70.

McLaughlin, E., Trewsdale, J. and McCay, N. (2001) 'The rise and fall of the UK's first tax credit', *Social Policy and Administration*, vol 35, no 2, pp 163-80.

Millar, J. (2000) *Keeping track on welfare reform: The New Deal programmes*, York: Joseph Rowntree Foundation.

Oliver, Wyman & Company (2001) *The future regulation of UK savings and investment*, London: Oliver, Wyman & Company.

Paxton, W. (2001) 'Assets: a third pillar of welfare', in S. Regan (ed) *Assets and progressive welfare*, London: IPPR.

Peck, J. (2001) 'Job alert', *Benefits*, issue 30, pp 11-15.

Pension Reform Group (2001) *Universal protected pension*, London: Institute of Community Studies.

Rake, K. (2001) 'Gender and New Labour's social policies', *Journal of Social Policy*, vol 30, no 2, pp 209-31.

Regan, S. (ed) (2001) *Assets and progressive welfare*, London: IPPR.

Rowlingson, K. (2000) *Fate, hope and insecurity*, London: Policy Studies Institute.

Ward, S. (2000) 'New Labour's pension reforms', in H. Dean, R. Sykes and R. Woods (eds) *Social Policy Review 12*, Newcastle: Social Policy Association, pp 157-83.

Wintour, P. (2001) '£1bn extra for poor in benefit reform', *The Guardian*, 3 August, p 12.

Working Brief (2001) 'In-work support up by 50%', issue 125, June, p 5.

ELEVEN

Toughing it out: New Labour's criminal record

Sarah Charman and Stephen P. Savage

Introduction

The Labour Party underwent far-reaching and radical changes to transform itself from a party that was increasingly being considered to be almost unelectable in the 1980s to one that won a landslide election victory in the 1997 General Election and a near repeat performance in 2001. Surely one of the more difficult challenges that the Labour Party faced was the attempt to transform itself from a party that was traditionally viewed as 'soft' on crime and 'soft' on offenders to a party that could challenge the Conservatives to the title of 'the party of law and order', not necessarily a desirable title. One of New Labour's most striking successes is in achieving this transformation so quickly and so smoothly (Charman and Savage, 1999).

The 'tough on crime, tough on the causes of crime' slogan was to be central to all New Labour's policies. It successfully negotiated the difficult balance between understanding the causes of crime yet demanding responsibility for actions – a difficult yet achievable combination of left- and right-wing thinking on crime and criminality. While the sentiments were sound, the dilemma lay in achieving harmony between those two somewhat contradictory aims. Whether the Labour Party would be able to square that circle when in government is the essence of this chapter.

A legitimate place was being carved out for 'action' against offenders. It was New Labour's way of avoiding the old accusation from the right that in focusing solely on the causes of crime it was in effect *excusing crime*. This was never a justified (or indeed logical) deduction. However, it was an accusation that New Labour was anxious to deflect. The counter-rhetoric was aimed at neutralising this potential Achilles' heel. 'Excusing crime' was to law and order policy what unilateral nuclear disarmament was to defence policy. Scotching this one would enable New Labour to claim, as it did in the Party Manifesto, that "Labour is the party of law and order in Britain today" (Labour Party, 1997). But it was always more than politically driven rhetoric, for the shift in New Labour's approach was also a clear acknowledgement that, unlike some other sections of the Left, New Labour was not prepared to 'talk down' crime by seeing crime problems as media-led exaggerations of reality, as nothing more than a 'moral panic'. It was a move to a left realist stance (see Young, 1997) that argued that crime really is a problem, and furthermore, crime is a problem that disproportionately harms the weakest and most vulnerable in the community.

Yet the dark art of politics was never far away in New Labour's approach. As Jack Straw took over as Shadow Home Secretary, the head-to-head with Howard became, if anything, more pronounced. Often to the dismay of liberals and sectors of the left, Straw waded into the game of out-gunning on rhetoric. What was often ignored by critics of Straw's stance was that, however inappropriate some of these sentiments might have been, they seldom got above the rhetoric. On matters of actual *policy*, an agenda very different in tone was emerging. Rightly or wrongly, Straw seemed to be using certain, easy, targets to win public support or at least neutralise the Tory's campaign.

Labour's success in establishing itself, at the very least, alongside the Conservative Party in terms of the public support towards law and order policies was a significant achievement, begun by Tony Blair as Shadow Home Secretary and continued by Jack Straw as Blair shifted to the top job. There were criticisms of their strategy in achieving that aim, most notably in the often crass way in which New Labour pandered to the tabloid press, but nonetheless crime, law and order were central stage in the months leading up to the 1997 General Election. This was a significant departure from earlier elections when the issue of crime had played a very low-key role in both Manifestos and campaigns (Goddard, 1997). New Labour was responding to public concern and beginning to understand, at least on crime issues, the mechanics of winning an election.

Promises

The particular pledges that are concerned with crime exhibit some of the potential contradictions of the twin-track approach to crime mentioned earlier. While wanting to reduce crime through tough policing and tough sentencing, emphasis is also placed on tackling the causes of crime, through crime prevention schemes and in areas of youth offending. Clearly, and as would be expected, the emphasis in the Election Manifesto is more concerned with fighting crime than with the more complicated issue of fighting the inequality that contributes to crime. Analysis of the actual performance of the government will undoubtedly reveal more about the second and equally important measure of tackling the causes of crime.

Youth crime was featured as one of the five promises on the pledge cards of the 1997 Election. Labour promised to halve the time taken from arrest to sentencing of persistent young offenders. In 1997, it took an average of 142 days by 2002, it was to take 71 days. This one measure in itself effectively outlines the dual approach that New Labour was intending to take. In order to crack down on crime, young offenders needed to be removed from the area of offending and dealt with as quickly as possible. Much of the offending taking place was as a result of the gap between arrest and sentencing. However, by speeding up the process, the intention was also to move the offenders into the care of the newly created youth offending teams as soon as possible (these teams will be discussed later).

Alongside this major election promise were five other, slightly less rigid, pledges contained in the 1997 Election Manifesto (Labour Party, 1997):

- fast-track punishment for persistent young offenders;
- Reform Crown Prosecution Service to convict more criminals;
- police on the beat, not pushing paper;
- crackdown on petty crimes and neighbourhood disorder;
- fresh parliamentary vote to ban all handguns.

Clearly the Labour Party was keen to concentrate on some areas, such as disorder and falling convictions, while giving less prominence to other areas, such as the prison population or violent crime. What follows now is an assessment of New Labour's successes and failures in relation to its stated pledges and its successes and failures and possible omissions in other key areas of crime and criminal justice.

Intrinsic evaluation

Evaluating any government's 'performance' on crime is fraught with difficulties. To begin with, there is the problem of access to reliable data on crime, given that, on all accounts, only around one quarter of actual crimes end up in the official crime statistics (Maguire, 1997). The official crime statistics are made up of police records of crime. Given that most offences are not reported to the police, and of those that are reported only are portion are formally recorded by the police, the official figures provide only a partial insight into the real extent of crime in the community. However, even when we can get close to assessing actual rates of crime, by means of victim surveys such as the British Crime Survey (HMSO, 2000a), we must be careful not to view these as measures of *government* action. Crime rates are reflections of a host of factors, many of which are outside of the scope of government intervention, such as demographic change (most notably how many young males there are in the population). While governments are quick to claim credit for declining crime rates, we know that it is not always appropriate that they do so.

Despite the methodological difficulties with evaluating a government's crime policy, New Labour's whole stance on crime demands that we attempt to do so. As we have already argued, New Labour chose to raise the stakes in the politics of law and order, thus exposing crime as a key issue on which it would have to be judged. Furthermore, New Labour elected to adopt a highly ambitious agenda for its crime policy, embracing the full machinery of law enforcement, criminal justice and the penal system. In many ways, this was a more comprehensive agenda for change than that pursued by any previous

British government. To what effect? We shall assess the out-turn of this agenda under a number of general headings: dealing with young offenders; disorder; policing; and the criminal process.

Dealing with young offenders

Dealing with youth crime was central to New Labour's new agenda for crime reduction. There is little doubt that there has been much activity in response to New Labour's pledges in this area. As regards the pledge on 'fast-tracking' for persistent young offenders, the government, by means of the 1998 Crime and Disorder Act (CDA), established statutory time limits that would apply to young offenders from their arrest to sentencing. As a consequence of this and related measures, year-on-year reductions in average time between arrest and sentence have been achieved, such that the target reduction from 142 days to 71 days seemed to be well on schedule for 2002 (HMSO, 2000b). It used to be said that 'justice delayed is justice denied'; it remains to be seen whether 'justice speeded up' is 'justice guaranteed'.

The government also controversially set out to change the system whereby young offenders could be given repeated formal cautions by the police before criminal charges were made. It was concerned that offering the same disposal after each alleged offence had failed to force offenders to confront their behaviour and wanted to introduce a graded response designed to prevent reoffending. The CDA replaced the old system of cautioning for juvenile offenders with one involving the stages of 'reprimand', 'final warning' and then prosecution. The original scheme of formal cautioning (which remains in place for adult offenders) was supported by many liberal academics and criminal justice practitioners because it provided opportunities for the *diversion* of offenders from the formal processes of criminal justice. However, concern had grown over time about persistent offenders who apparently exploited the system of repeat cautioning. It should be noted that the final warning scheme is attached to the work of Youth Offender Teams (YOTs). Offenders given the final warning are automatically referred to a YOT, which will make an assessment on whether a reparation or rehabilitation programme is appropriate to prevent reoffending. Early returns indicate that the new framework is proving successful, at least in terms of the extent of application: in 10 pilot areas chosen for the programme, the police issued 3,543 reprimands, 1,799 final warnings and 602 reparation orders (Travis, 1999).

The YOTs were created under the CDA as a requirement for each area. They are multiagency teams bringing together all of the key agencies with an involvement in young offenders – the police, social services, education, probation, and so on. They are aimed at realising the long-supported case for multiagency approaches to dealing with youth crime and extending the concept of 'joined-up government' to the youth justice system. The YOTs are charged with designing and implementing a Youth Justice Plan for their locality. They began on a pilot basis with nine schemes, but have since spread nationally – by 2000, some 154 schemes were in place. The Home Office commissioned evaluative research on the pilot schemes, which reached mixed, but generally positive, conclusions about the YOTs in practice (Holdaway et al, 2001). The research found that the YOTs had added value for offenders, victims and the courts by speeding up justice, opening access to a range of services, encouraging innovation in rehabilitative schemes, developing more systematic case management and enhancing transparency of process. However, there remained problems with the commitment of some partners to the joint working principle, with YOT funding and finances and with variations between the YOTs in the nature of service delivery – even Downing Street admitted that there had been a 'patchiness' evident in the results from early inspections of the work of the YOTs (Hinsliff, 2001). Nevertheless, the research held out the promise that a "distinctive culture for the delivery of youth justice" was beginning to emerge with the YOT idea (Holdaway et al, 2001, p 113). Support for New Labour's general approach to youth crime comes from other quarters. For example, Hoyle and Rose have commented that New Labour seems to be offering "a genuine commitment to a coherent national strategy for dealing with young offenders" (2001, p 77); they have also commended "an impressive regard for evidence-led policy" (2001, p 77) in New Labour's youth justice policy, particularly as regards the research-based initiatives for 'restorative justice' schemes for young offenders, which seek to bring offenders and victims closer together in repairing the harm caused by youth crimes.

Disorder

New Labour's pledges on youth crime overlap with a range of promises in the broad area of 'disorder'. The reception to the government's activities in this area has been less positive. In opposition, Labour chose to widen the debate on crime to include the more nebulous issue of 'social disorder'. This appeared to stem from a populist response to public concerns over 'noisy neighbours', 'rowdy youth', 'squeegee merchants' and the like, who had seemingly blighted the life of many communities, particularly in the cities. The 1997 Manifesto stated:

> The Conservatives have forgotten the 'order' part of 'law and order'. We will tackle the unacceptable level of anti-social behaviour and crime on our streets. Our 'zero-tolerance' approach will ensure that petty criminality among young offenders is seriously addressed. (Labour Party, 1997, p 23)

This stance was not purely of populist origin. It drew from branches of, mainly American, criminology associated with the 'broken windows' theory (Wilson and Kelling, 1982). This rests on the view that failure to deal with petty crimes and 'incivilities' can lead to general neighbourhood decline and ultimately to an escalation of social problems, such as serious and violent crime. By adopting a 'zero-tolerance' approach to small problems, the bigger problems can potentially be avoided. An important association is made in this respect between *non-criminal* disorders and *criminal* behaviour; not only can one lead to the other, but the 'policing' of the latter depends, so it is argued, on the 'policing' of the former. The shift from controlling *crime* to controlling *disorder* is a significant one and in many ways, as we shall see, a problematic one.

A number of measures were introduced in support of the pledge to deal with 'anti-social behaviour'. The CDA introduced Anti-Social Behaviour Orders, under which the courts could order parents of disorderly children to attend training sessions. However, despite the high priority given to this facility in New Labour's electoral discourse, very few orders have in practice been applied. By November 2000 only 132 Anti-Social Behaviour Orders had been issued (Toynbee and Walker, 2001, p 165), a result that must have come as an embarrassment for New Labour. The CDA also introduced Child Curfews, launched in 1998, and Parenting Orders and Child Safety Orders, both put into effect from June 2000. Child Curfew Orders allow the police and/or local authorities to declare an 'off the streets' curfew time for children under 10 in a particular area. Child Safety Orders are measures allowing the authorities to identify children under 10 who are 'at risk' of becoming involved in crime and to ban them from visiting certain places or people, or to confine them to home for specified periods. Parenting Orders can bind parents to attend 'parenting skills' programmes or require them to ensure that their children do not truant. All of these measures were aimed at enhancing controls over 'unruly' children and at increasing parental involvement and responsibility in the process. However, these orders would seem to be going the same way as Anti-Social Behaviour Orders. Not a single Child Curfew Order had been issued in the first year of its implementation. Only a handful of Child Safety Orders have been passed and in 10 pilot regions for the Parenting Orders only 21 orders were made, a quarter of them in one region (Travis, 1999).

Extent of usage should not, however, be the only measure of evaluating the new mechanisms introduced under the 'disorder' agenda. If there are dangers inherent in these new court orders, then underutilisation might be a positive benefit. There are indeed concerns with aspects of this agenda. While the apparent target of the Anti-Social Behaviour Orders was 'yob culture', it has been claimed that in so far as they have been used it is in relation to single parents and children. Furthermore, it has been claimed that the threat of punishment for non-compliance of the orders simply adds to the already heavily pressurised and disadvantaged lives of vulnerable and abused women (Campbell, 2000; Toynbee and Walker, 2001). More fundamentally, the 'disorder' agenda could serve to blur the lines between 'disruptive' and specifically *criminal* behaviour and drag more people into the clutch of the law-enforcement machinery. This is a form of what criminologists have called 'net-widening' (Cohen, 1985), the process by which not only offenders but those deemed 'at risk' of offending are brought within the remit of the social control agencies, one consequence of which is that *more*, rather than less, people find their way into the formal criminal justice process. As Anti-Social Behaviour Orders can be imposed for a wide range of non-criminal acts, and as non-compliance can lead to criminal sanction, a person can end up with imprisonment for what was initially only behaviour deemed 'unacceptable' (Hoyle and Rose, 2001). This process has been termed the 'criminalisation of social policy' (Gilling and Barton, 1997).

Policing

The task of *enforcement* of the youth crime and disorder agendas falls primarily on the *police* as the front line of law enforcement. In one sense, New Labour placed policing at the fore of its crime policy by including the police in its five core pledges on crime. The commitment to relieving the police of 'unnecessary bureaucratic burdens' in order to 'get more officers back on the beat' was a signal that the police were at the heart of New Labour's new agenda. Yet ironically, policing was to be a largely low-key dimension of New Labour's first term of office. As we shall see, radical moves on police reform were to figure much more in New Labour's agenda for a second term. Up until that point, most of the political discourse on policing from the government has been on *finances* and *police numbers*.

New Labour's early commitment to getting 'more officers on the beat' – the mantra destined to warm the hearts of 'middle England', attracted to reinventing the 'golden' and largely mythical past of British policing (Reiner, 2000) – was not supported by clear policies. It seemed to be based on the vague goal of 'cutting back on paperwork' rather than on new levels of investment – ironically, the government's wider agenda for enhanced performance management ran somewhat counter to that objective. Indeed, by 1998 the police were being told to make efficiency savings in order to make better use of the resources they had. The 1998 Spending Review asked for 2% efficiency savings from the police service for the forthcoming year. At that time the police service seemed destined for a period of tighter budgets after many years of 'generous' expenditure settlements – at least, generous relative to the rest of the public sector (Savage and Nash, 2001). However, New Labour's political sensitivity to accusations about declining police numbers and the perceived need to bolster its image as 'pro-police' meant that a renewed agenda of *increased* police funding was soon to reemerge. The 2000 Spending Review allowed for the police to receive an extra £1.24 billion over the following three years. The government also announced a new Crime Fighting Fund, much of which was to find its way into funding for the recruitment of an extra 5,000 officers. During 2000, political controversy raged over the allegation that this 5,000 would not cover the numbers actually *leaving* the police, so that in effect the new recruitment levels would hardly break even, an allegation that would later be addressed by the government with rather large increases in recruitment levels, entailing further increases in the police budget during 2001 (discussed later in this chapter). It is a moot point whether additional police numbers will actually mean 'more officers on the beat' in the traditional sense. It is even more debatable whether more officers, on the beat or not, will have any impact on crime, given the well-established view that increasing police officers makes little impact on crime levels (Reiner, 2000, pp 116-21). Nevertheless, as was clear from the 2001 General Election campaign, 'talking crime control' has become in political discourse 'talking police numbers', and all parties have seemed locked into this mind-set. 'Evidence-based' policy appears to have little impact in this regard.

However, beyond the rhetoric over police numbers, New Labour was responsible, at least indirectly, for the establishment of a more radical agenda for policing, one that, as we shall see later, is only just becoming explicit in New Labour's more recent plans for the modernisation of the police. Two inquiries were set up by New Labour to address quite specific issues: policing in Northern Ireland and the police response to the killing of Stephen Lawrence in London. Two reports followed, which, as well as tackling the particular questions both inquiries were charged to answer, contained messages that have much wider and longer-term resonance for British policing.

The Patten Commission was set up in 1998 as part of the Northern Ireland Peace Process to review the role of the Royal Ulster Constabulary, an organisation at the heart of negotiations between the various parties involved in the process. What was particularly significant was the choice of Commission members, two of whom, coming from very different backgrounds, were clearly oriented to a radical approach to policing. Sir John Smith, former Deputy Commissioner of the Metropolitan Police, had distinguished himself as very much a progressivist on matters relating to the future of policing. Professor Clifford Shearing was widely regarded as one of the leading academics on policing and someone who had argued openly for 'community-oriented' policing. It was hardly surprising, given the involvement of such individuals, that the commission would not be limited to the specific brief of policing in Northern Ireland; to a great extent it ended up as a 'mini-Royal Commission' on *policing* more generally. The Report of the Commission (HMSO, 1999) made a number of recommendations that were as applicable to policing outside of the province as inside. For example, it recommended a fully independent system for the handling of complaints against the police. As we shall see, this was to become an element in New Labour's 2001 modernisation agenda for British policing. It also recommended that a Policing Board be set up to oversee and govern the local police service. The Board was to have much more 'teeth' than the currently constituted 'local police authorities'. It was to have real powers to *direct* policing policy, powers that stood to challenge the traditional principle of 'constabulary independence', under which policing policy was very much the province of the chief police officer (see Savage et al, 2000, pp 206-8). The Patten Report thus laid down fundamental markers for the future of British policing that went well beyond the hotly contested issues relating specifically to policing in Northern Ireland; as such, its publication was something of a watershed.

Another important watershed was the publication, in the same year, of the MacPherson Report on the inquiry into the killing of Stephen Lawrence (MacPherson, 1999). Labour had promised in opposition to set up a public inquiry into the events relating to the death of Stephen Lawrence against the backcloth of allegations that the Metropolitan Police had mishandled the case. The final report was a devastating indictment of the way in which the police dealt with the killing. Again, as with Patten, the message was of much wider significance than the particular case at hand, however important that was in itself. Two issues in particular arose from the report. The first was the conclusion that the police had been guilty of 'institutionalised racism' in their handling of the case. This dimension of the MacPherson Report was directly influential in the new legislation that followed in 2000 with the Race Relations Amendments Act, which extended the scope of the Commission for Racial Equality to the police, prisons, local authorities and the NHS. This now meant that these institutions would be required to demonstrate that they were operating fair policies on race and anti-racism. The second key conclusion of the report was that the police had exhibited poor *management* and low levels of *competency* in their approach to the case. This could only help fuel concerns within the Home Office that there were problems of *leadership* and *quality* within British policing that called for a more radical agenda for policing in the future. It served to speed up the process by which New Labour's 'softly, softly' approach to policing, dictated in part by the desire to continue to appear as 'pro-police', was giving way to something more radical, as we shall see later.

The criminal process

There is little doubt that New Labour has honoured its pledge to be 'tough on crime'. A raft of measures have been introduced as evidence of this. The *probation service* has been reformed (and expanded substantially) to become more explicitly an arm of the courts and the penal system. A formal departure has been made from the notion that the probation officer was, at least in part, a 'befriender' of offenders, something reflected in major changes to the training of probation officers – they are no longer trained under a 'social work' framework but under a law/criminal justice framework. On a managerial level, a National Probation Service has replaced the 54 separate local probation services. Ironically, at the same time, the government was *decentralising* the Crown Prosecution Service to create 42 new service areas, to bring it in line geographically and managerially with the 42 police services of England and Wales. This move followed the recommendations of the Glidewell Report (HMSO, 1998).

Sentencing has undergone a range of changes, all in line with a 'tougher' stance. The government introduced mandatory sentences for repeat offenders convicted of burglary and serious crimes. It has also set up a Sentencing Advisory Panel that advises the Court of Appeal in framing sentencing guidelines. The ethos of these changes is to confront what the government considers to be 'over-lenient' sentencing, or at least inconsistencies in sentencing practice across the country. The consequence of such measures will most likely be an increase in the numbers of offenders who are sentenced to imprisonment. We shall return to this point.

A general measure to which the government seems committed is to *speed up* the processes of criminal justice and in particular the work of the criminal courts, following in part the recommendations of the Narey Report into delay in the courts system (Narey, 1997). By 2001, the government could claim to have reduced delays in the magistrates' courts by 15% and to have streamlined the administration of the magistrates' courts, by setting up Magistrates' Courts Committees in 42 'criminal justice areas' to match the distribution of Crown Prosecution Service (CPS) areas (HMSO, 2001, pp 60-1). These measures have been relatively non-controversial. Far more contentious, however, has been the determination to speed up justice by reducing the number of cases that can be tried by *juries*. On a number of occasions, the then Home Secretary Jack Straw attempted to introduce amendments to the right to trial by jury by ending the defendant's absolute right to elect for jury trial in 'triable either way' cases. It would have been left to magistrates rather than defendants to decide, in most cases, on the appropriateness of trial by jury where discretion was available. The aim was to reduce substantially the number of cases heard in the crown courts and to redirect them to the magistrates' courts – not just to speed up justice, but also to reduce the cost of justice. These plans have caused much controversy in all quarters of the legal, civil liberties and political spectrum; they have been rejected repeatedly in the House of Lords. At the time of writing, they live to fight another day.

Measures that have been more welcomed by both liberal and right-wing commentators relate to provisions for the *victims* of crime. The 'victims' lobby' had long argued that victims were treated as relatively peripheral participants in the criminal justice process (Zedner, 1997). New Labour pledged to remedy this situation and since 1997 has introduced a number of steps to provide better protection for victims and to allow victims more access to information about their cases. The 1999 Youth Justice and Criminal Justice Act included new measures to allow live video links in court and video-recorded evidence to be presented in court, both aimed at protecting vulnerable witnesses from some of the traumas of the trial process. It also disallowed defendants the right to cross-examine alleged victims in certain sexual offence cases. As another response to the Lawrence Inquiry, the government made new arrangements for police forces to establish family liaison schemes to ensure a better flow of information and better victim support for those suffering crimes against their family members. The move towards a fairer deal for victims of crime has been carried forward into New Labour's second term, as we shall see later. These are all measures to be broadly welcomed.

We have covered many, but not all, of the actions and outcomes relating to New Labour's 1997 Manifesto pledges. There are others areas, such as *drugs* policy and the law relating to the possession of handguns, where similarly wide-ranging initiatives have been implemented, including drugs testing and treatment for offenders, drug programmes for prisoners and so on. The government has also made a major commitment to *crime prevention*. The CDA created a statutory responsibility on local authorities to develop *partnerships*

Table 11.1: Progress against Manifesto/Annual Report targets for criminal justice

Pledge	New Labour's assessment	Score/10
67: Decentralise the CPS	Done	8
68: Halve the time from arrest to sentence for young offenders	On course	5
69:Youth Offender Teams in every area	On course	8
70: Streamline the youth courts system	On course	5
71:Audit the prison service resources	Done	9
72: Implement an effective sentencing policy	On course	3
73: Introduce Child Protection Orders	Done	8
74: Free vote on handguns	Done	10
75: Introduce Parental Responsibility Orders	Done	5
76: Introduce Community Safety Orders	Done	9
77: Make racial harassment and racially motivated violence criminal	Done	10
78.Appoint an anti drugs supremo	Done	2
79: Keep victims of crime fully informed about their cases	On course	10
80: Greater protection for rape victims	On course	10
81: Local authorities to develop crime prevention partnerships	Done	10
82: Pilot the use of compulsory drug testing for offenders	Done	4

between the key agencies, the police, probation and the health services, with the local authorities themselves, to audit crimes in their locality and to develop local crime plans to reduce crime, including steps to enhance crime prevention. This has been an important development and one that has been generally welcomed by academics and criminal justice managers alike (see Leishman et al, 2000, chs 8 and 18).

So how much of New Labour's pledges have been met and how many remain to be completed? The following table shows the government's answer to this question, based on its Annual Report and our own assessment of its performance. This is, of course, very difficult to quantify and even if this could be done satisfactorily, achievement of these particular pledges does not necessarily equate with a desirable set of criminal justice policies. Nevertheless the picture may look something like that shown in Table 11.1.

Extrinsic evaluation

With an agenda as wide as this, drawing up an overall assessment of New Labour's performance is extremely difficult. We might be tempted to use national *crime rates* as one indicator of success, but we have already highlighted the problems in this area. Nevertheless, it is the case that *aggregate* crime levels have *declined* during New Labour's period in office. Levels of recorded crime declined by more than 5% between 1997 and 1999 (HMSO, 2000). The major reductions were in the areas of burglary (down 13%) and crimes associated with vehicles – theft from, and of, vehicles (down 8%). These were both 'target' crimes for the Home Office. There were, however, *increases* in robbery (up 23%) and theft from the person (up 25%) – much of the latter may be due to the greater availability of mobile phones as 'targets' for crime. In the year from March 2000 to March 2001, burglary fell by 8% and thefts from, and of, vehicles fell by 7% (HMSO, 2001b). Robberies rose by 13% (HMSO, 2001b). In the past, fluctuations in recorded crime have been questioned because, as has been noted earlier, recorded crimes tell us only about a minority of actual crimes. However, the British Crime Survey, based on a national victim survey, broadly backs up these data. Indeed, the British Crime Survey for 2000 concluded that aggregate levels of crime may have declined by as much as 10% (HMSO, 2001b). It also found the same types of decreases and increases in particular areas of crime as the recorded crime statistics. However, we must be clear that crime rates, by both sets of measures, had been declining in aggregate since *before* New Labour came into office; since 1995, in fact. There are clearly wider forces at work here than government policy alone.

On a less positive note, New Labour also inherited and managed to oversee the continuation of another trend: the *rising prison population*. After reductions in the prison population in the late 1980s and early 1990s – to bring it to just over 40,000 – from 1995 onwards the prison population began to rise steadily under the Major government. By March 1997, it was just under 60,000. Under Labour, the prison population continued to rise so that by March 2001 it stood at over 65,000 (HMSO, 2001c). The continuation of a policy of placing custody at the forefront of penal policy, as we have already argued, has been a reflection of the populist ambitions of New Labour and linked to a political calculation of the public support such a stance will deliver. For this very reason, it remains as a weak link in New Labour's overall crime policy. At the very time when other areas of New Labour policy seek to address social *exclusion* (Woods, 2000), New Labour's crime policy (or at least parts of it), wrapped in the 'tough on crime' agenda, facilitates the *exclusion* of large numbers of offenders from the community through incarceration in penal institutions.

This raises the more general question of whether there is an appropriate *balance* in New Labour's record on crime, or indeed in the new agendas it is mapping out on crime policy, to be examined below. In a sense, the criminal justice process is always some form of balance between the need to control crime and to an extent that means convicting the offender, on the one hand, and protecting the rights of both suspects and those actually convicted of offences on the other. This has been expressed as the relationship, or dilemma, between *crime control* and *due process* (Packer, 1968). However simplistic this framework may be, it is useful as a reminder at least that crime policy has to balance a number of priorities at one and the same time in order to be both successful and *fair*. It should not be left to what Jack Straw labelled pejoratively 'Hampstead liberals' (Toynbee and Walker, 2001, p 153) to champion the cause of suspects' and defendants' rights. As the government that introduced the

1998 Human Rights Act, Labour might feel more at ease than has been apparent with balancing victims' rights, or the rights of the community to 'protection', with the rights of those either suspected or convicted on criminal offences. A worry is that, as New Labour signals the 'way ahead' for criminal justice, this is an area on which it continues, doggedly, to remain silent.

Next steps: New Labour and crime in 2001 and beyond

While it has been difficult to evaluate the success or otherwise of recently introduced measures during the last Labour government, it can only be mere speculation to assess what the future may hold for New Labour's second term. New Labour won the 2001 General Election with a majority only marginally smaller than its extremely successful election victory of 1997. One of New Labour's slogans of the election campaign was "A lot done, a lot more to do" (Labour Party, 2001, p 5) and there are many, particularly liberal supporters, who would agree with the latter part of this statement. Feelings were running high that with a second term under its belt New Labour would learn the confidence to trust research and trust its instinct, rather than trusting populism and the sentiments of the *Daily Mail*. An analysis of its 2001 Manifesto reveals that New Labour is still committed, at least on paper, to being tough on crime and tough on the causes of crime (Labour Party, 2001, p 31). Modernisation is the key to the New Labour government's plans for criminal justice – modernisation of the police, the courts, sentencing and much more. However, crime in New Labour's modern Britain no longer deserves a title in its Manifesto – instead we have "strong and safe communities" (p 30). Within the section on 'strong and safe communities' (which is quite clearly its section on crime, although phrased in as much more positive way), we see a commitment to increased numbers in two areas where increased numbers either make no difference or do much harm – an increase of police officers on the beat and an increase in the prison population. Both of these issues will be discussed here.

Renewing public services was a key message for New Labour and this time the criminal justice system will be subject to the same scrutiny that other public services have long been used to. We also see an increasing emphasis on tough strategies for persistent offenders, both young and adult offenders alike, an increase in drug detection and an increase in the technological strategies to fight crime. This will all take place under a revised and thoroughly modern criminal justice system. After the 2001 Election, the Home Office was given the heaviest legislative workload of all government departments. There are a huge quantity of new schemes, plans and strategies to deal with crime. Many of these can in this context only merit a mention. Much more comment and analysis is needed of these plans. These measures must represent one of the most fundamental attacks on crime (and to a lesser degree the causes of crime) seen in years. This is despite an overall decrease in crime of 7% (according to recent British Crime Surveys) over the last New Labour administration – one wonders what would have been seen if there had been an increase in crime.

What follows is an attempt to summarise briefly some of the main trends for criminal justice over the next parliament and distinguish the policy from the inevitable, and now well-recognised, spin and rhetoric.

After the 2001 Election Jack Straw became Foreign Secretary and, to the relief of many in the education sector, David Blunkett moved from Education Secretary to Home Secretary.

Blunkett wasted no time in letting the police know that he meant business. Within weeks of his appointment, he prompted Sussex police authority to consider sacking its chief constable after a raid in which an unarmed man was shot dead. The chief constable, Paul Whitehouse, resigned the next day. The police are centre stage again in the law and order debate. One of the key election promises of the 2001 Manifesto is to increase the number of uniformed officers – by 6,000 (despite comprehensive research from many countries showing that extra officers do not equate to a lower crime rate or even a higher detection rate (Reiner, 2001, pp 115-24). Police funding is also set to increase – by 20% to £9.3 billion. Under the Criminal Justice and Police Bill launched in 2001, there is a whole raft on new powers for the police including plans to attack so-called 'yob culture' (a favourite theme of the Prime Minister, Tony Blair). In all, there were 20 new police powers revealed in the Bill, the irony of which was that the renowned 'illiberal' shadow Home Secretary Ann Widdecombe raised concerns over its neglect of human rights and civil liberties (*The Guardian*, 20 January 2001). As part of the 10-year crime plan launched in February 2001, ideas about two-tier policing, 'super-bobbies' and civilian investigators were all touted. The themes of the plan placed a heavy onus on the police to reverse the long-term decline in detection and to break the cycle of reoffending. John Wadham, director of Liberty, argued that the police were "vacuuming up new powers" (Wadham, 2001). However, the trade-off for extra numbers and funds is modernisation and improved performance. The never-challenged yet unjustifiable amount of sickness and early retirement in the police service is to be subject to scrutiny. In addition, there is to be a new independent police complaints system. The targets that the police are being asked to meet are tough by any standards. Local police authorities are being asked to set five-year targets for cutting crime in three priority areas, to reduce burglary by 25%, to reduce car crime by 30% and to reduce robbery in major cities by 14%, all by 2005 (HMSO, 2000b).

In terms of crime itself, the focus is to be laid on persistent offenders, both young and adult offenders. Statistics abound to support the contention that a small number of both young and adult offenders account for a large proportion of crimes. One of New Labour's 10-year goals is to double the chance of a persistent offender being caught and punished, although it is difficult to ascertain how this will happen, given that the government expects increased police numbers to play their part. The length of the sentences for these offenders is set to rise, although these punishments are to be coupled with more education programmes and drug treatment. Given the very high levels of illiteracy among offenders, this measure appears to address the far more important causes of crime. David Ramsbotham, who was the Chief Inspector of Prisons until 2001, reported that, in one young offender institution, 70% of the inmates had a reading age of less then eight (Ramsbotham, 2001). Drug-related crime and organised crime are also to be priorities. Drug testing is to be expanded to every stage of the criminal justice system, with a newly created register of drug dealers (we can only hope that this will not result in the unfortunate security lapse of the sex offenders register – a copy for one area was found in a supermarket car park). Persistent youth offenders will be subjected to the newly created Intensive Supervision and Surveillance Programme, designed to track these offenders 24 hours a day, seven days a week using the latest technology. The list is seemingly endless for youth offending – there is the 'on-track' scheme, the 'youth inclusion' programme, the 'children's fund' and the extension of the seemingly unworkable Child Curfew, to name but a few. The message from the Manifesto is clear: "stay straight or you will stay supervised or go back inside" (Labour Party, 2001, p 32).

The 'tough on crime' ethos looks set to become even more firmly embedded. The courts will be functioning in the evening to allow the processing of ever more cases, the disclosure of a defendants' previous criminal record to juries before verdict is likely to be permitted, along with the dubious American principle of victim impact statements before sentencing. The automatic right of a defendant to choose their mode of trial is also likely to be restricted, although this measure has provoked fury in the House of Lords (as mentioned earlier). The practice of double jeopardy is likely to be changed, so that a person acquitted on a murder trial can stand trial again if sufficient new evidence comes to light. The onus of responsibility is set to return to the offender and not the offence, a strategy that has not been in favour since the early 1980s. Victims will have access to online checking of the offender and a Bill of Rights for victims which will include increased levels of compensation and higher amounts.

However, it is not only convicted offenders who need be concerned about New Labour's tough new plans. The DNA database is to be expanded to cover all active offenders by 2004 and these records will not be destroyed if the accused is subsequently acquitted or if no trial is brought. The police will have the powers to stop football fans from travelling abroad if they have reason to think that hooligan behaviour may result, even if there are no previous convictions of football hooliganism. In addition, those who are deemed dangerous and mentally ill are permitted to be detained without an offence taking place, and a suspect's assets are liable to be seized before trial. There is little evidence here that New Labour will pull back from the 'tough on crime' aspects of its crime policy and reset the balance in favour of more liberal measures.

This brings us to the prison system. As discussed elsewhere (see Charman and Savage, 1999), the New Labour government has proved to be fairly reticent on its attitudes towards the prison system and in particular the rising prison population. Commentators have expressed surprise over this stance, but one possible explanation was the need for strong-sounding rhetoric before the 1997 General Election. However, this optimism proved to be unfounded as has been discussed earlier. So what next for the prison system? As Home Secretary, Jack Straw clashed very publicly with many experts in penal affairs – at the beginning of 2001 the Chief Inspector of Prisons, the Prison Director General and the Lord Chief Justice all called for the sparing use of imprisonment. Straw responded by arguing that:

> If we are to get on top of this problem of persistent criminality and are to process more through the system then prison numbers may well have to rise.
> (*The Guardian*, 1 February 2001)

With a prison population that, per head of population, exceeds every other European country bar Portugal, and with measures for part-time prison for repeat offenders plus longer sentences, we are set to see the prison population rise further. Prison will no longer be viewed as a 'last resort' as we saw in the 1980s. Rather, prison is now a central part of New Labour's penal and sentencing strategy. We are also set to see an increase in the number of private prisons and more secure training places for young offenders. However, New Labour intends to improve drug treatment and education for young offenders in prison, as well as supervision and support on release, to the tune of £200 million. However, in 2001, the Prison Service reported that it had failed to meet some of its very modest targets – in particular, its commitment to provide for each prisoner 24 hours a week of education, work or treatment (Toynbee and Walker, 2001, p 161). If New Labour is so committed to the idea of 'what matters is what works', then it is difficult to understand why the prison remains such a central option within the penal system. Crime reduction strategies have been shown to be far more successful. For every £1 spent on crime reduction or on prison, the former is 36 times more successful in reducing crime (*The Guardian*, 19 May 2000). The government must realise that an increasing prison population is not economically, socially or morally justifiable. If leaked reports from the Home Office are correct (*The Guardian*, 17 May 2001), and there will need to be an extra 9,500 prison places, then the Chancellor must surely have to question where the extra £650 million will be coming from.

Conclusion

Taking the whole New Labour package on law and order together, one is presented with a rather uneven, if not contradictory, picture. On the one hand, we have a strategy for 'community safety' that draws upon criminologically sound principles such as social crime prevention, social control networks and early intervention. It is surrounded by notions of coherence, coordination, research-based planning and concerted action. Likewise, in the new proposed legislation, there are commendable and positive ideas designed to address the causes of crime. There are New Deals for the unemployed, literacy and numeracy schemes, increased awareness and strategies to combat school truancy, support for families under stress and neighbourhood renewal. In much of New Labour's plans, there are measures that make eminent good sense and which are based on good research. Yet instead of laying emphasis on the more positive measures that New Labour has adopted to reduce crime, including helping to make people's houses more secure against crime, better use of police budgets and a much improved policy towards youth offending, Straw, in the run-up to the General Election, preferred to wheel out his "I'm the toughest on crime" party piece, which he played with Howard/Major in 1997 and again with Widdecombe/Hague in 2001.

Yet, on the other hand, we have a penal strategy that is still all too inseparable from the policies Labour inherited. We have yet to see a radical attack on the prison system to equate with the radicalism of the community safety agenda. There would seem to be a dilemma, in that the liberal heart says move in one direction but the political head says go the other. To date, it is the political head, still seemingly lacking in confidence despite another huge Commons majority, that is winning. Hugo Young, one of the most eminent centre-left commentators, has said about New Labour's policy that "the politics of law and order are entirely about spin. Not just partly. Entirely" (*The Guardian*, 27 February 2001). Until New Labour feels politically comfortable to 'think the unthinkable' about the custodial end of law and order policy, the picture will remain an uneven one.

Britain has one of the highest rates of crime in Europe (HMSO, 2000c). If it leads the way on both crime and the size of its prison population, it might convince some that perhaps imprisonment is not the best way to tackle crime. Given that, on the evidence, only 3% of all crimes actually lead to conviction, what happens to those convicted should not necessarily be a priority. This points to the conclusion that what matter are the social and cultural forces that cause crime, not finding more and more severe ways to punish the small percentage of offenders who are actually detected and convicted. Politics should not be allowed to cloud that fact.

References

Campbell, B. (2000) 'Missing the target', *The Guardian*, 3 July.

Charman, S. and Savage, S.P. (1999) 'The new politics of law and order: labour, crime and justice', in M. Powell (ed) *New Labour, new welfare state?: The 'third way' in British social policy*, Bristol: The Policy Press, pp 191-212.

Cohen, S. (1985) *Visions of social control*, Cambridge: Polity Press.

Gilling, D. and Barton, A. (1997) 'Crime prevention: a new home for social policy?', *Critical Social Policy*, vol 17, no 1, pp 63-83.

Goddard, J. (1997) 'New Labour: the party of law and order?', Unpublished paper presented to Political Studies Association Conference, April.

Hinsliff, G. (2001) 'Young to face impact of their crimes', *Observer*, 22 April.

HMSO (Her Majesty's Stationery Office) (1998) *Review of the Crown Prosecution Service* ('Glidewell Report'), London: HMSO.

HMSO (1999) *The Report of the Independent Commission on Policing for Northern Ireland: A new beginning*, London: HMSO.

HMSO (2000) *The British Crime Survey 2000*, London: HMSO.

HMSO (2000b) *The Government's Annual Report 1999/2000*, London: HMSO.

HMSO (2000c) *International Crime Victims Survey 2000*, London: HMSO.

HMSO (2001) *Criminal justice: The way ahead*, London: HMSO.

HMSO (2001b) *Recorded crime: England and Wales, 12 Months to March 2001*, London: HMSO.

HMSO (2001c) *Prison population brief: England and Wales: March 2001*, London: HMSO.

Holdaway, S., Davidson, N., Dignan, J., Hammersley, R., Hine, J. and Marsh, P. (2001) *New strategies to address youth offending: The national evaluation of pilot Youth Offending Teams*, London: RDS Occasional Paper No 69.

Hoyle, C. and Rose, D. (2001) 'Labour, law and order', *Political Quarterly*, vol 72, no 1, pp 76-85.

Labour Party (1995) *New Labour, new Britain: The pocket guide*, London: Labour Party.

Labour Party (1997) *Labour Party Manifesto*, London: Labour Party.

Labour Party (2001) *Labour Party Manifesto*, London: Labour Party.

Leishman, F., Loveday, B. and Savage, S. (eds) (2000) *Core issues in policing*, London: Pearson Education.

MacPherson, Sir William of Clurry (1999) *The Stephen Lawrence Inquiry*, Cm 4262-1, London: The Stationery Office.

Maguire, M. (1997) 'Crime statistics, patterns and trends' in M. Maguire, R. Morgan and R. Reiner (eds) *The Oxford handbook of criminology*, Oxford: Oxford University Press, pp 135-88.

Narey, M. (1997) *Review of delay in the criminal justice system*, London: The Stationery Office.

Packer, H. (1968) *The limits of criminal sanction*, Stanford, CA: Stanford University Press.

Ramsbotham, D. (2001) 'The state of our prisons', Lecture at Church House, 19 June.

Reiner, R. (2000) *The politics of the police* (3rd edn), Oxford: Oxford University Press.

Savage, S. and Nash, M. (2001) 'Law and order under Blair: New Labour or Old Conservatism?', in S. Savage and R. Atkinson (eds) *Public policy under Blair*, Basingstoke: Palgrave, pp 102-22.

Savage, S., Charman, S. and Cope, S. (2000) *Policing and the power of persuasion: The changing role of the Association of Chief Police Officers*, London: Blackstone Press.

Toynbee, P. and Walker, D. (2001) *Did things get better?*, London: Penguin Books.

Travis, A. (1999) 'Child curfews flop with courts', *The Guardian*, 17 August.

Wadham, J. (2001) 'Bad laws, little order', *The Guardian*, 15 March.

Wilson, J.Q. and Kelling, G. (1982) 'Broken windows', *Atlantic Monthly*, March, pp 29-38.

Woods, R. (2000) 'Social housing: managing multiple pressures', in J. Clarke, S. Gewirtz and E. McLaughlin (eds) *New managerialism, new welfare?*, London: Sage Publications, pp 128-47.

Young, J. (1997) 'Left Realist criminology: radical in its analysis, realist in its policy', in M. Maguire, R. Morgan and R. Reiner (eds) *The Oxford handbook of criminology*, Oxford: Oxford University Press, pp 473-98.

Zedner, L. (1997) 'Victims', in M. Maguire, R. Morgan and R. Reiner (eds) *The Oxford handbook of criminology*, Oxford: Oxford University Press, pp 577-612.

TWELVE

Conclusion

Martin Powell

Introduction

Existing verdicts give a mixed but generally positive evaluation on New Labour's welfare reforms. On the one hand, Rawnsley (2001, p 382) writes that the five promises of the pledge card, supposedly easy and early, had proved difficult and slow to deliver. A generally negative verdict is given in *Critical Social Policy* (2001). On the other hand, Toynbee and Walker (2001, p 7) claim that the five pledges have "all just about been realised, without too much equivocation". They conclude that "things did get better" (2001, p 240). According to Rawnsley (2001, pp 382-3), the achievement is "quite considerable". He continues that, compared with many governments, this was well above average record. By the measure of the expectations aroused by the size of the majority, New Labour's transformatory rhetoric and the ambitions that Blair had trumpeted, his government looked less impressive. The vital and virtually unquantifiable issue is clearly individual expectations. As Philip Gould put it, "If I'd have gone to a focus group on April 29th 1997 and said this Labour government is going to run the economy more competently than any other, it's going to invest unprecedented amounts in public services plus it will create a million jobs plus it will lift a million people out of poverty, they would have thought I was mad. It was difficult enough getting them to believe our five pledges. They would have called me a Martian!" (in Rawnsley, 2001, p 383). Glennerster (2001) gives New Labour's social policy an 'alpha minus': alpha for the strategy, gamma for presentation, beta for some of the detail. Summarising the contributions to his edited text, Seldon (2001) points to major change in 'selective universality in welfare', public expenditure (from 1999-2000), constitutional reform and devolution, primary education and employment. He views 'some change' in secondary education, local government, criminal policy, family policy, higher education and health. Finally, he sees continuity in a flexible labour market and public expenditure (until 1999/2000). Similarly, he categorises some areas such as constitutional reform, and some redistribution of income and reduction of poverty, as 'positive policy'. However, the exaggerated promises, the two-year spending freeze and the obsession with meeting 'targets' is viewed as 'poor or indifferent' policy. On the whole, Seldon regards the net record as positive.

He states, but does not explain, that some areas, such as crime, pensions and social security, saw considerable activity, but positive progress was hampered by factors largely outside the government's control. He concludes, "the government outshines in achievement over that of all other Labour administrations, except 1945-50" (Seldon 2001, p 597).

Giddens (2002, p 23) differentiates Labour's first term into 'successes' (marginalising the Conservatives, economic policy, welfare reform, high employment, redistribution, and some key aspects of education policy), 'half-way houses' (constitutional reform, the NHS, crime and punishment, EU, and the environment) and 'failures' (the Dome, PR and communications, and the promotion of corporate responsibility).

Much of the focus has been on intrinsic evaluation. The BBC (2002) carried out a 'major research project' into New Labour's 1997 Manifesto pledges. It examines 229 pledges (compared to 177 in the Annual Reports), dividing them into 'pledge met', 'pledge not met', 'pledge partly met', 'on course', and 'debatable'. It is stressed that the decisions on whether or not a pledge has been met do not include judgements as to the inherent value of any of the pledges or the quality of its delivery. Therefore, the government has been measured against the letter rather than the spirit of its Manifesto commitments. In other words, the analysis is, in our terms, intrinsic. Overall, nearly 80% of the pledges were met. However, this hides a varied pattern of success. The areas of great success were welfare, housing and pensions (92.3% pledges met) and education (86.4%), while the areas of least success were the constitution (47.4%) and foreign and defence policy (53.8%). This variable pattern is confirmed by an opinion poll carried out for the BBC, which suggests that voters trust New Labour on the economy, but little else. They believe that New Labour failed to deliver on key areas such as transport, crime and the NHS. Toynbee and Walker (2001, p 238) write that it is hard at the end of the day to compile a single balance sheet, but they argue that, in the narrow sense, the obvious starting point is New Labour's own pledges. They note (2001, p 7) that this was a targeted government. However, they go on to say that some of the 1997 pledges were pretty vacuous. Timmins (2001, pp 556-7) considers the pledges to be 'minimalist', but some were 'unmeasurable', and the NHS waiting list pledge was termed 'crazy' by New Labour's first Secretary of State for Health, Frank Dobson. Nevertheless, the pledges were incorporated in Annual Reports, which were joined by Public Service Agreements (PSAs), Performance Assessment Frameworks (PAFs), and a host of other PAP (promises, aspirations, pledges). All this provides a vast mine of information that can – and has – been quarried selectively by government and opposition, resulting in many unheard debates (not least by the MPs themselves) and unread papers.

This concluding chapter aims to place the contributions to this book in a wider context. It begins with intrinsic evaluation, or examining the degree of success in achieving the government's own stated aims. After an overview of the various targets, a summary of the contributors' assessments of the achievement of the Manifesto pledges is presented. This leads to a critical examination of whether New Labour's targets were SMART (specific, measurable, achievable, relevant and timed) (HM Treasury 1998a, 1998b). This broader focus on intrinsic evaluation leads to extrinsic evaluation, where success is examined with reference to wider criteria. In other words, this provides some perspective on what aims the contributors consider that the government should have set rather than on those it did set.

Intrinsic evaluation

As we saw in Chapter One of this volume, the New Labour government has placed great emphasis on performance and delivery. It has ambitiously argued that it is concerned with outputs and outcomes rather than inputs (see Chapter Three of this volume). For example, according to the Comprehensive Spending Review (HM Treasury, 1998b), PSA targets are of a new kind. As far as possible, they are expressed in terms of end results (for example, reductions in crime) or service standards (for example, smaller class sizes). Similarly, *Modernising government* (Prime Minister, 1999a) points to a new focus on delivery. It criticises the traditional concern of governments with inputs rather than outcomes. Public services are awash with performance data, but it can be argued that we are data-rich and information-poor (see Talbot, 2000). There are many sources of performance data: manifestos, Annual Reports, PSAs, PAFs, Green and White Papers (for example, DSS, 1998), as well as ad hoc targets such as increasing spending on the NHS to the EU average, ending child poverty and achieving full employment (see Chapter One of this volume). Which targets are most important? Which have been the subject of most scrutiny? Are they compatible with each other? As Talbot (2000, p 64) points out, the official 'scripts' about performance say different things, at different times, with different emphases and different definitions.

If not full of promise, manifestos are often full of promises. New Labour set out its five 'early pledges' in the 'Road to the Manifesto' in 1996 (Gould, 1998, pp 266-72; Powell, 1999, p 7). As New Labour pollster Philip Gould explains (1998, p 267), these were derived from focus groups and perceptions of what rival manifestos might say. The New Labour Manifesto would contain very simple, very basic, claims: the simpler the claim, the more powerful the communication. People wanted smaller promises that they could believe in, not larger ones that sound incredible. He writes that "the pledges worked better than anything else I have ever tested in politics. People loved them although politicians and media commentators did not take to them easily" (1998, p 270). They are "central to government. They are being used by the people and the media to hold the government to account, which is how it should be. When Labour meets its pledges, a contract will have been kept, trust in politics restored a little" (1998, p 271). The public wanted smaller, more concrete and credible promises. They have established a new pattern that will not be broken: hard, concrete, accountable promises that are, effectively, a binding contract with the electorate (1998, p 272).

The five pledges became the core of the 1997 Election pledge card, and were incorporated in the Manifesto as the 'pledge card 5', along with the 'covenant 10' (Labour Party, 1997; see Chapter One of this volume). They contained a mix of specific pledges, such as "we will raise the proportion of national income spent on education" (Labour Party, 1997, p 9), and grand intention, such as "we will save the NHS" (p 20). Some of the promises should be seen as signalling broad intentions in the realm of symbolic politics, being so vague that they would be almost impossible to measure. On the other hand, others appear to be more measurable. Nevertheless, they still contain much room for interpretation (cf Timmins, 2001). For example, claiming to "cut NHS waiting lists by treating an extra 100,000 patients as a first step by releasing £100 million saved from NHS red tape" (Labour Party, 1997, p 20) does not clearly equate into the conventional interpretation of reducing waiting lists by 100,000. The figure refers to treating extra patients – crudely an activity measure – that would only lead to reducing waiting lists by 100,000 if demand remained constant. It would be possible to treat an extra 100,000 patients and waiting lists might still rise. Indeed, this is the very broad story of the 50-year history of the NHS (for example, Powell, 1997). Moreover, what does the 'first step' mean? It surely cannot refer to the whole Parliament, as this precludes a second step, and the term of first step becomes redundant. What is the definition of waiting lists? Is it only the inpatient list? What about waiting to get on a waiting list? Note that this was one of the more precise pledges. The New Labour 'wonderkids' who drafted this should perhaps be forced to attend David Blunkett's literacy hour, and be given extra homework.

The Manifesto formed the basis for the innovation of the government's Annual Reports (Prime Minister, 1998, 1999b, 2000). Civil servants scoured the Manifesto, producing 177 'measurable' pledges. Each one is then given a verdict, usually 'kept', 'done' or 'on course', with a few lines of explanation. In addition to being debated in parliament, the government made a real effort to provide the information to the electorate, styled as shareholders in UK PLC, with information posted on the internet and copies being sold in stores for £5.95. Unfortunately, many copies remained unsold and were pulped, which was also the fate of subsequent reports priced at £2.99. This means that the parallel with a shareholders' meeting was fairly accurate: most shareholders took little interest, the information provided was insufficient to constitute a decent audit and there were few mechanisms to hold the board to account.

In the introduction to the first Annual Report (Prime Minister, 1998), Tony Blair claims that Labour has set a 'cracking pace', with 50 of the 177 commitments carried out and 119 under way and on course, leaving only eight yet to be timetabled. The then Conservative leader, William Hague, presented an alternative account of New Labour's first Annual Report: will it "tell the real story of the last year – that welfare bills are higher than a year ago; that waiting lists are higher; that class sizes are higher; that taxes are higher; that interest rates are higher; that inflation is higher; that exports are falling; that unemployment is rising; that output is stagnating...?" (*Hansard*, 29 July 1998, col 365).

In his introduction to the second Annual Report (Prime Minister, 1999b, pp 6-7), Tony Blair claims that "we will try to deliver every one of our 177 manifesto commitments. If there are any commitments we fail to meet, we will have the honesty to say so". He goes on to state that "today the total number of promises kept or done stands at 90, with 85 on course to deliver and only 2 which have still to be timetabled. We have also set over 600 testing performance and efficiency targets to transform the way the public services operate. We will report progress on every one, every year" (1999b, p 7).

Jill Sherman in the *Times* (27 July 1999) considered the report 'over-generous'. In a commentary in the same paper, Peter Riddell argued that the distinction between decision and implementation is blurred. Too often, passing a law or setting up a programme is presented as the same as fulfilling a Manifesto commitment. He reported the Tories' alternative assessment of 54 not yet delivered, 45 fudged, 33 failed and 45 done (of which three out of four are damaging in their effects or are completely pointless). *The Guardian* editorial (27 July 1999) focused on the objectivity of the report: "A pat on the back is always welcome, but it tends to count for less when the back you pat is your own.... Here and there independent observers might take a less rosy view of the government than the government does of itself". It concluded by suggesting that the views of "good old impartial civil servants" might be replaced by "independent observers" or a new organisation on the model of inspectorates such as OFSTED that might be termed 'OFGOV'. More critically, Derek Brown (*The Guardian*, 26 July 1999) wrote that the New Labour government has gazed into the mirror, and found the prospect pleasing: "What is serious about this drivel" of this "preening, self-congratulatory" report is "its very superficiality and weasel language".

In his introduction to the third Annual Report (Prime Minister, 2000), Blair reports "steady progress ... promises made becoming promises kept. We are on the way to meeting our five election pledges and ten-point contract with the people". He states that "these are the facts. People can make their own judgement on them. But my assessment is that most of the key measures are going in the right direction". The report concluded that "This year an expanded version of the government Annual Report is being published on the internet at www.annualreport.gov.uk" (p 64). This gives more details, listing the exact wording of each of the 177 commitments and reports progress on each one in much more detail than has been possible in previous years in the printed version of the report. However, this seems to have subsequently disappeared, and an e-mail and a letter to the addresses listed have not produced any result.

No Annual Report appears to have been produced for the year 2000/01, and in October 2001 the idea of Annual Reports was quietly dropped. However, the Labour Party Election Manifesto (Labour Party, 2001) gives some details on progress. This claims that three of the five pledges have been completed early, and that all will be completed within five years "as we promised". Turning to the ten-point contract, it is admitted that "not everything" has been completed, "it never does" but "we are getting there".

Blair's view that people make judgements on the 'facts' is problematic on two counts. First, the facts must be available. This illustrates the dangers of a paperless world. Books may be burnt at 451^0 Fahrenheit, but they cannot disappear like information on internet sites. If information is the lifeblood of accountability, then www.annualreport.gov.uk urgently requires a transfusion. Second, 'facts' are not as innocent as Mr Blair believes. The most obvious example of this concerns the timescale for the promises. As early as 22 February 1998, the *Sunday Telegraph* considered the promises as flexible as the cards they were written on. Some 'early pledges' were first transformed into the lifetime of the Parliament, and then into a five-year plan. Malcolm Bruce, the Liberal Democrat Treasury spokesperson, stated that the backsliding on the pledges reminded him of the pigs in George Orwell's *Animal farm*, who changed the animals' 10 commandments. In British politics, without fixed-term Parliaments, it is generally understood that election pledges are for the term of office rather than for a meaningless maximum five-year period. At the launch of the 1997 Manifesto, Blair said of the pledges: "Hold us to them. If we deliver, we can come back the election after next [ie 2001/02] and say 'Trust us again' because we kept our promises". As the 1998/99 Annual Report clearly puts it, "These are the five key pledges of the government for this Parliament" (Prime Minister, 1999b, p 3). The changing timescale may be seen in other government sources. In his foreword to the Spending Review document (HM Treasury, 1998b), Blair lists the PSAs that include key manifesto pledges. The timescale of the pledge to cut class sizes was given as September 2001, while that of reducing NHS waiting lists was by the end of the Parliament. As these pledges were originally given together, it seems difficult to justify their different timescales. It is not 'SMART' (specific, measurable, achieveable, relevant and timed; see below) to treat similar pledges in different ways. Subsequently, Blair (Prime Minister, 1999a) reported the timescales of the pledges as September 2001 for class sizes, but May 2002 for waiting lists. The reason for the different timescales appears to be simple expediency in assessing the figures in terms of the targets rather than vice versa. A government with a record majority that argues that it could not fulfil its pledges because it has called an early election shows audacity in inverse proportion to veracity. The *Sunday Telegraph* (18 June 2000) reported that the government "watered down the pledges, apparently recognising that it is unable to deliver them all". It sent a "redrafted" pledge card to members, with "cast iron guarantees" replaced by "vague policy pronouncements".

The pledge cards were critically examined in the 2001 Election campaign. The *Sunday Telegraph* (13 May 2001) presented "Labour 1997-2001: the audit". With a photograph of Tony Blair, it asks "Has this man delivered?". The audit was carried out by the Centre for Policy Studies, "Britain's most respected think tank" (at least by the *Sunday Telegraph*). It considered that the five pledges were all achieved with the exception of the one on young offenders ("not quite"). It pointed to a large number of caveats ("achieved but ..."). For example, waiting lists were reduced, but there are more people now waiting to go on waiting lists, and there has also been a possible distortion of clinical priorities. Similarly, class sizes for those aged five to seven were cut to 30 or under, but 30% more pupils in secondary schools are now in classes of more than 30. This illustrates the problems of opportunity costs and externalities. Even with New Labour's creative accountancy of double and triple counting expenditure, it is possible to spend money only once. Prioritising spending in some areas means that there is less to spend in other areas (to be discussed later in this chapter). More important than the views of a few newspaper columnists is the greater number of newspaper readers and voters. There is some evidence to show that the voters did not believe that the pledges had been achieved. For example, the *Sunday Telegraph* (14 January 2001) presents a MORI opinion poll of over 1,000 people. Analysed by the respected John Curtice, it shows 52% saying they would vote Labour if an election were held the next day. However, relatively few people considered that the pledges had been met: 32% for class sizes, 17% for young offenders, 34% on young unemployed, 30% on NHS waiting lists. The only pledge perceived as kept was on tax, with a bare majority of 51%.

The New Labour Election Manifesto (Labour Party, 2001) claims that three of five pledges were completed early, and that all would be completed within five years, "as we promised". It admits that not everything in the 10-point contract was carried out: "it never does" but "we are getting there". According to my count, there are 43 'we will now' pledges. Some promise legislation such as a new Pension Credit. Others promise more inputs, such as more nurses, doctors, teachers and police. Yet more promise more outputs, such as expanding childcare places to provide for 1.6 million children, helping 750,000 adults with basic skills, and providing a good-quality nursery place for every three-year-old. For an outcome-orientated government (HM Treasury, 1998b; Prime Minister, 1999a; cf 6, 1997), there are few clear outcome targets. It discussed 25 steps to a better Britain, and set 10 goals for 2010, including long-term economic stability; rising living standards for all; expanded higher education as we raise standards in secondary schools; a healthier nation with fast, free treatment at the point of use; full employment in every region; opportunity for all children, security for all parents; a modern criminal justice system; strong and accountable local government; British ideas leading a reformed and enlarged Europe; and global poverty and climate change tackled. Some of these are important and radical, but they are also long term and so are not timed to be completed by the 2005/06 General Election. Moreover, they may be ART (achievable, relevant and timed), but are not SM (specific, measurable).

According to the *Times* (12 May 2001), the five pledge card promises of 1997 were derided immediately as insubstantial and unambitious: "The ambition may have been limited but the pledges proved difficult to fulfil". It claims that two – on class sizes and young offenders – were missed, implicitly assuming a parliamentary rather than a five-year timescale, while the waiting-list pledge was secured "yesterday". It adds that pledges should be precise, sensible and have quantifiable outcomes. On those measures, New Labour's pledge card comprehensively failed. The 2001 pledges were dismissed as being equally unambitious and meaningless, and as unquantifiable, unsuitable or misleading as the waiting-list pledge.

Less attention has been focused on PSAs (but see, for example, Chapters Three, Five and Seven of this volume). Toynbee and Walker (2001, p 7) mention and dismiss them in one breath. It was claimed in 2000 that 90% of the 1998 PSAs had been met. The obvious response was, so what? Talbot (2000, p 65) points out that the 600 or so PSAs of 1998 were reduced to about 200 in 2000. This makes it difficult to compare achievement over time. Is the new reduced set more focused, better specified or merely easier to achieve? The links between PSAs and Manifesto pledges are not clear. We have two different reporting systems in the PSAs and the Annual Reports, as well as more specific systems such as the Annual Report on poverty (for example, DSS, 1999). Although there are overlaps in that some of the Manifesto pledges are incorporated in PSAs, the overlap is far from complete. Put simply, is success in government achieved through the 177 Manifesto pledges in the Annual Reports or the 600 old or 200 new PSAs?

PAFs are important in sectors such as health and social care (see Chapters Seven and Nine of this volume), and there has been some examination of them (for example, Boyne et al, 2003). Labour claims that its system of performance assessment is a more rounded and balanced scorecard than the Conservatives' one-dimensional focus on a narrow definition of efficiency (for example, Newman, 2000). In many ways, PAFs monitor implementation at the local level. There is some excitement from newspapers and concern among the producers of public services on the unveiling of league tables of local authorities, hospitals, schools and universities. This has clear links with the problem of accountability (discussed later in this chapter). If local producers fail to meet government standards, they can be 'named and shamed' and dismissed as a little local difficulty on implementation rather than any general failure in central policy making.

The balanced scorecard

The contributors to this book have added breadth and depth to the broad picture. They have provided more detail than has been available in previous accounts, and have explored some of the less familiar territory such as the PAFs and PSA for some sectors. There is no need to repeat in any detail the conclusions reached in each chapter. However, some attempt will be made to pull some of the main threads together. One of the tasks given to the contributors was to score out of 10 the relevant Manifesto commitments. Clearly, on one level this is a crude and impressionistic exercise to be regarded 'just for fun' like the famous swingometer on election nights. However, on another level, it is no less crude and impressionistic than the verdicts provided by the civil servants in the Annual Reports. Indeed, in a number of ways it can be seen as superior.

Table 12.1: Summary of Manifesto pledges

Sector	Pledges*	Mean	Range
Education	14	6	3-10
Housing	10	3	0-8
Health	13	6	3-7
Social security	14	6	2-10
Social care	8	8	5-10
Criminal justice	16	7	2-10
Family	5	7	5-10
Independent sector	7	6	4-9
All sectors	76	6	0-10

*The number of pledges do not add to the total, as some pledges were examined in two different chapters.

First, it enables a more fine-grained judgement than the 'done' or 'on-course' verdicts that dominate the Annual Reports. Second, the judgements can be seen as more independent. Some of the contributors may be more sympathetic to New Labour than others. Nine pledges were examined in more than one chapter. There is a significant degree of agreement between the contributors on these. The only exceptions are for Child Benefit (pledge 85; Chapters Five and Ten) and the Royal Commission on Long-Term Care (pledge 100; Chapters Four and Nine). While it is a moot point how the scores for individual policy areas in this book might compare with those of other experts in the field, the contributors can exercise greater freedom than the civil servants. In short, this book goes some way to meet the independent audit called for by some newspapers (see above). Third, they attempt to justify their argument. 'Showing their working' in this way enables others to examine the rationale or justification for the verdict. As noted earlier, commentators such as Glennerster (2001), the BBC (2002) and Giddens (2002) tend to regard social policy as a successful policy area. There is no easy way of directly comparing these judgements to the ones reached by the contributors to this book. However, very broadly, while there is general agreement that the NHS is not an outstanding example of delivery, the contributors in this book tend to see the areas of welfare, housing, pensions and education as less successful than the more favourable verdicts of the other commentators.

Table 12.1 gives information on 76 social policy pledges, nearly half of the total of 177 pledges. It gives the arithmetic mean (assuming equal weighting) and the range of scores. While there are a range of scores both between and within areas, it is hardly surprising that there are fewer 'perfect 10s' than implied in the Annual Reports. Brian Lund (Chapter Six) terms New Labour's achievement in housing an 'insipid attempt to achieve modest objectives'. He notes that the Manifesto was terse on housing policy, and that housing did not feature in the five or 10 high-profile pledges. The government passed no primary legislation in its first term, leaving New Labour in the embarrassing position of having to repeat much of the housing section of the 1997 Manifesto in its 2001 Manifesto. Mark Baldwin (Chapter Nine) gives an overall 5 (less than the arithmetic equally weighted mean of 8.5) as the government did not reach many of its stated social care targets, and the implied ones are still a long way from fruition. He regards some targets as proxies for their implied targets. For example, the target to reduce the time for youth justice is viewed by the government as a means to an end of reducing youth crime. The generally good marks for the original social care pledges must be seen in the context of their limited scope and relevance, as easily achievable and soft targets. Similarly, for health, Calum Paton (Chapter Seven) writes that the government may have met its limited objectives, but failed to achieve much. The fact that most of the health pledges were met before the NHS Plan of 2000 suggests that meeting limited pledges did not add up to a thriving NHS. Some contributors point to differential levels of success in meeting the pledges. Edward Brunsdon and Margaret May (Chapter Four) point to mixed success in meeting the goals that the government set itself. Rajani Naidoo and Yolande Muschamp (Chapter Eight) argue that the education targets were often either vague or narrowly defined, but give their lowest marks for the pledges concerned with equity. Martin Hewitt (Chapter Ten) notes a complex picture of new and old targets and strategies for different groups. Jane Millar and Tess Ridge (Chapter Five) conclude that New Labour's family policy contains many paradoxes – it is visible and invisible, radical and cautious, stigmatising and inclusive. For Sarah Charman and Steve Savage (Chapter Eleven), criminal justice policy presents a rather uneven, if not contradictory picture: New Labour certainly upheld its promise to be 'tough on crime', but put less emphasis on being 'tough on the causes of crime'. They warn that achieving the Manifesto pledges does not necessarily equate with a desirable set of criminal justice policies (as I discuss later). John Rouse and George Smith (Chapter Three) divide accountability into two main components of democratic renewal and enhanced performance management. They argue that in spite of grand claims, the programme for democratic renewal may be faulted for its lack of cohesion and half-heartedness in diffusing power to citizens. In particular, the steps towards democratic regional government have been slight. This pledge (140) was one of the few given as 'not yet time-tabled' in the 1998/99 Annual Report (Prime Minister, 1999b, p 80): the government remains committed to its undertaking "in time". The other was to introduce Commonhold (91) for which "draft legislation is in preparation" (1999b, p 77: see Chapter Six of this volume).

SMART targets?

This section examines whether New Labour's targets were SMART. Some of the contributors have considerable doubts about this. According to Lund (Chapter Six), some housing PSAs are moving targets, frequently imprecise, often expressed in outputs not outcomes and with fulfilment dates set for the distant future. Similarly, for Baldwin (Chapter Nine), social care targets are less

SMART than contradictory, reactive, unclear, disconnected and excessive. Each element will now be examined in more detail.

Specificity differentiates the grand, symbolic promises of the Manifesto from more precise claims. Promises to 'rebuild the NHS' and 'help build strong families' belong more to the realm of symbolic politics – 'words that succeed' (Edelman, 1964) rather than specific pledges. Similarly, the PSAs contain a hierarchy of broad, overall aims, key objectives that pursue these aims, and more specific targets (for example, HM Treasury, 1998b). In some cases, initial vague promises became more precise in office. For example, Millar and Ridge (Chapter Five) note that the original pledge of helping single parents back to work became SMART-er in 2000 with the setting of a 70% target. However, they also note that there is no more detail in the pledge to provide affordable and high-quality childcare.

A measurable target has clear links with statistical reliability. In other words, will different commentators arrive at the same measure? One of the obvious points here is the difference between quantitative targets. Generally speaking, it is easier to measure quantitative targets. Charman and Savage (Chapter Eleven) note particular problems in the area of criminal justice. They point out that, since much crime goes unreported, the relationship between the recorded crime rate and the 'real' crime rate is problematic. However, it should be relatively simple to count expenditure, staff and activity. Even here, seemingly simple statements such as we will spend more 'in real terms' on a service is problematic as it is not clear which inflation rate will be used. Does a promise of extra staff refer to full-time, part-time or 'full-time equivalents'? Similarly, is it gross or net? For example, does 'extra' police refer to recruitment figures or the total number, including new entrants to replace those who resign or retire? Moreover, most measures focus on inputs and activity rather than outcomes or results. Nevertheless, the most significant problems relate to qualitative issues. As Baldwin (Chapter Nine) points out, the PAF for social care is a "monumental statistical exercise", but it largely consists of crude quantitative measures, and it remains to be seen whether it will have any worth in providing evidence of service quality. Similarly, Paton (Chapter Seven) uses the example of the inquiry into the Bristol Royal Infirmary to illustrate the problems in assessing high-quality medical care. In spite of the stress on 'quality public services' and outcomes (Prime Minister, 1999a), there is still relatively little information on these dimensions.

An achievable target is problematic as judgements on feasibility vary. As previously pointed out (cf Gould, 1998; Rawnsley, 2001; Timmins, 2001), New Labour deliberately chose a set of limited promises. Nevertheless, many critics consider the targets too modest and timid. Paton argues that the 1997 Manifesto was modest as regards its intentions for the NHS. For example, the promise to spend more money in real terms on the NHS was quite modest, in that nearly all governments had raised spending on the NHS in real terms since 1948. Similarly, the pledge to 'retain Child Benefit' probably led to few sleepness nights for the New Labour Cabinet. However, there are pledges that few could regard as trivial, such as those on achieving 'full employment', reducing child poverty and narrowing health inequality. They are longer-term objectives, and it is possible to have reservations about whether they will be achieved, but they are significant and radical. Similarly, it is possible to criticise the level of the National Minimum Wage, but as the government has pointed out, this has been an unachieved aim of Labour Party policy for the best part of a century. Many critics point to the 'two wasted years' of keeping within the Conservative spending limit. Lund (Chapter Six) refers to these as "fallow years". In this sense, spending increases after this time were too late to contribute substantially to improving public services (for example, Toynbee and Walker, 2001). However, this ignores the fact that some improvements are not necessarily linked with extra spending, and treats the perceived taxation constraint a lot less seriously than the government did (see, for example, Gould, 1998). A further point is that New Labour inherited a broadly positive economic environment. As both Paton and Hewitt (Chapters Seven and Ten) point out, the extent to which financing public services and full employment respectively will be successful in a harsher economic climate is not clear.

Achievability is linked to two further 'As' – attribution and accountability. Attribution will be discussed later in terms of the relevance dimension. Accountability focuses on who is responsible for reaching the targets. In many areas of the classic Westminster model, central government makes policy and local agencies implement it. With a large parliamentary majority, it is relatively simple to pass legislation. However, it is sometime more difficult to make it work. This is often seen in terms of an 'implementation gap' (for example, Marsh and Rhodes, 1992), but it is unclear whether failure to meet a target is a 'formulation failure' of central government or an 'implementation failure' at local level (for example, Wolman, 1981). For whatever reason, Charman and Savage (Chapter Eleven) show that by November 2000, only 132 Anti-Social Behaviour Orders were made. Not a single Child Curfew Order was made in the first year of implementation. Only a handful of Child Safety Orders and Parenting Orders were made. From a central perspective, these pledges were kept by passing the legislation, but they have made a very limited impact on the ground. As Rouse and Smith (Chapter Three) point out, the government's democratic renewal and performance management agendas show some tensions. New Labour is very happy to centralise credit and decentralise blame. Local managers may lose their jobs if they fail to achieve targets, but few Ministers have felt the need to resign for their failures. Paton (Chapter Seven) points to the problem of 'initiative-itis', with the endless setting up of initiatives, task forces and agencies at central levels. Local agencies are deluged with endless central orders, with little apparent consideration as to whether some may be more easily achieved in some contexts than others.

A relevant target may be seen broadly in terms of statistical validity. In other words, the issue is whether the target is appropriate: will fulfilling the pledge solve the problem? This has clear links with evidence-based policy, with its central problem of attribution and causality (Wolman, 1981; Davies et al, 2000).

For example, Charman and Savage (Chapter Eleven) point out that the government claims credit for the falling crime rate, but many factors such as demographic changes (most notably how many young males are in the population) are outside the scope of government intervention. Moreover, the fall began before New Labour's term of office. To take a longer-term example, the infant mortality rate has been declining for about 150 years irrespective of changes in government. In order to determine the 'value-added' of Labour or the 'Labour effect', it may be necessary to look for a variation in the rate of change over time or a 'break of slope', or a reversal of direction (for example, hospital waiting lists rising under the Conservatives and falling under Labour). This is related to the problem of time lags. It is unlikely that policy changes will have instantaneous effects. They may take different amounts of time to filter into the system. For example, an increase in petrol duty takes effect in a matter of hours, but training more doctors or building new hospitals in the NHS takes years. Similarly, any change of 'culture' surrounding benefits will be long term, as will a Sure Start programme that makes children more healthy adults. There is also likely to be a limit on the time in which New Labour can blame the previous Conservative government for measures such as increasing hospital waiting lists. However, the converse does not occur: New Labour has not thanked the previous government for any positive inheritances such as a broadly sound economic situation. Millar and Ridge (Chapter Five) point to the issue of additionality in terms of whether unemployed people would have found jobs without the New Deal. Another way of addressing this issue is through the counterfactual of what would have happened without the policy. Miller and Ridge report research indicating a "small but appreciable effect" at a modest net cost. In short, we are not certain of the links between mechanisms and outcomes (Pawson and Tilley, 1997) and which policy levers we should pull (Powell, 2000) in many areas of public policy.

The temporal dimension is usually viewed in terms of whether a clear timescale exists for the pledge. As we saw above, there are at least some questions as to whether some policy goals have been scored late in time added on. There is also the issue of whether pledges are consistent over time. Sometimes pledges are made more precise. At other times, existing pledges may be amended, and new pledges added. Hewitt (Chapter Ten) notes that the discourse in the early period of the Labour government was concerned with social exclusion, but more recently there has been a revived emphasis on poverty. Pledges may become watered down or more challenging over time. Lund (Chapter Six) considers that graded against the performance criteria that New Labour set in government, it deserves a higher mark than the fulfilment of its manifesto pledges but this is awarded more for elevated vision than for achievement. Finally, Millar and Ridge (Chapter Five) use the example of the child poverty pledge to point to the problems of long timescales. First, the first groups lifted out of poverty tend to be those in least poverty, and future gains may be more difficult. Second, without cross-party support, the 20-year pledge to abolish child poverty is vulnerable to a possible change in administration.

Extrinsic evaluation

The strengths of intrinsic evaluation have already been outlined. It evaluates an organisation on its own terms, with the result that any failing carries great force, as the organisation has failed to achieve its own stated aims. The organisation cannot claim that it is being judged by failing to reach unreasonable goals if it set the goals itself. Comparing promises with delivery is of central importance to New Labour (Gould, 1998). Toynbee and Walker claim that "the fairest judgements must be based on what New Labour itself promised" (2001, p 232; cf BBC 2002) .

However, there are also a number of possible deficiencies. First, a limited set of promises may be made and more challenging ones avoided in order to maximise success. We saw earlier ('SMART targets?') that, while the pledges may include some soft or easy targets, some of the longer-term promises appear to be more radical. Second, the pledges may be concentrated in certain areas rather than providing a balanced scorecard (see Chapter Three). Put another way, the shopping list may not cover the full range of political goods. There may be sins of omission and of commission. Some promises that critics consider important may not be on the list, while it might contain promises that critics consider should not appear. Finally, the shopping-list approach presents 177 apparently independent promises. However, it is important to consider trade-offs and externalities. There are opportunity costs in that spending money on promise x means that there is less to spend on promise y, and potential promise z is completely omitted. Moreover, achieving target a may have some positive impact on promise b, but a negative impact on promise c. In economic terms, it is necessary to approach the whole Manifesto from the point of view of allocative efficiency rather than view each item in terms of narrow technical efficiency.

In line with the new and distinctive nature of third way (Blair, 1998; see Powell, 1999), it might be expected that the pledges would be distinctive from both the 'old left' and the 'new right', and include a mix of old and new targets. Carter et al (1992) locate the roots of performance management in the USA in the 1960s. The Conservatives seized on the concept, resulting in an explosion of interest in performance. However, it can be claimed that the Conservatives' interests were partial and simplistic. First, they tended to examine the 3Es of economy, effectiveness and efficiency. New Labour claims that its performance measures are wider (Chapter Three of this volume; see also Newman, 2000). In particular, it has concentrated more on equity. Second, the Conservatives used one-dimensional PIs such as the simplistic and much-criticised efficiency measure in the NHS. They also used simple league tables. For example, schools were ranked by outcome measures such as examination passes. However, most critics pointed out that examination success depends heavily on school intake. In order to compare like with like, league tables should compare actual examination success with expected success given the composition of the school. This could result in a school with a low proportion of passes performing better than expected, and showing 'value-added'. In opposition, Labour criticised raw league tables, but official 'value-added' tables have been slow to be produced. Nevertheless, it is clear that PIs have evolved over time, and were more sophisticated by the end of the Conservatives' term of office. It appears that while New Labour's PIs may have more breadth, they are not significantly different in depth.

While New Labour's scorecard may be more balanced than the Conservatives', some of the contributors still consider that there are few measures focused on concerns such as equity and service quality. In terms of specific pledges, Hewitt (Chapter Ten) notes a new emphasis on individual savings, with emphasis on Individual Savings Accounts (ISAs) and Asset-Based Welfare. Naidoo and Muschamp (Chapter Eight) suggest that New Labour has diluted its traditional opposition to selection in education and has embraced diversity and competition. They raise the spectre of a two-tier higher education system, which has a certain irony given New Labour's opposition to a two-tier NHS. Several of the contributors remark on the limited emphasis on redistribution. While a note a caution must be sounded in saying that New Labour has abandoned redistribution (Chapter Two of this volume), there are certainly marked differences from 'Old Labour' Manifestos.

New Labour has stressed joined-up government (Chapter Three of this volume; cf 6, 1997; Wilkinson and Appelbee, 1999). For example, it is necessary to design policy around shared goals and carefully defined results rather than around organisational structures or existing functions. A focus on outcomes will encourage departments to work together where this is necessary to achieve a desired result. The keystones are inclusiveness and integration (Prime Minister, 1999a). However, a cross-cutting approach remains unusual, with most policies still falling down 'silos' from centre to locality. Some of the contributors note that pledges are not independent. For example, Baldwin (Chapter Nine) notes that anti-poverty pledges have implications for social care. Charman and Savage (Chapter Eleven) consider that the best route to reduce crime may not be found in the 'tough on crime' pledges. They point out that Britain has one of the highest crime rates and prison populations in Europe. Certainly, given that only 3% of all crime leads to conviction, sentencing policy alone is unlikely to lead to a reduction in crime. However, such a cross-sectional comparison neglects the counterfactual that we do not know what the crime rate in Britain might be with a different sentencing regime.

Performance targets may lead to a concentration on how to meet the target rather than solve the problem. For example, there is a rather sterile debate about whether meeting waiting-list targets has distorted clinical need (Chapter Seven of this volume) as maximum reductions result from treating, say, 10 in-growing toenails rather than performing one heart bypass operation. Charman and Savage (Chapter Eleven) point out that in an overall reduction in crime rates, there are reductions in 'targeted' crime; but increases in other categories.

At one level, it is easy to criticise some of New Labour's pledges as narrow and limited. Others may not work in terms of evidence-based policy. For example, Charman and Savage (Chapter Eleven) suggest that the pledge to put more police officers on the beat has more to do with responding to public opinion than with evidence that this strategy works in terms of reducing crime. However, pledges must ultimately succeed at the level of political strategy. Some of the contributors implicitly or explicitly suggest a more traditional agenda based on equality and redistribution. Similarly, some criticise the two years based on Conservative spending limits. However, all this is with the benefit of hindsight, and from the easy position of external critic rather than from the more difficult perspective of seeking office (see Gould, 1998; Rawnsley, 2001). For better or worse, it was New Labour rather than the contributors to this book who were elected to govern.

Conclusions

The main aim of this book was to provide some evaluation of New Labour's welfare reforms. There are a number of different answers in response to different questions. Different degrees of success might come from a concentration on different sources such as the pledge card five, the covenant 10, the Manifesto 177, the PSAs, the PAFs and other ad hoc promises. On the most examined source of the Manifesto, the answer seems to be that – hardly surprisingly – the evaluation is not as positive as the civil servants made out in the Annual Reports, but hardly a failure either. The pledges were not particularly SMART, although they did become a little SMART-er over time. Some of the initial pledges were trivial or unmeasurable. However, some important, long-term pledges were made later, such as reducing health inequalities, abolishing child poverty and creating full employment. Inevitably, the jury will still be out on these pledges, assuming that juries will still be allowed to decide on matters in the future.

Contrasting with their broadly positive line on intrinsic evaluation, many of the contributors are more critical in considering extrinsic evaluation. They point out that many of the pledges were limited. They note sins of omission and of commission. Some consider that New Labour has dropped some 'old' pledges, such as redistribution via the tax and benefit system. Others argue that some pledges may have negative implications (for example, Chapter Eleven).

A detailed consideration of the government's second term is beyond the scope of this book. At a very general level, the twin themes are investment and reform. More investment will be put into key services such as the NHS. The 2002 Budget revised 'taxes on income' (rather than income tax) through increasing national insurance contributions equivalent to adding 3p to the standard rate of income tax. However, there will continue to be 'modernisation' and organisational change in areas such as health and social care, and the criminal justice system. Nevertheless, spotting clear policy directions may be no easier here than in the first term. There is speculation about at least a partial de facto renationalisation of the rail system. However, in other areas the direction is less obvious. New Labour will have 'zero tolerance' for 'failing' organisations, but whether any resulting takeovers will be from 'successful' public sector organisations or from the private sector is yet to be fully established. Tony Blair is currently alternating between 'good cop and bad cop' on the public sector: the workers who inflicted scars on his back turned into heroes when criticised by the Conservative leader, and then back into villains in the form of 'wreckers'. There may be a 'strategic shift' in the balance of responsibilities between the state and the individual, notably in the broad shape of asset-based welfare within a regulated environment (Chapters Four, Ten).

The government hopes that the second term will remedy any perceived implementation deficit of the first term as the seeds of investment and reform of the first term bear fruit. The main theme for the second term is said to be 'delivery, delivery, delivery'. Progress can be monitored against a number of long-term objectives, such as increasing health spending to the EU average, reducing health inequalities and abolishing child poverty. However, it is not clear whether achieving these pledges will be contingent on favourable economic conditions.

This book has highlighted many of the problems of evaluation, illustrating the rudimentary state of the art. Although it has provided probably the most comprehensive analysis of welfare reform in New Labour's first term, it is perhaps no more than a partial and incomplete evaluation of an unfinished revolution.

References

6, P. (1997) *Holistic government*, London: Demos.

BBC (2002) 'Has Labour kept its promises?' (http://news.bbc.co.uk/hi/english/uk_politics/newsid_1961000/1961522.stm).

Blair, T. (1998) *The third way*, London: Fabian Society.

Boyne, G., Farrell, C., Law, J., Powell, M. and Walker, R. (2003: forthcoming) *Evaluating public management reforms*, Buckingham: Open University Press.

Carter, N., Klein, R. and Day, P. (1992) *How organisations measure success*, London: Routledge.

Critical Social Policy (2001) In and against New Labour (special issue), vol 21, no 4.

Davies, H., Nutley, S. and Smith, P. (eds) *What Works?: Evidence-based policy and practice in public services*, Bristol: The Policy Press.

DSS (Department for Social Security) (1998) *A new contract for welfare: New ambitions for our country*, London: The Stationery Office.

DSS (1999) *Opportunity for All: Tackling poverty and social exclusion*, London: The Stationery Office.

Edelman, M. (1964) *The symbolic use of politics*, Urbana, IL: University of Illinois Press.

Giddens, A. (2002) *Where now for New Labour?*, Cambridge: Polity Press.

Glennerster, H. (2001) 'Social policy', in A. Seldon (ed) *The Blair effect*, London: Little, Brown & Company, pp 383-403.

Gould, P. (1998) *The unfinished revolution*, London: Little, Brown & Company.

Hansard (1998) House of Commons, 29 July.

HM Treasury (1998a) *Modern public services for Britain*, London: The Stationery Office.

HM Treasury (1998b) *Public services for the future*, London: The Stationery Office.

Labour Party (1997) *New Labour because Britain deserves better* (Election Manifesto), London: Labour Party.

Labour Party (2001) *New ambitions for our country* (Election Manifesto), London: Labour Party.

Marsh, D. and Rhodes, R. (eds) (1992) *Implementing Thatcherite policies*, Buckingham: Open University Press.

Newman, J. (2000) 'Beyond the new public management?', in J. Clarke, S. Gewirtz and E. McLaughlin (eds) *New managerialism, new welfare?*, London: Sage Publications, pp 45-61.

Pawson, R. and Tilley, N. (1997) *Realistic evaluation*, London: Sage Publications.

Powell, M. (1997) *Evaluating the National Health Service*, Buckingham: Open University Press.

Powell, M. (ed) (1999) *New Labour, new welfare state?: The 'third way' in British social policy*, Bristol: The Policy Press.

Powell, M. (2000) 'Something old, something new, something borrowed, something blue', *Renewal*, vol 8, no 4, pp 21-31.

Prime Minister (1998) *The government's Annual Report*, London: The Stationery Office.

Prime Minister (1999a) *Modernising government*, London: The Stationery Office.

Prime Minister (1999b) *The government's Annual Report 98/99*, London: The Stationery Office.

Prime Minister (2000) *The government's Annual Report 99/00*, London: The Stationery Office.

Rawnsley, A. (2001) *Servants of the people*, Harmondsworth: Penguin.

Seldon, A. (2001) 'The net Blair effect', in A. Seldon (ed) *The Blair effect*, London: Little, Brown & Company, pp 593-600.

Talbot, C. (2000) 'Performing "performance"', *Public Money and Performance*, vol 20, no 4, pp 63-8.

Timmins, N. (2001) *The five giants* (2nd edn), London: HarperCollins.

Toynbee, P. and Walker, D. (2001) *Did things get better?*, Harmondsworth: Penguin.

Wilkinson, D. and Appelbee, E. (1999) *Implementing holistic government: Joined-up action from the ground*, Bristol: The Policy Press.

Wolman, H. (1981) 'The determinants of program success and failure', *Journal of Public Policy*, vol 1, no 4, pp 433-64.

Index